Official and Economic Statistics

Official and Economic Statistics

Pankaj Dutta

RANDOM

RANDOM PUBLICATIONS

NEW DELHI (INDIA)

Official and Economic Statistics

ISBN 978-93-5111-228-0

Published in 2014 in India by

RANDOM PUBLICATIONS

4376-A/4B, Gali Murari Lal, Ansari Road
New Delhi-110 002
Phone : +91-11-43580356, +91-11-23289044
e-mail: randomexports@gmail.com, sales@randompublications.com, info@randompublications.com

Type Setting by : Keystoneprintads, Delhi-110051
Printed at : Sanat Printers

Preface

Economists have been grousing a good deal lately about the deteriorating quality of basic economic statistics-official data on prices, incomes, employment, productivity, and poverty, among other things-and about the lack of government funding to remedy the problem.

Economic statistics is a topic in applied statistics that concerns the collection, processing, compilation, dissemination, and analysis of economic data. It is also common to call the data themselves 'economic statistics', but for this usage see economic data. The data of concern to economic statistics may include those of an economy of region, country, or group of countries. Economic statistics may also refer to a subtopic of official statistics for data produced by official organizations. Analyses within economic statistics both make use of and provide the empirical data needed in economic research, whether descriptive or econometric. They are a key input for decision making as to economic policy. The subject includes statistical analysis of topics and problems in microeconomics, macroeconomics, business, finance, forecasting, data quality, and policy evaluation. It also includes such considerations as what data to collect in order to quantify some particular aspect of an economy and of how best to collect in any given instance.

Business statistics is the science of good decision making in the face of uncertainty and is used in many disciplines such as financial analysis, econometrics, auditing, production, and operations including services improvement, and marketing research. These sources feature regular repetitive publication of series of data. This makes the topic of time series especially important for business statistics. It is also a branch of applied statistics working mostly on data collected as a by-product of doing business or by government agencies. It provides knowledge and skills to interpret and use statistical techniques in a variety of business applications. A typical business statistics course is intended for business majors, and covers statistical study, descriptive statistics, probability, and the binomial and normal distributions, test of hypotheses and confidence intervals, linear regression, and correlation. But I wonder. Having used official economic statistics from time to time for some thirty-five years, I would miss them if they were to disappear. Yet, however put out I might be as an economic analyst, I suspect that the world would be a happier place had these figures never been created. Certainly the statistics are often inaccurate or otherwise flawed, and hence misleading. An even more serious consideration, however, is that the official statistics help to provide rationales for pernicious policy making.

I thank all members of my team who have helped in the preparation of the book. My special thanks go to "Random Publications" who have published the book.

– ***Pankaj Dutta***

Contents

1

Overview of Statistics

Statistics is a set of tools used to organize and analyse data. Data must either be numeric in origin or transformed by researchers into numbers. For instance, statistics could be used to analyse percentage scores English students receive on a grammar test: the percentage scores ranging from 0 to 100 are already in numeric form. Statistics could also be used to analyse grades on an essay by assigning numeric values to the letter grades, *e.g.*, A=4, B=3, C=2, D=1, and F=0.

Employing statistics serves two purposes:

- Description
- Prediction.

Statistics are used to describe the characteristics of groups. These characteristics are referred to as variables. Data is gathered and recorded for each variable. Descriptive statistics can then be used to reveal the distribution of the data in each variable.

Statistics is also frequently used for purposes of prediction. Prediction is based on the concept of generaliz-ability: if enough data is compiled about a particular context (*e.g.*, students studying writing in a specific set of classrooms), the patterns revealed through analysis of the data collected about that context can be generalized (or predicted to occur in) similar contexts. The prediction of what will happen in a similar context is probabilistic. That is, the researcher is not certain that the same things will happen in other contexts; instead, the researcher can only reasonably expect that the same things will happen.

Prediction is a method employed by individuals throughout daily life. For instance, if writing students begin class every day for the first half of the semester with a five-minute freewriting exercise, then they will likely come to class the first day of the second half of the semester prepared to again freewrite for the first five minutes of class. The students will have made a prediction about the class content based on their previous experiences in the class: Because they began all previous class sessions with freewriting, it would be probable that their next class session will begin the same way. Statistics is used to perform the same function; the difference is that precise probabilities are determined in terms of the percentage chance that an outcome will occur, complete with a range of error. Prediction is a primary goal of inferential statistics.

REVEALING PATTERNS USING DESCRIPTIVE STATISTICS

- Descriptive statistics, not surprisingly, "describe" data that have been collected. Commonly used descriptive statistics include frequency counts, ranges (high and low scores or values), means, modes, median scores, and standard deviations. Two concepts are essential to understanding descriptive statistics: *variables* and *distributions*.

Variables

Statistics are used to explore numerical data. Numerical data are observations which are recorded in the form of numbers. Numbers are variable in nature, which means that quantities vary according to certain factors. For examples, when analyzing the grades on student essays, scores will vary for reasons such as the writing ability of the student, the students' knowledge of the subject, and so on. In statistics, these reasons are called variables.

Variables are divided into three basic categories:

1. Nominal Variables
2. Ordinal Variables
3. Interval Variables

Distributions

A distribution is a graphic representation of data. The line formed by connecting data points is called a frequency distribution. This line may take many shapes. The single most important shape is that of the bell-shaped curve, which characterizes the distribution as "normal." A perfectly normal distribution is only a theoretical ideal. This ideal, however, is an essential ingredient in statistical decision-making. A perfectly normal distribution is a mathematical construct which carries with it certain mathematical properties helpful in describing the attributes of the distribution. Although frequency distribution based on actual data points seldom, if ever, completely matches a perfectly normal distribution, a frequency distribution often can approach such a normal curve.

The closer a frequency distribution resembles a normal curve, the more probable that the distribution maintains those same mathematical properties as the normal curve. This is an important factor in describing the characteristics of a frequency distribution. As a frequency distribution approaches a normal curve, generalizations about the data set from which the distribution was derived can be made with greater certainty. And it is this notion of generalizabilityupon which statistics is founded. It is important to remember that not all frequency distributions approach a normal curve. Some areskewed. When a frequency distribution is skewed, the characteristics inherent to a normal curve no longer apply.

MAKING PREDICTIONS USING INFERENTIAL STATISTICS

Inferential statistics are used to draw conclusions and make predictions based on the descriptions of data. In this section, we explore inferential statistics by using an extended example of experimental studies.

Key concepts used in our discussion are:

1. Experiments
2. Probability
3. Population
4. Sampling
5. Matching.

Experiments

A typical experimental study involves collecting data on the behaviors, attitudes, or actions of two or more groups and attempting to answer a research question (often called a hypothesis). Based on the analysis of the data, a researcher might then attempt to develop a causal model that can be populations.

A question that might be addressed through experimental research might be "Does grammar-based writing instruction produce better writers than process-based writing instruction?" Because it would be impossible and impractical to observe, interview, survey, etc.

All first-year writing students and instructors in classes using one or the other of these instructional approaches, a researcher would study a sample—or a subset—of a population. Sampling—or the creation of this subset of a population—is used by many researchers who desire to make sense of some phenomenon. To analyse differences in the ability of student writers who are taught in each type of classroom, the researcher would compare the writing performance of the two groups of students.

Two key concepts used to conduct the comparison are:

1. Dependent Variables
2. Independent Variables

Probability

Beginning researchers most often use the word *probability* to express a subjective judgment about the likelihood, or degree of certainty, that a particular event will occur. People say such things as: "It will probably rain tomorrow." "It is unlikely that we will win the ball game." It is possible to assign a number to the event being predicted, a number between 0 and 1, which represents *degree of confidence* that the event will occur. For example, a student might say that the likelihood an instructor will give an exam next week is about 90 per cent, or.9. Where 100 per cent, or 1.00, represents certainty.9 would mean the student is almost certain the instructor will give an exam.

If the student assigned the number.6, the likelihood of an exam would be just slightly greater than the likelihood of no exam. A rating of 0 would indicate complete certainty that *no* exam would be given. The probability of a particular outcome or set of outcomes is called a*p-value*.

In our discussion, a p-value will be symbolized by a *p* followed by parentheses enclosing a symbol of the outcome or set of outcomes. For example, p(X) should be read, "the probability of a given X score" (Shoeninger). Thus p(exam) should be read, "the probability an instructor will give an exam next week."

Population

A *population* is a group which is studied. In educational research, the population is usually a group of people. Researchers seldom are able to study every member of a population. Usually, they instead study a representative sample—or subset—of a population. Researchers then generalize their findings about the sample to the population as a whole.

Sampling

Sampling is performed so that a population under study can be reduced to a manageable size. This can be accomplished via random sampling, or via matching.

Random sampling is a procedure used by researchers in which all samples of a particular size have an equal chance to be chosen for an observation, experiment, etc. There is no predetermination as to which members are chosen for the sample. This type of sampling is done in order to minimize scientific biases and offers the greatest likelihood that a sample will indeed be representative of the larger population. The aim here is to make the sample as representative of the population as possible. Note that the closer a sample distribution approximates the population distribution, the more generalizable the results of the sample study are to the population. Notions of probability apply here. Random sampling provides the greatest probability that the distribution of scores in a sample will closely approximate the distribution of scores in the overall population.

Matching

Matching is a method used by researchers to gain accurate and precise results of a study so that they may be applicable to a larger population. After a population has been examined and a sample has been chosen, a researcher must then consider variables, or extrinsic factors, that might affect the study.

2

Describing Data: Numerical Measures

MEASURES OF CENTRAL TENDENCY

In describing a set of data, we are interested in the numerical measures of centre and spread. the centre of the data appears to be a cycle time of 21 days. That is formally called the measure of central tendency of the data. There are two classic ways to measure the centre of a distribution of data: the mean and the median.

Mean

The mean or average is the arithmetic measure of central tendency, and is simply the sum of all of the observations in a set of data divided by the total number of observations. So, the mean of seven cycle times with values 21, 23, 19, 22, 20, 22, 20 is:

$$\text{Mean} = (21 + 23 + 19 + 22 + 20 + 22 + 20)/7 = 21$$

You will read in statistics texts that this is the formula for both the population mean (its symbol is the Greek letter mu) and the sample mean (its symbol is an x with a bar over it, or x-bar). Don't get alarmed - this is not a course with a lot of formulas, symbols and computations - we will let the computer do it.

I just want to highlight the computations for the classic measures in descriptive statistics. You will also read in textbooks that measures based on a population are called parameters, and measures based on a sample are called statistics.

Median

The median is called the location measure of central tendency since it is the middle value of an ordered array of observations - 50% of the observations in a set of data fall below the median provided the data is in an ordered array. Since we have to account for 100% of the data, 50% of the observations fall above the median. So, given the cycle times of 21, 23, 19, 22, 20, 22, 20; first created an ordered array (sorted list of the numbers):

Ordered array = 19, 20, 20, 21, 22, 22, 23

The median is the ordered or ranked observation that appears at location = (n + 1)/2, where n is the symbol for the number of numbers in the set of data. For this ordered array: Median = (7 + 1)/2 = 4th ordered observation, which is the number 21.

Do you note that the mean and the median are equal? They will be approximately equal (such as within 5% of each other) as long as the distribution of the set of data is somewhat symmetric without extreme values (signals or outliers) to one side or the other. This is an important point. Suppose we had an outlier or signal cycle time of 38 instead of 23. Let's calculate the mean and the median:

Mean = (19, 20, 20, 21, 22, 22, 38)/7 = 23.14

Median = (7 + 1)/2 = 4th ordered observation, which is 21: The mean was "pulled" to the outlier value of 38 - the mean is not resistant to extreme values, but the median is since it is a location and not arithmetic measure. Note that the mean is about 10% greater than the median: 21 is more representative of the centre when the distribution is not symmetric. As an aside, economists generally use the median when reporting the measure of centre for housing values since sets of housing data are often skewed by high or low extreme values.

It would be misleading or even unethical to report the mean housing value as a measure of centre when there are extreme values on the high side - the median is more representative of centre in that case. Also note that when the mean > median, the distribution is skewed right . Similarly, when the mean < median, the distribution would beskewed left . Before we go on, let me show you how to compute the median with an even set of data. Suppose we have the numbers 19, 20, 20, 21, 22, 22, 23, and 23.

The median is:

Median = (n + 1)/2 = (8 + 1)/2 = 4.5th ordered observation; the number at the 4.5th location is the average between the 4th and 5th numbers or 21.5 Let's return to the made up one more example of the quiz on which you made a three discussed previously in the module Introduction to Central Tendency and shown in Table.

Table. Three Possible Datasets for the 5-point Make-up Quiz.

Student	Dataset 1	Dataset 2	Dataset 3
You	3	3	3
John's	3	4	2
Maria's	3	4	2
Shareecia's	3	4	2
Luther's	3	5	1

For Dataset 1, the median is three, the same as your score. For Dataset 2, the median is 4. Therefore, your score is below the median. This means you are in the lower half of the class. Finally for Dataset 3, the median is 2. For this dataset, your score is above the median and therefore in the upper half of the distribution. Computation of the Median: When there is an odd number of numbers, the median is simply the middle number. For example, the median of 2, 4, and 7 is 4. When there is an even number of numbers, the median is the mean of the two middle numbers.

Thus, the median of the numbers 2, 4, 7, 12 is:

4 + 7

2

= 5.5.

Mode

Sometimes you hear of the mode as a measure of central tendency. However, the mode is simply the most frequently appearing number in a data set, so there are actually two modes in the above distribution, 20 and 22. We will not be using the mode as a measure of central tendency, but only to help in general examination of shape.

The mode is the most frequently occurring value. For the data in the table, Number of touchdown passes, the mode is 18 since more teams (4) had 18 touchdown passes than any other number of touchdown passes. With continuous data such as response time measured to many decimals, the frequency of each value is one since no two scores will be exactly the same. Therefore the mode of continuous data is normally computed from a grouped frequency distribution. The Grouped frequency distribution table shows a grouped frequency distribution for the target response time data. Since the interval with the highest frequency is 600-700, the mode is the middle of that interval (650).

Table. Grouped Frequency Distribution

Range	Frequency
500-600	3
600-700	6
700-800	5
800-900	5
900-1000	0
1000-1100	1

Pause and Reflect

The mean and the median are measures of centre. The mean and median will be approximately equal for symmetric sets of data. The median is resistant to extreme values, whereas the mean is pulled towards them. When the mean > median, the distribution is skewed right by an extreme value(s) > mean. When the mean < median, the distribution is skewed left by an extreme value(s) < mean.

Thus, for sets of data with extreme values, the median is more representative of the centre, and is the preferred measure. Alternatively, the extreme values could be removed from the data for separate study, and a new, more accurate arithmetic mean can then be computed.

MEASURES OF VARIATION

Range

Equally important to describing the centre of a set of data with a numerical measure, is describing the spread or variation in a set of data. There are three classic ways to measure variation.

The simplest measure of spread is the range. In the data set, 19, 20, 20, 21, 22, 22, 23.

Range = Maximum Number—Minimum Number = 23–19 = 4

So there is a spread of four days between the smallest and largest cycle times.

Standard Deviation

The range is not very rich - it ignores all but two numbers. If the distribution is approximately normal or a symmetric bell-shape, the classic measure of variation is the standard deviation. To set the stage for the standard deviation, recall that the mean of these numbers is 21. The number 19 varies from 21 by – 2, the number 20 varies by -1, the number 23 by +2, and so forth.

The standard deviation is simply a measure of the average of these deviations. To compute the standard deviation for a population of numbers 19, 20, 20, 21, 22, 22, 23; first find the mean (we already did that, it is 21).

Now subtract each number from the mean, square the result (to get rid of plusses and minuses), sum the resulting squared deviations, and divide by the number of numbers. This is called the variance of the population.

The standard deviation of the population (the symbol is the Greek letter sigma) is the square root of the variance:

Mean = (19 + 20 + 20 + 21 + 22 + 22 + 23)/7 = 21

Sum of Squared Deviations = $(19 - 21)^2 + (20 - 21)^2 + (20 - 21)^2 + (21 - 21)^2 + (22 - 21)^2 + (22 - 21)^2 + (23 - 21)^2 =$ 4+1+1+0+1+1+4 = 12

Variance = 12/7 = 1.714

Standard Deviation = Square Root of 1.714 = 1.3

The standard deviation for a sample (the symbol is the letter s) is similar to the above, but the variance is computed by dividing the sum of squared deviations by the number of numbers minus one (n – 1).

We will adjust the sample size to n – 1 again, and refer to this as degrees of freedom. For large sample sizes, the impact of dividing by n – 1 versus dividing by n is negligible. For small samples, it makes a difference so dividing by n – 1 gives a larger or more conservative estimate of the spread. If the above set of data is a sample, the variance and standard deviation are:

Mean = 21

Sum of Squared Deviations = 12

Variance = 12/(7 – 1) = 2

Standard Deviation = S = Square Root of 2 = 1.4

The standard deviation is interpreted with respect to the mean. For symmetric bell-shaped sets of data, the interpretation of the standard deviation is:

95% (most) of the observations fall between the mean + 2 Std Dev

This can be combined with areas incorporating 1 and 3 standard deviations to completely describe a set of approximately symmetric, bell-shaped data:

68% of the observations fall between the mean + 1 Std Dev

95% of the observations fall between the mean + 2 Std Dev

99.7% (almost all or 100%) of the observations fall between the mean + 3 Std Dev

This very important property is called the Empirical Rule - it applies to all symmetric bell shaped sets of data. We will apply it later when we get to a larger example.

Interquartile Range

The third measure of spread or variation is the interqu-artile range (IQR). To compute this measure, we need the 1st and 3rd quartiles (Q1 and Q3, respectively). Twenty five per cent of the ordered observations in a set of data is contained within a quartile, so 25% of the observations are below the first quartile, 50% of the observations are below the 2nd quartile (Q2, also called the Median), and 75% of the observations are below the 3rd. The IQR is simple Q3 – Q1. Here are the computations, using the numbers 19, 20, 20, 21, 22, 22, 24.

Q1 = (n + 1)/4 ordered observation = 0.25 (7 + 1) = 2nd ordered observation which is the first number 20.

where "*" is symbol for multiplication

Q3 = 3 (n + 1)/4 ordered observation = 0.75 (7 + 1) = 6th ordered observation which is the second number 22 in the ordered array.

IQR = Q3 – Q1 = 22 – 20 = 2 days

The middle 50% of the data falls within the IQR. Sometimes, analysts like to expand the location measure of spread by reporting the five number summary: Minimum, Q1, Median, Q3, Maximum

Pause and Reflect Pause and Reflect

The standard deviation and the interquartile range are measures of spread or variation. The standard deviation is associated with the mean and is an accurate measure of spread for symmetric bell-shaped distributions.

The IQR is generally associated with the median, and is an accurate measure of spread for non-symmetric distributions. With two numerical measures (mean and standard deviation; or median and IQR) we gain much knowledge about a data set - even data sets of thousands of numbers.

RELATIVE MEASURES

Symmetry

There are some quick numerical measures than can be used to supplement frequency distribution charts to determine if the distribution is symmetric, bell-shaped or skewed.

They are:

- Set of Data is skewed to left if mean < median
- Set of Data is skewed to right if mean > median
- Set of Data is symmetric, bell shaped if:
  - Mean is approximately equal to median
  - Empirical rule is met

$$IQR = 1.33 \times \text{Standard Deviation(Approx.)}$$

We will try the above rules of thumb when we illustrate the Excel descriptive statistics with a larger sample later.

Variation

The coefficient of variation is a useful tool when comparing the variation of one distribution to that of another, especially if the distributions have different units of measurement.

Coefficient of variation = (standard deviation/mean) × 100%

For the example: (1.4/21) ×100% = 6.67%

Suppose another company experiences mean cycle time of 21 in their supply chain as well, but the standard deviation is 7 days. The coefficient of variation in this case is 33%, which reflects a process with much greater variability than one with 6.67% coefficient of variation.

Observations

Relative measures of observations are useful to give observations context within a data set. The percentile is a relative measure of location for a number in an ordered array. We already discussed examples of percentiles, since the first quartile is actually the 25th percentile - 25% of the data in an ordered array are below the 25th percentile. Perhaps you recall your percentile score on college entrance exams. If you scored in the 90th percentile on the SAT, 90 per cent of the ordered scores were below yours.

To find the 90th percentile, order the observations, then compute 90th percentile = 0.90 (n + 1) to find the ordered observation of interest. If n = 780, then we would be looking for the 703rd number. For distributions that are approximately symmetric, bell-shaped, the Z–Score or Z– Value is a powerful relative measure for observations. The Z-Score is simply the number of standard deviations an observation is from the mean. So when we find the Z -Score of a number, we standardize that number. What is the Z-Score for the number 19.6 in a distribution with a mean of 21 and standard deviation of 1.4?

Z = (observation - mean)/standard deviation = (19.6 – 21)/1.4 = –1

We would say that the number 19.6 is 1 standard deviation from (to the left of) the mean of 21. Z-Scores have associated probabilities. Do you recall that 68% of the observations in a symmetric bell-shaped distribution fall between the mean and + 1 standard deviation? That "1" standard deviation is the Z-Score!

Note also the 68% - we can find the probability for getting any Z-Score as long as the set of data is normal or is approximately symmetric bell-shaped. For example, what is the probability of getting an observation less than 19.6 days? We know that theoretically, the range of data from 19.6 to 22.4 days includes 68% of the data, and since we have to have 100% of the data accounted for, 100% - 68% or 32% of the data must include numbers up to 19.6 and above 22.4.

Since we assume these distributions are symmetric, 16% of the data is up to 19.6 and 16% is above 24. So, for a symmetric bell shaped distribution with mean of 21 and standard deviation of 1.4, the probability of observing a number less than 19.6 is 0.16 or 16%.; the probability of observing a number greater than 19.6 is simply 100% - 16% or 84%.

USING EXCEL FOR THE COMPUTATIONS

We will use the Data Analysis Tool and Statistical Functions to produce the descriptive statistics we have discussed thus far. The quickest way to generate a family of descriptive statistics is to use the Data Analysis Descriptive Statistics Tool. First create a column of the cycle times as shown in that Worksheet (or if you saved that example, copy C1:C31 to a new area of your worksheet past the histogram, such as Column J). I placed the numbers in column J, starting with the title "Time" in Row 1, and the 30 cycle times in J2 to J31. The data doesn't have to be sorted to compute the descriptive statistics, but it can be.

Now select Tools from the Standard Toolbar, then Data Analysis from the pulldown menu, then select Descriptive Statistics and follow the dialog box requests as you did in creating the histogram. For output options, select summary statistics and Confidence Level for the Mean, leaving the confidence level default at 95%. I also like to put the output close to my data and histogram if I created a histogram for the data. Remember that you only have to enter one cell location for the Output Range, such as L1, and that cell will define the upper left-hand corner of the range of cells needed for the output - just be sure that the worksheet is clear below and to the right of the cell you select. Note that you can put your output on a separate worksheet or even in a separate workbook if you like.

You should get Worksheet 1 below:

Worksheet:

Time	
Mean	21.07
Standard Error	0.54
Median	21
Mode	21
Standard Deviation	2.94
Sample Variance	8.62
Kurtosis	0.90
Skewness	0.89
Range	13
Minimum	16
Maximum	29
Sum	632
Count	30
Confidence Level(95.0%)	1.10

We have discussed the Mean, Median, Mode, Standard Deviation, Sample Variance, Range, Minimum, Maximum, Sum and Count (number of observations). You may ignore Kurtosis (a mathematical measure of the concentration of data around the centre compared to the tails of the distribution) and Skewness (a mathematical measure of the symmetry of the distribution).

The Descriptive Statistics tool provides everything we have discussed then, except Q3 and Q1. To get these, we need to use the Function feature of Excel. As for all Excel Functions, position the cursor in a cell or select the cell in which you want the quartile, for example M31. Select Insert from the Standard Toolbar, then Function, then Statistical(in left box of Paste Function dialog screen), then Quartile (scroll down to find Quartile in right box of dialog screen), then follow the dialog screen by inserting the cell range for your data (*e.g.*, L2:L30), and 1 for Q1.

The resulting cell formula is =QUARTILE(L2:L30, 1).

Note that no labels are allowed so I started the cell range with L2 rather than L1. You should get the results in Worksheet 2 repeated this process for the third quartile, Q3, which I placed in M32. I also added the formula =(M32 – M31) in cell M33 to get the interquartile range. I added the labels in cells L31, L32, and L33 for clarity since the function feature does not insert the title of the function.

Worksheet:

First Quartile, Q1 = 19

Third Quartile, Q3 = 22
Interquartile Range = 3

Lets use the above descriptive statistics to completely describe the set of data.

Location Measures of Centre and Spread

Fifty per cent of the ordered observations fall below the median of 21 days. Twenty-five per cent of the ordered observations fall below the first quartile of 19 days; and 75% of the ordered observations fall below the third quartile of 22 days. The interquartile range is 3 days from 19 to 22, representing the middle 50% of the ordered observations. The five number summary is complete when we add the minimum value of 16 and maximum of 29 days.

Arithmetic Measures of Centre and Spread

The mean is 21.07, or simply 21 days depending on the accuracy we need for reporting purposes. The standard deviation is 2.94 or, rounded, 3 days. The interpretation: most or 95% of the observations fall within the interval:

$$\text{Mean} + 2s = 21 + (2 \times 3) \text{ or } 15 \text{ to } 27 \text{ days.}$$

To use the Empirical Rule to completely summarize a set of data which is approximately symmetric and bell-shaped, and having a mean of 21 and standard deviation of 3:

68% of the observations are within 21 ± (1 × 3): 18 to 24 days.
95% of the observations are within 21 ± (2 × 3): 15 to 27 days.
100% of the observations are within 21 ± (3 × 3): 12 to 30 days.

From the above, we would not expect any observations below 12 days or above 30. Such observations would be outliers.

Percentile

To find the percentile using Excel, select Insert on the Standard Toolbar, then Function, then Statistical, then Percentile, and then respond to the dialogue box by entering the cell range for your numbers and the desired percentile. For example, to get the 25th percentile for this illustration, the resulting cell formula will be: = Percentile (L2: L31, 0.25). The percentile will be placed in your spread sheet wherever you have the cursor (active cell).

The Z-Score

What is the Z-Score for the number 18?

$$\text{Z-Score} = (\text{number} - \text{mean})/\text{standard deviation} = (18 - 21)/3 = -1$$

So, 18 is one standard deviation to the left of the mean of 21. What is the Z-Score for the number 24?

$$\text{Z-Score} = (24 - 21)/3 = 1$$

The number 24 is one standard deviation to the right of the mean. To get the Z-Score from Excel, we use the Standardize function. Position the cursor or point and click in a cell in which you want to place the Z-Score, such as

Q2. Select Insert from the Standard Toolbar, then Function, then Statistical, then Standardize and respond to the dialog box questions. You should replicate the cell formula = Standardize (18,21,3) which gives a Z-Score of – 1. I actually prefer to use the cell address for the number 18 so that I can copy the standardize cell reference to standardize a whole row or column of numbers.

This would be = Standardize (L6,21,3). I then add a title to the column, such as "Z-Scores." The fifth requirement in Project Assignment 1 is to standardize (generate Z-Scores) for your column of data. Z-Scores are very handy ways of identifying outliers. Any Z-Score below -3 or above +3 would identify a number more than 3 standard deviations from the mean. The sixth requirement in Project Assignment 1 is to remove any outliers from your data, and re-compute the descriptive statistics. Outliers are quickly identified by Z-Scores. Removing an outlier from a real data set doesn't mean we can ignore it for analysis - it just means we should analyse it separately from the data.

A side note: To remove a data element from a column of numbers in Excel means to remove it, not type over the number with a zero. To remove a number, point and click to it, selectEdit on the Standard Toolbar, then Clear from the pulldown menu, then select Contents. This creates a blank space where the number once resided. If you want to remove the number and the space, select Edit, then Delete from the pulldown menu, then check Shift cells up if you have a column of data, or Shift cells left if you have a row of data.

The Probability for the Z-Score

Excel has a statistical function that automatically computes the probabilities for Z-Scores. Let's find the probability of getting a cycle time below 18 days (remember, time is a continuous variable, so a number below 18 could be 17.9999). If you know the Z-Score for a number, the NORMSDIST function will give a cumulative probability for the area under a symmetric bell-shaped distribution up to that Z-Score. Normsdist stands for Standardized Normal Distribution. Position the cursor or point and click in a cell in which you want the probability.

Select Insert, then Function, then Statistical, then Normsdist and simply enter the Z-Score of -1. You should get 0.158655 or 0.16 or 16%. The probability of obtaining an observation less than 18 days is 0.16 or 16%. What is the probability of obtaining an observation greater than 18?

You guessed it: 100% – 16% = 84%.

The seventh item in Project Assignment 1 is to compute the probability of exceeding the 45th ordered (sorted) observation in your data set. If you have more or less than 50 observations, compute the process capability for the 5th from the last ordered observation. There are some alternative Excel procedures and manipulations, but we have described the important basics.

What if you want the probability of getting a cycle time below 18 days but do not know the Z-Score? Use the Excel Function Normsdist function.

Point and click to a cell where you want the probability, select Insert from the Standard Toolbar, thenFunction, then Statistical, then NORMDIST and respond to the dialog box questions by entering the number, mean, standard deviation and the work TRUE). The cell formula would look like this: = Normsdist (18,21,3,TRUE).

The Normal Distribution

Before we close this set of notes with one more example, let me say a few words about the normal distribution. The mean, standard deviation, Z-Scores and normal probabilities or probabilities for Z-Scores all depend on the distribution being approximately symmetric bell-shaped or "Normal". The distributions will never be perfectly bell-shaped in real life, but they don't have to be - approximately normal is fine, especially if we have at least 30 observations. So, how do you know if the distribution is normal?

Here are some general rules of thumb:

- Check the histogram to see if it has a symmetric bell shape, without outliers (any observation with a Z-Score greater than +3 or less than –3).
- The mean should be approximately equal to the median. For this example, 21.07 is approximately equal to 21.
- The interquartile range should be close to 1.33 times the standard deviation. Here, the IQR of 3 is fairly close to 1.33 times 2.94 (3.9) although we would like this somewhat closer.
- Check theoretical ranges of the empirical rule and compare them to the actual data.
  - 68% of the data should be between 18 and 24. The actual count is 26 out of 30 or 80%.
  - 95% of the data should be between 15 and 27. The actual count is 29 out of 30 or 96.7%.
  - 100% of the data should be between 12 and 30. The actual count is 30 our of 30, or 100%.
  - Most of the rules of thumb work for this cycle time example. Lets look at an example where there is an outlier.

PUTTING IT TOGETHER WITH ONE MORE EXAMPLE

What if the 31st observation was 38? We already know that 100% of the observations should fall within the range of 12 to 30, so 38 is more than 3 standard deviations from the mean - do you remember what we called that - yes, an outlier or a signal.

Process Control Chart

Suppose you created a process control chart to monitor the cycle time process based on the original 30 observations. The mean of the chart is 21, the upper control limit for a process is the mean plus three standard deviations or 21 + (3 × 3) = 30. The lower control limit is the mean minus three standard deviations or 21 – (3 × 3) = 12. These are upper and lower control limits for processes since we expect nearly 100% of the observations generated by a process to be within the area of the mean + 3 Std Dev. The Upper Specification Limit of 24 is set by the boss or the customer, or whomever - it is not set by statistics.

Here is the process control chart:

Worksheet:

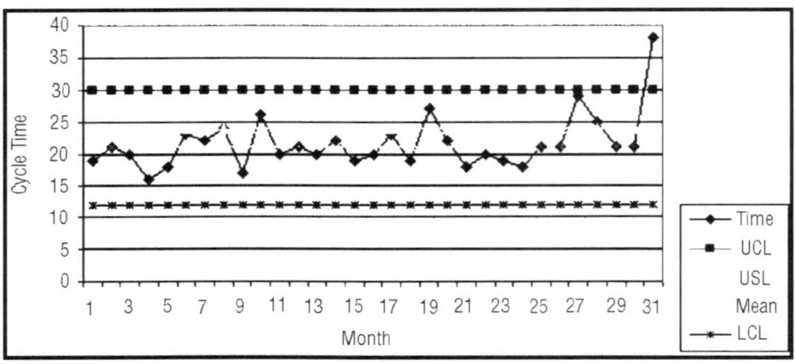

Fig. Cycle Time Process Control Chart

Note that the 31st observation is above the UCL and would justify investigation as a signal that the process has gone out of control. Let's confirm this with finding the probability of getting an observation of 38 or greater, with a process mean of 21 and standard deviation of 3. First, the Z-Score computation:

Z-Score = (number – mean)/Std Dev = (38 – 21)/3 = 5.67

Now, find the probability using NORMSDIST function of Excel.

The cell formula is: =NORMDIST(5.67) = 0.99999999

Recall, this is the cumulative probability of observing a number LESS than 38. So to get the probability of observing a number greater than 38, take 1.0 –.99999999 = 0.00000001 or there is a 0% probability of observing a 38 if the mean is 21 and the standard deviation is 3 - that's why its called a signal or outlier.

Before leaving the process control chart, let's focus for a moment on the upper specification limit set usually by the boss or customer. The USL is 24. Way back at the beginning of this note set, we indicated that there is no way we can please the boss with an upper specification limit of 24. Now you should be able to say why that is so. With a mean of 21 and a standard deviation of 3, we know that 24 is +1 standard deviations from the mean (z- score = (24 – 21)/3 = + 1). The probability of getting an observation above 24 is found by first getting the probability of a number less than 24: = Normsdist (+1) = 0.84 This process is only capable of satisfying the customer 84% of the time - that is a measure of process capability.

Now, to get the probability of finding a number above 24: 1.0 – 0.84 = 0.16. There is a 16% probability of getting an observation above 24 – that is why the customer will not be pleased. An upper specification limit one standard deviation above the mean is a 1 sigma process – GE's goal is to have Six sigma processes - specification limits 6 standard deviations from the mean.

Descriptive Statistics

What if you were just starting out and collected 31 observations and had no prior knowledge of the mean, standard deviation, median, IQR or histogram. You would first generate the histogram, as shown in Worksheet 4 below.

Worksheet:

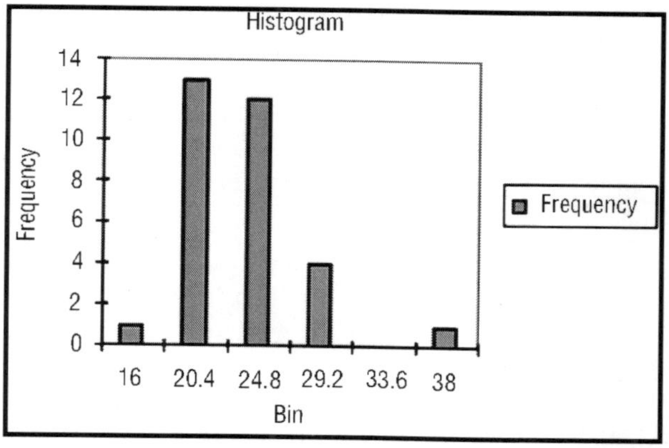

By observation, we would say there is an outlier to the right of the range of the data, thus making a distribution that is skewed right. If we needed to report the centre and spread of the skewed distribution we would use the...that's right, the median and interquartile range.

Here are the descriptive statistics:

Worksheet:

Time	
Mean	21.61
Standard Error	0.75
Median	21
Mode	21
Standard Deviation	4.19
Sample Variance	17.58

Kurtosis	7.04
Skewness	2.22
Range	22
Minimum	16
Maximum	38
Sum	670
Count	31
Confidence Level(95.0%)	1.54
1st Quartile =	19
3rd Quartile =	22.5
Interquartile Range =	3.5

Using this data, we see that the mean is now greater than the median, confirming the right skew. Note that the median remains 21, as with the original data set. The mean is larger since the outlier is pulling it to the right. Note also the standard deviation is 4.19 or 4.2 which is considerably inflated from the original data with its standard deviation of 3. Outliers always increase the standard deviation.

To confirm that 38 is an outlier with this data, we standardize: = Standardize(38,21.6,4.2) = 4.05 Thirty-eight is more than 3 standard deviations from the mean. In a real project, we would segregate the 38 from the rest of the data, investigate and make corrections, and redo the descriptive analysis without the outlier.

This is precisely what you may have to do with your data in Project Assignment 1. Item 5 is to standardize your data, Item 6 is to remove outliers and re-compute the descriptive statistics. Data without outliers is likely to be symmetric, bell shaped if there was no bias in data collection. Inferential statistics for the mean of a distribution, which includes confidence intervals and tests of hypothesis, work best with symmetric bell shaped distributions.

OPTIONAL MATERIAL ON THE MEAN

Here focused on the arithmetic mean, the typical measure of central tendency, and the measure used in inferential statistics. There are two other means I should briefly mention: the weighted mean, and the geometric mean.

Weighted Mean

The weighted mean is a special case of the arithmetic mean used when there are several observations of the same value. Suppose you had cycle times of 21, 23, 19, 22, and 20, which gives an arithmetic mean of 21 days. But suppose further that cycle time 21 happened 20 times, 23 happened 5 times, 19 happened 50 times, 22 happened 10 times, and 20 happened 15 times. The mean cycle time weighted by frequency of occurrence, or simply the weighted mean is:

- Weighted mean = sum of weights × observation/sum of weights where weights are frequency of occurrence in this example.
- Weighted mean = (21 × 20 + 23 × 5 + 19 × 50 + 22 × 10 + 20 × 15)/100 = 20

Geometric Mean

The geometric mean applies when we are interested in computing the mean for interest and growth rates, percentages, and ratios. Suppose you have a CD paying 10% interest in Year 1, and then 4% interest in Year 2.

The arithmetic mean interest rate is:

Mean interest rate, i = (0.10 + 0.04) /2 = 0.07 or 7%

However, to take into account the compounding effect, the geometric mean gives a more precise outcome:

Geometric mean = (1 + i) = nth root [(1+i) × (1+i)]

= square root [(1+0.10) × (1+0.04)] = 1.0696 or 6.958 %

Let's check this with $95,000:

95,000 × 0.10 = 9500 (Year One)

(95000 + 9500) × 0.04 = 4180 (Year Two)

Total Interest = 9500 + 4180 = 13680

The geometric mean: 95000 × 0.6958 = 6610

(95000 + 6610) × 0.04 = 7070

Total Interest = 6610 + 7070 = 13680

The arithmetic mean: 95000 × 0.07 = 6650

(95000 + 6650) × 0.07 = 7115

Total Interest = 6650 + 7115 = 13765

The geometric mean gives the truer figure in recognition of the compounding effect. In general: geometric mean = nth root [$x_1x_2...x_n$] where all x values must be positive.

A second application of the geometric mean is to find the per cent increase, or growth rate, over time. Suppose the University gave the College of Business the following head count growth targets: 182 MBA students in 2001 and 344 MBA students in 2005.

The geometric mean per cent increase over time is:

= (n–1) root of [value at end of period/value at beginning of period] – 1

= (5 years – 1) or 4th root of [344/182] – 1

= .1725 or 17.25%

3

Describing Data: Displaying and Exploring Data

Pie charts, bar charts, and histograms are graphic displays of numerical data—simple collections of numbers made more understandable by use of visuals. As an example, consider the yearly expenditures of a college undergraduate. After collecting her data (expense records) for the past year, she finds the expenditures shown in Table.

Table. Yearly Expenses of a College Undergraduate.

Item	Amount
Tuition fees	$5,000
Room and board	9,000
Books and lab	2,000
Clothes/cleaning	1,000
Transportation	2,000
Insurance and miscellaneous	1,000

These figures, although presented in categories, do not allow for easy analysis. The reader must expend extra effort in order to compare amounts spent or relate individual proportions to the total. For ease of analysis, these data can be presented pictorially.

BAR CHART

In presentation graphics, a type of graph in which different values are represented by rectangular bars. A bar chart is made up of columns or rows plotted on a graph. Here is how to read a bar chart made up of columns. The columns are positioned over a label that represents a categorical variable.

The height of the column indicates the size of the group defined by the column label. And here is how to read bar chart made up of rows. The rows extend from labels that represent a categorical variable. The length of the row indicates the size of the group defined by the row label.

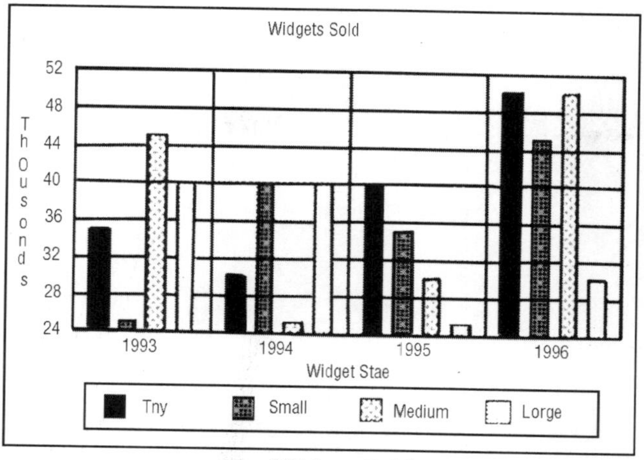

Fig. Widget Sold

Example: The following table lists the number of seats allocated to each party group in European elections in 1999 and 2004.

The results of 1999 have been multiplied by 1.16933, to compensate for the change in number of seats between those years. This bar chart shows both the results of 2004, and those of 1999:

DOT PLOTS: A USEFUL ALTERNATIVE TO BAR CHARTS

Readers make a number of judgments when reading graphs: they may judge the length of a line, the area of a wedge of a circle, the position of a point along a common scale, the slope of a line, or a number of other attributes of the points, lines, and bars that are plotted.

A dotplot is a type of graphic display used to compare frequency counts within categories or groups.

DOTPLOT OVERVIEW

As you might guess, a dotplot is made up of dots plotted on a graph. Here is how to interpret a dotplot. Each dot can represent a single observation from a set of data, or a specified number of observations from a set of data.

The dots are stacked in a column over a category, so that the height of the column represents the relative or absolute frequency of observations in the category.

The pattern of data in a dotplot can be described in terms of symmetry and skewness only if the categories are quantitative. If the categories are qualitative (as they often are), a dotplot cannot be described in those terms.

Compared to other types of graphic display, dotplots are used most often to plot frequency counts within a small number of categories, usually with small sets of data.

DOTPLOT EXAMPLE

Here is an example to show what a dotplot looks like and how to interpret it. Suppose 30 first graders are asked to pick their favourite colour. Their choices can be summarized in a dotplot, as shown below.

<table>
<tr><td>*</td><td></td><td></td><td></td><td></td><td></td><td></td></tr>
<tr><td>*</td><td></td><td></td><td></td><td></td><td></td><td></td></tr>
<tr><td>*</td><td></td><td></td><td></td><td>*</td><td></td><td></td></tr>
<tr><td>*</td><td></td><td></td><td></td><td>*</td><td></td><td></td></tr>
<tr><td>*</td><td></td><td></td><td>*</td><td>*</td><td></td><td></td></tr>
<tr><td>*</td><td></td><td></td><td>*</td><td>*</td><td></td><td></td></tr>
<tr><td>*</td><td></td><td>*</td><td>*</td><td>*</td><td></td><td>*</td></tr>
<tr><td>*</td><td>*</td><td>*</td><td>*</td><td>*</td><td></td><td>*</td></tr>
<tr><td>*</td><td>*</td><td>*</td><td>*</td><td>*</td><td>*</td><td>*</td></tr>
<tr><td>Red</td><td>Orange</td><td>Yellow</td><td>Green</td><td>Blue</td><td>Indigo</td><td>Violet</td></tr>
</table>

Each dot represents one student, and the number of dots in a column represents the number of first graders who selected the colour associated with that column. For example, Red was the most popular colour (selected by 9 students), followed by Blue (selected by 7 students). Selected by only 1 student, Indigo was the least popular colour. In this example, note that the category (colour) is a qualitative variable; so it is not appropriate to talk about the symmetry or skewness of this dotplot. The dotplot in the next section uses a quantitative variable, so we will illustrate skewness and symmetry of dotplots in the next section.

TEST YOUR UNDERSTANDING OF THIS LESSON

Problem

The dot plotted below shows the number of televisions owned by each family on a city block.

<table>
<tr><td></td><td></td><td>*</td><td></td><td></td><td></td><td></td><td></td><td></td></tr>
<tr><td></td><td></td><td>*</td><td>*</td><td></td><td></td><td></td><td></td><td></td></tr>
<tr><td></td><td>*</td><td>*</td><td>*</td><td>*</td><td></td><td></td><td></td><td></td></tr>
<tr><td></td><td>*</td><td>*</td><td>*</td><td>*</td><td>*</td><td></td><td></td><td></td></tr>
<tr><td>*</td><td>*</td><td>*</td><td>*</td><td>*</td><td>*</td><td>*</td><td>*</td><td>*</td></tr>
<tr><td>0</td><td>1</td><td>2</td><td>3</td><td>4</td><td>5</td><td>6</td><td>7</td><td>8</td></tr>
</table>

Which of the following statements are true?

- The distribution is right-skewed with no outliers.
- The distribution is right-skewed with one outlier.
- The distribution is left-skewed with no outliers.
- The distribution is left-skewed with one outlier.
- The distribution is symmetric.

Solution

The correct answer is (A). Most of the observations are on the left side of the distribution, so the distribution is right-skewed. And none of the observations is extreme, so there are no outliers.

PIE CHART

A pie chart is a way of summarizing a set of categorical data or displaying the different values of a given variable (*e.g.*, percentage distribution). This type of chart is a circle divided into a series of segments. Each segment represents a particular category. The area of each segment is the same proportion of a circle as the category is of the total data set. Pie charts usually show the component parts of a whole. Often you will see a segment of the drawing separated from the rest of the pie in order to emphasize an important piece of information.

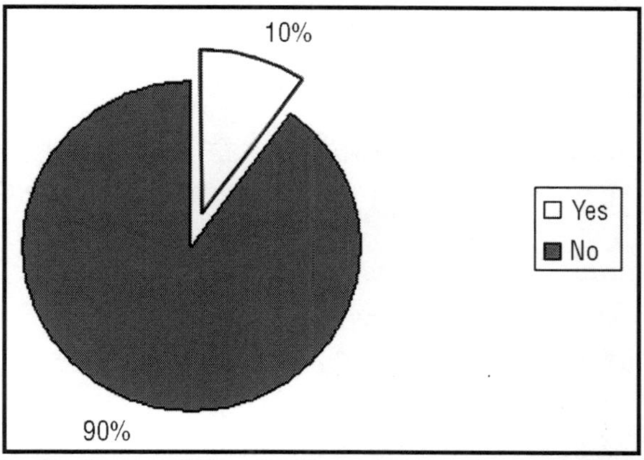

Fig. Student and Faculty Response to the Poll 'Should Avenue High School Adopt Student Uniforms?'

The pie chart above clearly shows that 90% of all students and faculty members at Avenue High School do not want to have a uniform dress code and that only 10% of the school population would like to adopt school uniforms. This point is clearly emphasized by its visual separation from the rest of the pie.

The use of the pie chart is quite popular, as the circle provides a visual concept of the whole (100%). Pie charts are also one of the most commonly used charts because they are simple to use. Despite its popularity, pie charts should be used sparingly for two reasons. First, they are best used for displaying statistical information when there are no more than six components only—otherwise, the resulting picture will be too complex to understand. Second, pie charts are not useful when the values of each component are similar because it is difficult to see the differences between slice sizes.

A pie chart uses percentages to compare information. Percentages are used because they are the easiest way to represent a whole. The whole is equal to 100%. For example, if you spend 7 hours at school and 55 minutes of that time is spent eating lunch, then 13.1% of your school day was spent eating lunch. To present this in a pie chart, you would need to find out how many degrees represent 13.1%.

This calculation is done by developing the equation:

Per cent ÷ 100 x 360 degrees = the number of degrees

This ratio works because the total per cent of the pie chart represents 100% and there are 360 degrees in a circle. Therefore 47.1 degrees of the circle (13.1%) represents the time spent eating lunch.

Constructing a Pie Chart

A pie chart is constructed by converting the share of each component into a percentage of 360 degrees. In Figure 2, music preferences in 14- to 19-year-olds are clearly shown.

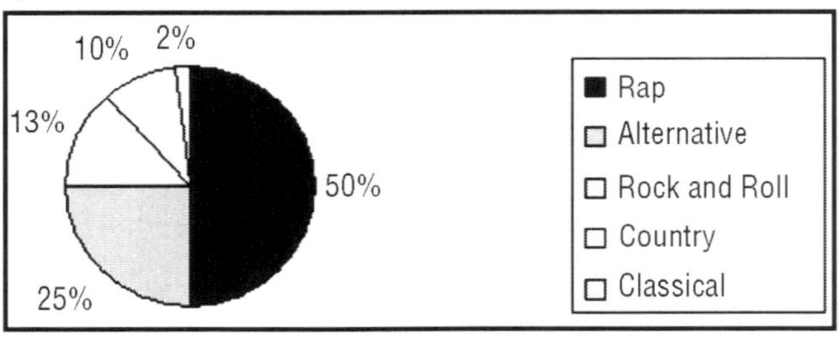

Fig. Music Preferences in Young Adults 14 to 19

The pie chart quickly tells you that:

- The majority of students like rap best (50%), and
- The remaining students prefer alternative (25%), rock and roll (13%), country (10%) and classical (2%).

In order to reproduce this pie chart, follow this step-by-step approach: If 50% of the students liked rap, then 50% of the whole pie chart (360 degrees) would equal 180 degrees.

- Draw a circle with your protractor.
- Starting from the 12 o'clock position on the circle, measure an angle of 180 degrees with your protractor. The rap component should make up half of your circle. Mark this radius off with your ruler.
- Repeat the process for each remaining music category, drawing in the radius according to its percentage of 360 degrees. The final category need not be measured as its radius is already in position.

Labeling the segments with percentage values often makes it easier to tell quickly which segment is bigger. Whenever possible, the percentage and the category label should be indicated beside their corresponding segments. This way, users do not have to constantly look back at the legend in order to identify what category each colour represents.

Pie Charts Versus Bar Graphs

When displaying statistical information, refrain from using more than one pie chart for each figure. Figure 6 is an example of a double pie chart.

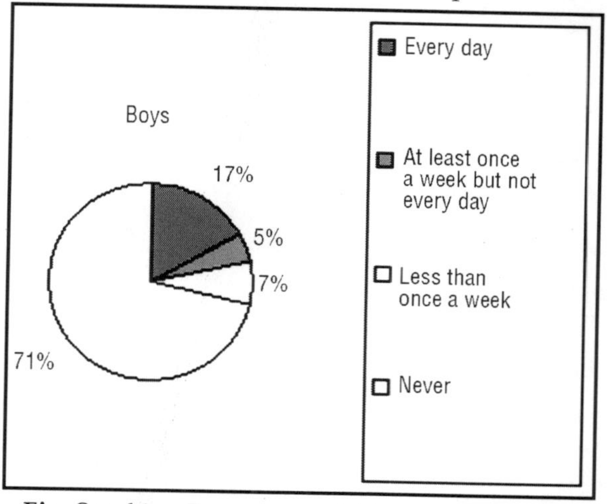

Fig. Smoking Frequency of 15-year-olds on the Parkview Secondary School Track and Field Team

Figure shows two pie charts side-by-side, where a split bar graph (two bar graphs back-to-back) would have shown the information more clearly. A user might find it difficult to compare a segment from one pie chart to the corresponding segment of the other pie chart. However, in a split bar graph, these segments become bars which are lined up back-to-back, making it much easier to make comparisons.

OGIVE (CUMULATIVE LINE GRAPH)

Data may be expressed using a single line. An ogive (a cumulative line graph) is best used when you want to display the total at any given time. The relative slopes from point to point will indicate greater or lesser increases; for example, a steeper slope means a greater increase than a more gradual slope. An ogive, however, is not the ideal graphic for showing comparisons between categories because it simply combines the values in each category and thus indicates an *accumulation*, a growing or lessening total. If you simply want to keep track of a total and your individual values are periodically combined, an ogive is an appropriate display.

For example, if you saved $300 in both January and April and $100 in each of February, March, May, and June, an ogive would look like below Figure .

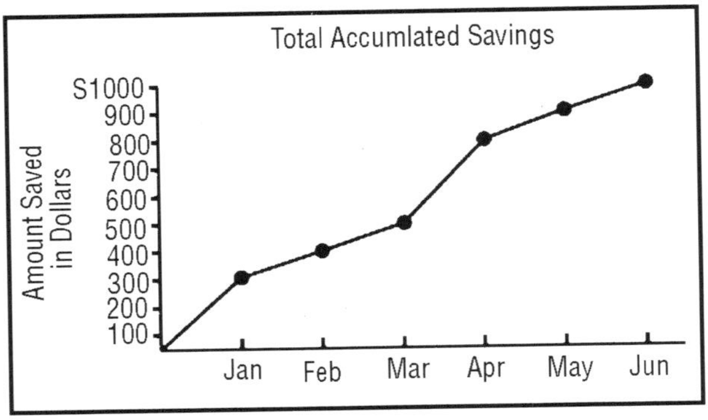

Fig. Ogive of Accumulated Savings for one year.

An ogive displays a *running total.* Although each individual month's savings could be expressed in a bar chart (as shown in Figure), you could not easily see the amount of total growth or loss, as you can in an ogive.

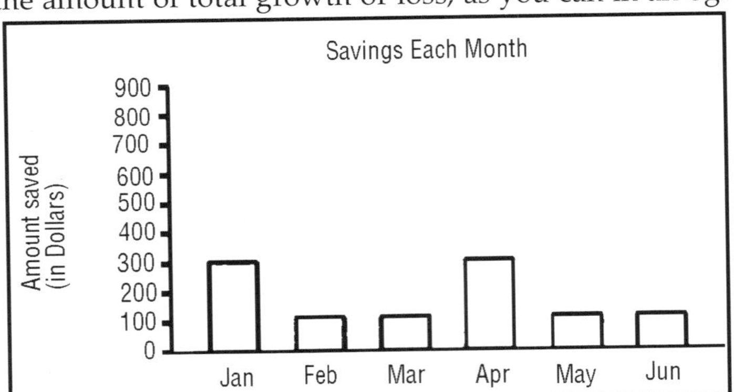

Fig. Vertical Bar Chart of Accumulated Savings for one year.

Th choice of graphic display, therefore, depends on what information is important for your purposes: percentages (parts of the whole), running total, comparisons of categories, and so forth.

FREQUENCY HISTOGRAM

One of the more commonly used pictorials in statistics is the frequency histogram, which in some ways is similar to a bar chart and tells how many items are in each numerical category. For example, suppose that after a garage sale, you want to determine which items were the most popular: the high-priced items, the low-priced items, and so forth. Let's say you sold a total of 32 items for the following prices: $1, $2, $2, $2, $5, $5, $5, $5, $7, $8, $10, $10, $10, $10, $11, $15, $15, $15, $19, $20, $21, $21, $25, $25, $29, $29, $29, $30, $30, $30, $35, $35.

The items sold *ranged* in price from $1 to $35. First, divide this range of $1 to $35 into a number of categories, called class intervals. Typically, no fewer than 5 or more than 20 class intervals work best for a frequency histogram. Choose the first class interval to include your lowest (smallest value) data and make sure that no *overlap* exists so that one piece of data does not fall into two class intervals.

For example, you would not have your first class interval be $1–$5 and your second class interval $5–$10 because the four items that sold for $5 would belong in both the first and the second intervals. Instead, use $1–$5 for the first interval and $6–$10 for the second. Class intervals are mutually exclusive.

First, make a table of how your data is distributed. The number of observations that falls into each class interval is called the class frequency.

Table Distribution of Items Sold at Garage Sale

Class	Interval	Frequency
1	$1-$5	8
2	$6-$10	6
3	$11-$15	4
4	$16-$20	2
5	$21-$25	4
6	$26-$30	6
7	$31-$35	2

Note that each class interval has the same width. That is, $1–$5 has a width of five dollars, inclusive; $6–$10 has a width of five dollars, inclusive; $11–$15 has a width of five dollars, inclusive, and so forth.

From the data, a frequency histogram would look like that shown in Figure:

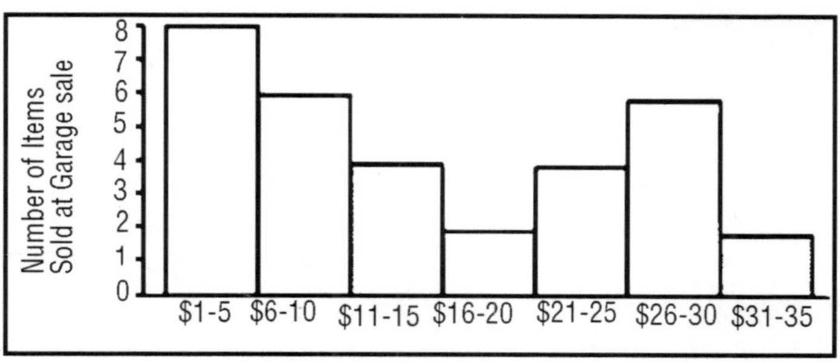

Fig. Frequency Histogram of Items Sold at a Garage Sale.

Unlike in a bar chart, the class intervals are drawn immediately adjacent to each other.

RELATIVE FREQUENCY HISTOGRAM

Relative Frequency Histogram

A relative frequency histogram compares each class interval to the total number of items. For example, the first interval ($1–$5) contains 8 out of the total of 32 items, so the relative frequency of the first class interval is 8/32. See Table.

Table. Distribution of Items Sold at Garage Sale, Including Relative Frequencies

Class	Interval	Frequency	Relative Frequency
1	$1-$5	8	.25
2	$6-$10	6	.1875
3	$11-$15	4	.125
4	$16-$20	2	.0625
5	$21-$25	4	.125
6	$26-$30	6	.1875
7	$31-$35	2	.0625

FREQUENCY POLYGON

Frequency polygons are a graphical device for understanding the shapes of distributions. They serve the same purpose as histograms, but are especially helpful for comparing sets of data. Frequency polygons are also a good choice for displaying *cumulative frequency distributions.*

To create a frequency polygon, start just as for histograms, by choosing a *class interval.* Then draw an X-axis representing the values of the scores in your data. Mark the middle of each class interval with a tick mark, and label it with the middle value represented by the class. Draw the Y-axis to indicate the frequency of each class. Place a point in the middle of each class interval at the height corresponding to its frequency. Finally, connect the points. You should include one class interval below the lowest value in your data and one above the highest value. The graph will then touch the X-axis on both sides.

A frequency polygon for 642 psychology test scores is shown in Figure. The first label on the X-axis is 35. This represents an interval extending from 29.5 to 39.5. Since the lowest test score is 46, this interval has a frequency of 0. The point labeled 45 represents the interval from 39.5 to 49.5. There are three scores in this interval.

There are 150 scores in the interval that surrounds 85. You can easily discern the shape of the distribution from Figure. Most of the scores are between 65 and 115. It is clear that the distribution is not symmetric inasmuch as good scores (to the right) trail off more gradually than poor scores (to the left). In the terminology of (where we will study shapes of distributions more systematically), the distribution is *skewed*

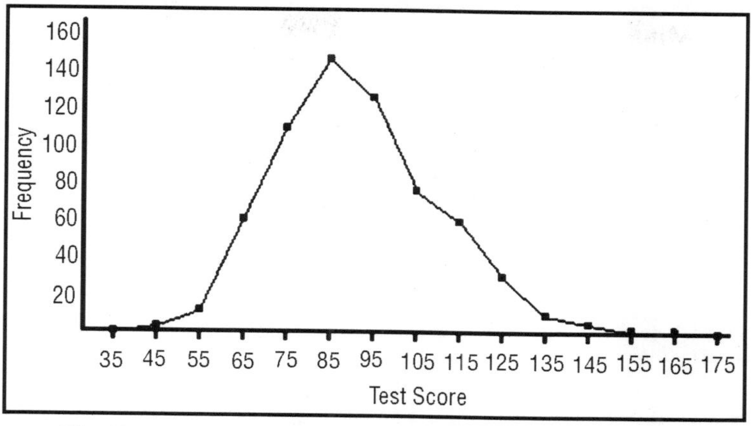

Fig. Frequency Polygon for the Psychology Test Scores.

A *cumulative frequency polygon* for the same test scores is shown in Figure. The graph is the same as before except that the Y value for each point is the number of students in the corresponding class interval plus all numbers in lower intervals.

For example, there are no scores in the interval labelled "35," three in the interval "45,"and 10 in the interval "55."Therefore the Y value corresponding to "55" is 13. Since 642 students took the test, the cumulative frequency for the last interval is 642.

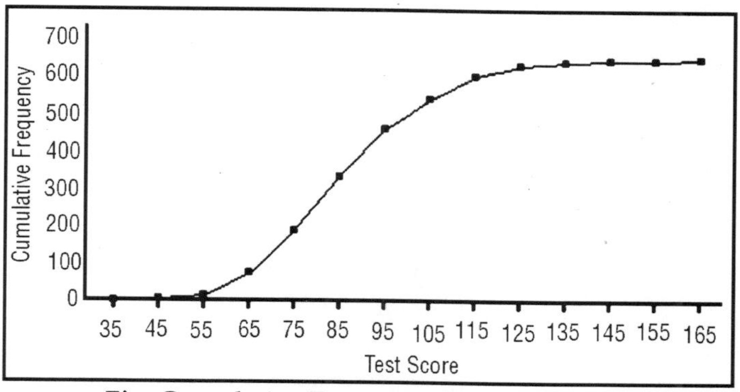

Fig. Cumulative Frequency Polygon for the Psychology Test Scores.

Frequency polygons are useful for comparing distri-butions. This is achieved by overlaying the frequency polygons drawn for different data sets. Figure 3 provides an example. The data come from a task in which the goal is to move a computer mouse to a target on the screen as fast as possible. On 20 of the trials, the target was a small rectangle; on the other 20, the target was a large rectangle. Time to reach the target was recorded on each trial.

The two distributions (one for each target) are plotted together in Figure. The figure shows that although there is some overlap in times, it generally took longer to move the mouse to the small target than to the large one.

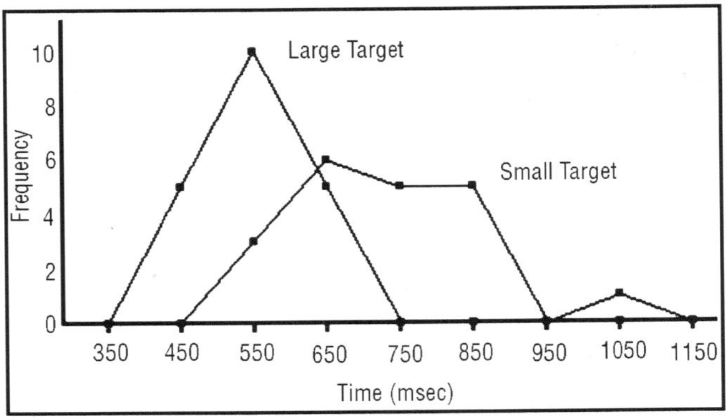

Fig. Overlaid Frequency Polygons.

It is also possible to plot two cumulative frequency distributions in the same graph. This is illustrated in Figure using the same data from the mouse task. The difference in distributions for the two targets is again evident.

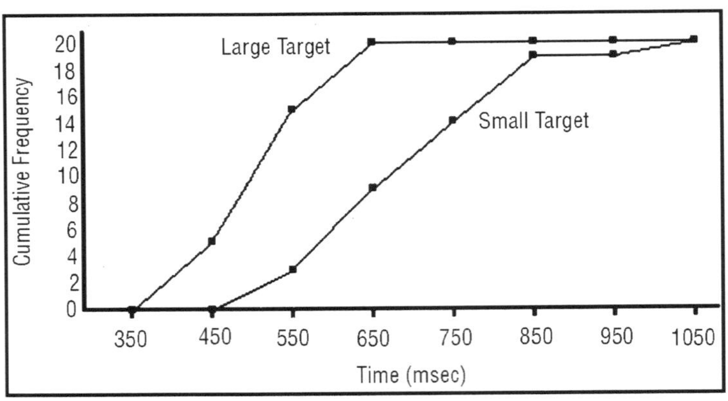

Fig. Overlaid Cumulative Frequency Polygons.

You might be curious about your own performance in the mouse task. Try the task yourself, and to compare your times with ours.

FREQUENCY DISTRIBUTION

Consider the following set of data which are the high temperatures recorded for 30 consequetive days. We wish to summarize this data by creating a frequency distribution of the temperatures.

Table. Data Set - High Temperatures for 30 Days.

50	45	49	50	43
49	50	49	45	49
47	47	44	51	51
44	47	46	50	44
51	49	43	43	49
45	46	45	51	46

To create a frequency distribtion from this data we proceed as follows:

- Identify the highest and lowest values in the data set. For our temperatures the highest temperature is 51 and the lowest temperature is 43.
- Create a column with the title of the variable we are using, in this case temperature. Enter the highest score at the top, and include all values within the range from the highest score to the lowest score.
- Create a tally column to keep track of the scores as you enter them into the frequency distribution. Once the frequency distribution is completed you can omit this column. Most printed frequency distributions do not retain the tally column in their final form.
- Create a frequency column, with the frequency of each value, as show in the tally column, recorded.
- At the bottow of the frequency column record the total frequency for the distribution proceeded by N = 30
- Enter the name of the frequency distribution at the top of the table.

If we applied these steps to the temperature data we would have the following frequency distribution.

Table. Frequency Distribution for High Temperatures

Temperature	Tally	Frequency
51	////	4
50	////	4
49	//////	6
48		0
47	///	3
46	///	3
45	////	4
44	///	3
43	///	3
	N = 30	

CUMMULATIVE FREQUENCY DISTRIBUTION

A cummulative frequency distribution can be created from a frequency distribution by adding an additional column called "Cummulative Frequency." For each score value the cummulative frequency for that score value is the frequency up to and including the frequency for that value. In the cummulative frequency distribution for the high temperatures data below, notice that the cummulative frequency for the lowest temperature (43) is 3, and that the cummulative frequency for the temperature 44 is 3+3 or 6.

The cummulative frequency for a given value can also be obtained by adding the frequency for the value to the cummulative value for the value below the given value.

For example the cummulative frequency for 45 is 10 which is the cummulative frequency for 44 (6) plus the frequency for 45 (4). Finally, notice that the cummulative frequency for the highest value (51 in the current case) should be the same as the total of the frequency column (30 in the case of the temperature data).

Table. Cummulative Frequency Distribution for High Temperatures

Temperature	Tally	Frequency	Cummulative Frequency
51	////	4	30
50	////	4	26
49	//////	6	22
48		0	16
47	///	3	16
46	///	3	13
45	////	4	10
44	///	3	6
43	///	3	3
	N = 30		

In summary then, to create a cummulative frequency distribution:

- Create a frequency distribution
- Add a column entitled cummulative frequency
- The cummulative frequency for each score is the frequency up to and including the frequency for that score
- The highest cummulative frequency should equal N (the total of the frequency column)

GROUPED FREQUENCY DISTRIBUTION

In some cases it is necessary to group the values of the data to summarize the data properly. For example, you wish to create a frequency distribution for the IQ scores in your class of 30 pupils. The IQ scores in your class range from 73 to 139. To include these scores in a frequency distribution you would need 67 different score values (139 down to 73). This would not summarize the data very much. To solve this problem we would group scores together and create a grouped frequency distribution. If your data has more than 20 score values, you should create a grouped frequency distribution by grouping score values together into class intervals.

To create a grouped frequency distribution:

- Select an interval size so that you have 7-20 class intervals
- Create a class interval column and list each of the class intervals
- Each interval must be the same size, they must not overlap, there may be no gaps within the range of class intervals
- Create a tally column (optional)
- Create a midpoint column for interval midpoints
- Create a frequency column
- Enter N = some value at the bottom of the frequency column

Look at the following data of high temperatures for 50 days. The highest temperature is 59 and the lowest temperature is 39. If we were to create a simple frequency distribution of this data we would have 21 temperature values. This is greater than 20 values so we should create a grouped frequency distribution.

Table. Data Set - High Temperatures for 50 Days

57	39	52	52	43
50	53	42	58	55
58	50	53	50	49
45	49	51	44	54
49	57	55	59	45
50	45	51	54	58
53	49	52	51	41
52	40	44	49	45
43	47	47	43	51
55	55	46	54	41

If we use this data and follow the suggestions for creation of a grouped frequency distribution, we would create the following grouped frequency distribution.

Note that we use an interval size of three so that each class interval includes three score values. Also note that we have included an interval midpoint column, this is the middle of each interval.

Table. Grouped Frequency Distribution for High Temperatures

Class Interval	Tally	Interval Midpoint	Frequency
57-59	//////	58	6
54-56	///////	55	7
51-53	///////////	52	11

48-50	/////////	49	9
45-47	///////	46	7
42-44	//////	43	6
39-41	////	40	4
		N = 50	

CUMULATIVE GROUPED FREQUENCY DISTRIBUTION

It is a simple matter to create a cumulative grouped frequency distribution. We just add a cumulative frequency column to the grouped frequency distribution and we have a cumulative grouped frequency distribution. The cumulative grouped frequency distribution below was created by adding a cumulative frequency column.

Table. Cumulative Grouped Frequency Distribution for High Temperatures

Class Interval	Tally	Interval Midpoint	Frequency	Cumulative Frequency
57-59	//////	58	6	50
54-56	///////	55	7	44
51-53	///////////	52	11	37
48-50	/////////	49	9	26
45-47	///////	46	7	17
42-44	//////	43	6	10
39-41	////	40	4	4
		N = 50		

STEM AND LEAF

The stem-and-leaf is a useful pictorial. It is similar to a histogram in that it shows the range of data, where the data are concentrated, if there are any outliers (occasional extremely high or extremely low scores), and the general shape of the distribution. For example, look at the following data—test scores of 17 high school students: 69, 75, 77, 79, 82, 84, 87, 88, 89, 89, 89, 90, 91, 93, 96, 100, 100. The stem-and-leaf takes the first digit of each score as the stem and uses the remaining digits as the leaf.

As an example, for the score of 69, the 6 is the stem and the 9 is the leaf; for the next three grades (75, 77, and 79), 7 is the stem, and 5, 7, and 9 are the leaves. Note, too, that along the extreme left side of the chart is a vertical column that keeps a running count or total. (Some stem-and-leafs do not include this running total.) Having a running total enables the reader to locate quickly the median.

The completed stem-and-leaf for the high school students' test scores looks like that shown in Table. Table Stem-and-Leaf Display of Students' Test Scores*Running CountStemLeaves*169475 7 91182 4 7 8 9 9 91590 1 3 617100 0

Notice that, like a histogram, each stem determines a class interval and, also like a histogram, the class intervals are all equal. (In this case, each interval width is from a possible low of 0 to a possible high of 9.) All 17 scores are displayed in the stem-and-leaf so that you can see not only the frequencies and the shape of the distribution but also the actual value of every score.

BOX PLOT (BOX AND WHISKERS)

Box plots, sometimes called box-and-whiskers, take the stem-and-leaf one step further. A box plot will display a number of values of a distribution of numbers:

- The median value
- The lower quartile (Q_1)
- The upper quartile (Q_3)
- The interquartile range or *IQR* (distance between the lower and upper quartiles)
- The symmetry of the distribution
- The highest and lowest values
- Use the set of values in Table to examine each of the preceding items.

Table. Verbal SAT Scores of 20 High School Students

280,	340,	440,	490,	520,	540,	560,	560,	580, 580,	600,	610,	630,	
650,	660,	680,	710,	730,	740,	740						

The median (the middle value in a set that has been ordered lowest to highest) is the value above which half of the remaining values fall and below which the other half of the remaining values fall. Because there are an even number of scores in our example (20), the median score is the average of the two middle scores (10th and 11th)—580 and 600—or 590.

The lower quartile (Q_1 or 25th percentile) is the median of the bottom half. The bottom half of this set consists of the first 10 numbers (ordered from low to high): 280, 340, 440, 490, 520, 540, 560, 560, 580, 580. The median of those 10 is the average of the 5th and 6th scores—520 and 540—or 530. The lower quartile score is 530. The upper quartile (Q_3 or 75th percentile) is the median score of the top half. The top half of this set consists of the last 10 numbers: 600, 610, 630, 650, 660, 680, 710, 730, 740,740. The median of these 10 is again the average of the 5th and 6th scores—in this case, 660 and 680—or 670. So 670 is the upper quartile score for this set of 20 numbers. A box plot can now be constructed as follows: The left side of the box indicates the lower quartile; the right side of the box indicates the upper quartile; and the line inside the box indicates the median. A horizontal line is then drawn from the lowest value of the distribution through the box to the highest value of the distribution. (This horizontal line is the "whiskers.") Using the Verbal SAT scores in Table, a box plot would look like Figure.

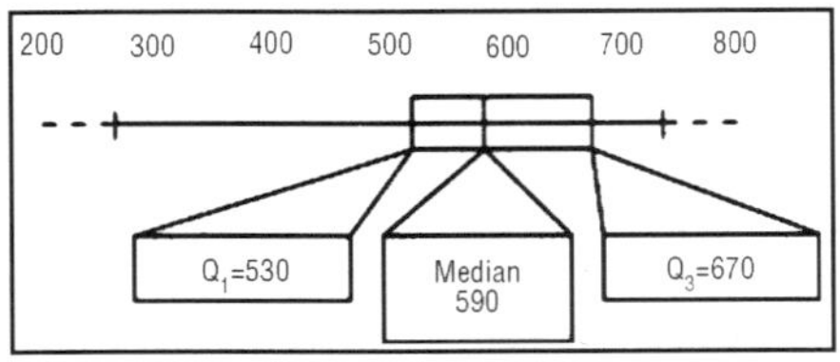

Fig. A Box Plot of SAT Scores Displays Median and Quartiles.

Without reading the actual values, you can see by looking at the box plot in Figure that the scores range from a low of 280 to a high of 740; that the lower quartile (Q_1) is at 530; the median is at 590; and the upper quartile (Q_3) is at 670. Because the median is slightly nearer the lower quartile than the upper quartile and the interquartile range is situated far to the right of the range of values, the distribution departs from symmetry.

SCATTER PLOT

Scatter plots are similar to line graphs in that they use horizontal and vertical axes to plot data points. However, they have a very specific purpose. Scatter plots show how much one variable is affected by another. The relationship between two variables is called their correlation .

Scatter plots usually consist of a large body of data. The closer the data points come when plotted to making a straight line, the higher the correlation between the two variables, or the stronger the relationship. If the data points make a straight line going from the origin out to high x- and y-values, then the variables are said to have a positive correlation . If the line goes from a high-value on the y-axis down to a high-value on the x-axis, the variables have a negative correlation .

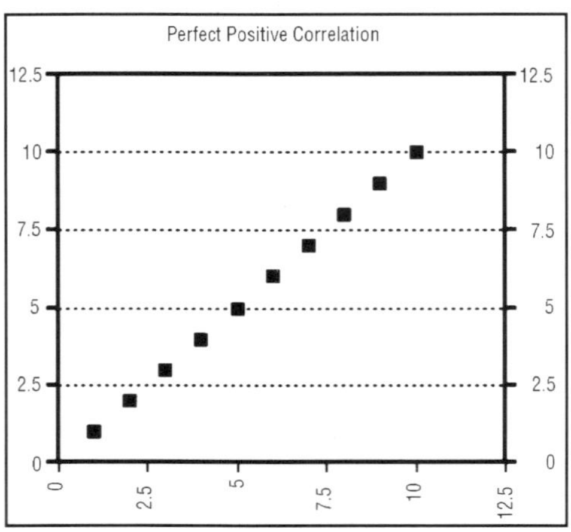

A perfect positive correlation is given the value of 1. A perfect negative correlation is given the value of -1. If there is absolutely no correlation present the value given is 0. The closer the number is to 1 or -1, the stronger the correlation, or the stronger the relationship between the variables.

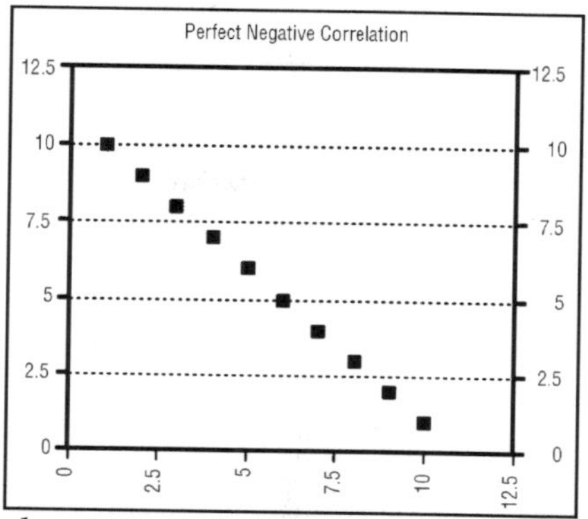

The closer the number is to 0, the weaker the correlation. So something that seems to kind of correlate in a positive direction might have a value of 0.67, whereas something with an extremely weak negative correlation might have the value –21. An example of a situation where you might find a perfect positive correlation, as we have in the graph on the left above, would be when you compare the total amount of money spent on tickets at the movie theater with the number of people who go. This means that every time that "x" number of people go, "y" amount of money is spent on tickets without variation. An example of a situation where you might find a perfect negative correlation, as in the graph on the right above, would be if you were comparing the speed at which a car is going to the amount of time it takes to reach a destination. As the speed increases, the amount of time decreases. On the other hand, a situation where you might find a strong but not perfect positive correlation would be if you examined the number of hours students spent studying for an exam versus the grade received. This won't be a perfect correlation because two people could spend the same amount of time studying and get different grades. But in general the rule will hold true that as the amount of time studying increases so does the grade received. Let's take a look at some examples. The graphs that were shown above each had a perfect correlation, so their values were 1 and -1. The graphs below obviously do not have perfect correlations. Which graph would have a correlation of 0? What about 0.7? –0.7? 0.3? –0.3?

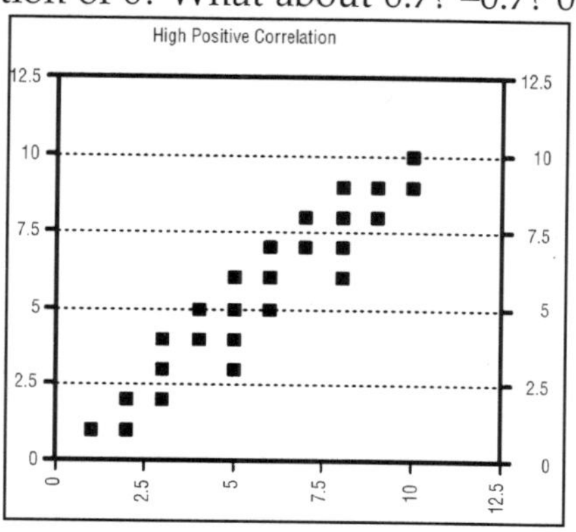

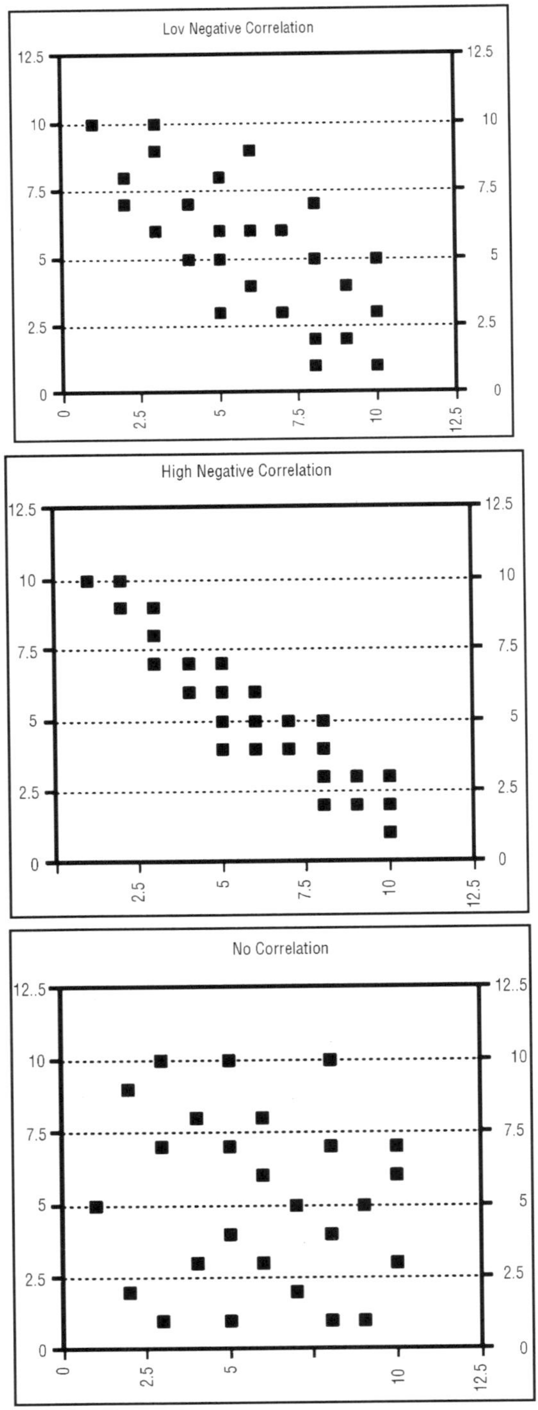
Lov Negative Correlation
High Negative Correlation
No Correlation

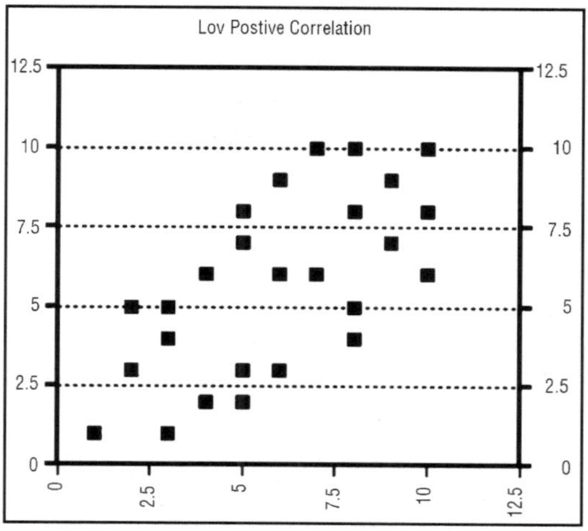

QUARTILES, DECILES AND PERCENTILES

Percentile "Ranks"

- Scores of students are arranged in rank order from lowest to highest
- The scores are divided into 100 equally sized groups or bands
- The lowest score is "in the 1st percentile" (there is no 0 percentile rank)
- The highest score is "in the 99th percentile"
  (you can't score in the 100th percentile because you can't beat your own score)

If you "scored in the 66th percentile", you scored "as well as or better than" 66% of the group. If your score was the same as "the mean" for that test, you scored in the 50th percentile.(The mean is the middle of a distribution, and the 50th percentile is the same...the middle of the group.)

If 700 people took a test, how many people would be in each percentile band? *(Divide 700 by 100 bands/ranks):* If only one student is taking the diagnostic achievement test, how do we determine his/her percentile ranking? Who do we compare him/her against? (The norm groups...kids who have taken the test previously... provided by the test)

Deciles ("Deca" Means "Ten")

- Scores of students are arranged in rank order from lowest to highest
- The scores are divided into 10 equally sized groups or bands (instead of 100 as with percentiles)
  (Or divide the percentiles into bands of 10 percentile ranks)
- The lowest score is "in the 1st decile"

- The highest score is "in the 10th decile"

This "ile" is the most difficult to visualize and state. For example, the 62nd percentile rank falls in the 7th decile rank (remember to add "1" to the tens column of the percentile rank to get the decile rank) (The first decile includes the first to 9.99th percentile, so that's why you add a "1" to the tens column to find the decile) The 4th deciles goes up to the 39.9th percentile. The 40th percentile start the 4th decile.

Quartiles

- Scores of students are arranged in rank order from lowest to highest
- The scores are divided into 4 equally sized groups or bands (Or divide the percentiles into bands of 25 percentile ranks)
- The lowest score is "in the 1st quartile"
- The highest score is "in the 4th quartile"
  - 1st quartile is 1st to 24.9th percentile
  - 2nd quartile is 25th to 49.9th percentile etc.

Definitions

- First quartile (designated Q1) = lower quartile = cuts off lowest 25% of data = 25th percentile
- Second quartile (designated Q2) = median = cuts data set in half = 50th percentile
- Third quartile (designated Q3) = upper quartile = cuts off highest 25% of data, or lowest 75% = 75th percentile

The difference between the upper and lower quartiles is called the interquartile range.

Computing Methods

There is no universal agreement on choosing the quartile values. The formula for locating the position of the observation at a given percentile, y, with n data points sorted in ascending order is:

$$Ly = (n)\left(\frac{y}{100}\right)$$

- Case 1: If L is a whole number, then the value will be found halfway between positions L and L+1.
- Case 2: If L is a decimal, round up to the nearest whole number. (for example, L = 1.2 becomes 2).

Example

Method 1

Example: Boxplot (with quartiles and an interquartile range) and a probability density function (pdf) of a normal $N(0,1s^2)$ population,

- Use the median to divide the ordered data set into two halves. Do not include the median into the halves.
- The lower quartile value is the median of the lower half of the data. The upper quartile value is the median of the upper half of the data.

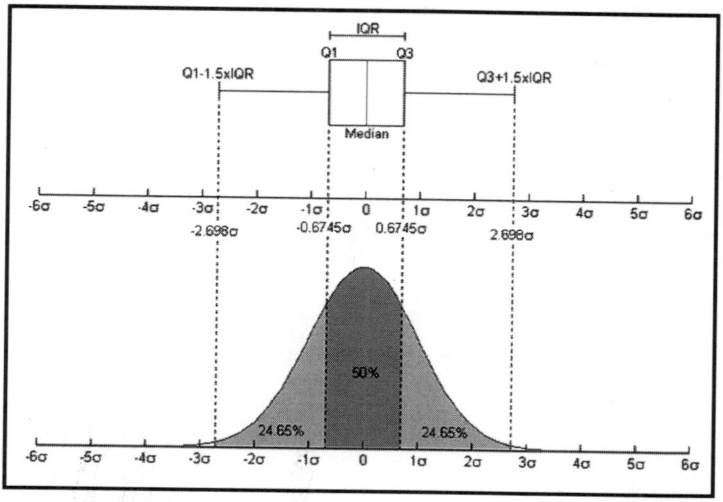

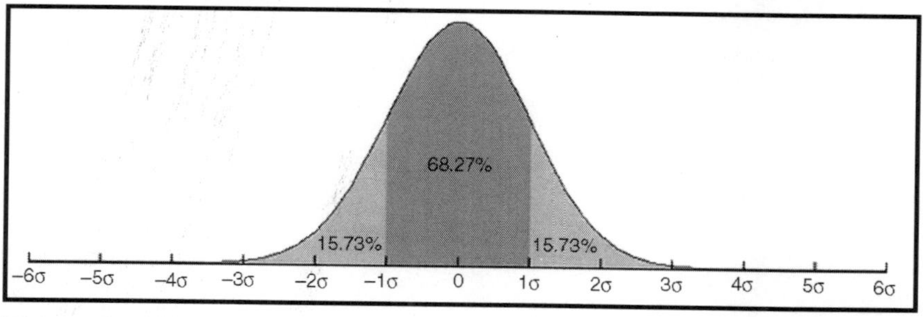

This rule is employed by the TI-83 calculator boxplot and 1-Var Stats functions.

Method 2

- Use the median to divide the ordered data set into two halves. Include the median into the halves.
- The lower quartile value is the median of the lower half of the data. The upper quartile value is the median of the upper half of the data.

Example 1:

Data set: 6, 47, 49, 15, 42, 41, 7, 39, 43, 40, 36

Ordered data set: 6, 7, 15, 36, 39, 40, 41, 42, 43, 47, 49

Method 1	Method 2
$\begin{cases} Q_1 = 15 \\ Q_2 = 40 \\ Q_3 = 43 \end{cases}$	$\begin{cases} Q_1 = 25.5 \\ Q_2 = 40 \\ Q_3 = 42.5 \end{cases}$

Example 2: Ordered Data Set: 7, 15, 36, 39, 40, 41

Method 1	Method 2
$\begin{cases} Q_1 = 15 \\ Q_2 = 37.5 \\ Q_3 = 40 \end{cases}$	$\begin{cases} Q_1 = 25.5 \\ Q_2 = 37.5 \\ Q_3 = 39.5 \end{cases}$

Example 3:
Ordered data set: 1, 2, 3, 4

Method 1	Method 2
$\begin{cases} Q_1 = 1.5 \\ Q_2 = 2.5 \\ Q_3 = 3.5 \end{cases}$	$\begin{cases} Q_1 = 2 \\ Q_2 = 2.5 \\ Q_3 = 3 \end{cases}$

In line with the definition of the median as; P(X<=m)>=0.5 and P(X>=m)>=0.5, it seems sensible to define the lower quartile, l, as P(X<=l)>=0.25 and P(X>=l)>=0.75.

This means that for;

4n-3 pieces of data, the LQ is the n th value,

4n-2 pieces of data, the LQ is the n th value,

4n-1 pieces of data, the LQ is the n th value,

but for 4n pieces of data, the LQ is not uniquely defined, by this, it could be the n th value, or the n+1 th value.

It would be sensible to take the average of these two values in this case. The Upper Quartile, u, is similarly defined a; P(X<=u)>=0.75 and P(X>=u)>=0.25. It is then easier to count the same number, from the RIGHT.

SKEWNESS AND KURTOSIS

Consider the distribution in the figure. The bars on the right side of the distribution taper differently than the bars on the left side. These tapering sides are called *tails*, and they provide a visual means for determining which of the two kinds of skewness a distribution has:

- Negative skew: The left tail is longer; the mass of the distribution is concentrated on the right of the figure. It has relatively few low values. The distribution is said to be *left-skewed*. Example (observations): 1,1000,1001,1002,1003
- Positive skew: The right tail is longer; the *mass* of the distribution

is concentrated on the left of the figure. It has relatively few high values. The distribution is said to be *right-skewed*. Example (observations): 1,2,3,4,100.

In a skewed (unbalanced, lopsided) distribution, the mean is farther out in the long tail than is the median. If there is no skewness *i.e.* the distribution is symmetric then the mean = the median = the mode. Many textbooks teach a rule of thumb stating that the mean is right of the median under right skew, and left of the median under left skew.

This rule fails with surprising frequency. It can fail in multimodal distributions, or in distributions where one tail is long but the other is heavy. Most commonly, though, the rule fails in discrete distributions where the areas to the left and right of the median are not equal. Such distributions not only contradict the textbook relationship between mean, median, and skew, they also contradict the textbook interpretation of the median.

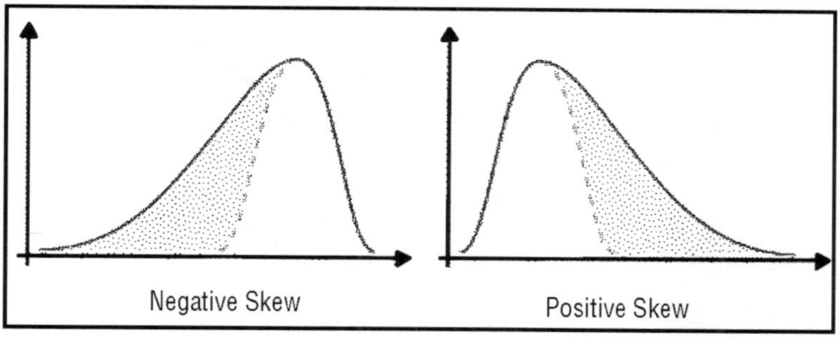

A fundamental task in many statistical analyses is to characterize the *location* and *variability* of a data set. A further characterization of the data includes skewness and kurtosis. Skewness is a measure of symmetry, or more precisely, the lack of symmetry. A distribution, or data set, is symmetric if it looks the same to the left and right of the centre point. Kurtosis is a measure of whether the data are peaked or flat relative to a normal distribution. That is, data sets with high kurtosis tend to have a distinct peak near the mean, decline rather rapidly, and have heavy tails.

Data sets with low kurtosis tend to have a flat top near the mean rather than a sharp peak. A uniform distribution would be the extreme case. The histogram is an effective graphical technique for showing both the skewness and kurtosis of data set. For univariate data Y_1, Y_2..., Y_N, the formula for skewness is:

$$\text{Skewness} = \frac{\sum_{I=0}^{N}(Y_i - \overline{Y})^3}{(N-1)S^3}$$

where Y is the mean, N is the standard deviation, and *N* is the number of data points. The skewness for a normal distribution is zero, and any symmetric data should have a skewness near zero. Negative values for the skewness indicate data that are skewed left and positive values for the skewness indicate data that are skewed right. By skewed left, we mean that the left tail is long relative to the right tail. Similarly, skewed right means that the right tail is long relative to the left tail. Some measurements have a lower bound and are skewed right.

For example, in reliability studies, failure times cannot be negative. *For univariate data Y_1, Y_2..., Y_N, the formula for kurtosis is*:

$$\text{Kurtosis} = \frac{\sum_{I=0}^{N}(Y_i - \overline{Y})^3}{(N-1)S^4}$$

where Y is the mean, S is the standard deviation, and N is the number of data points. The kurtosis for a standard normal distribution is three.

For this reason, some sources use the following defition of kurtosis:

$$\text{Kurtosis} = \frac{\sum_{I=0}^{N}(Y_i - \overline{Y})^3}{(N-1)S^4} - 3$$

This definition is used so that the standard normal distribution has a kurtosis of zero. In addition, with the second definition positive kurtosis indicates a "peaked" distribution and negative kurtosis indicates a "flat" distribution. Which definition of kurtosis is used is a matter of convention. When using software to compute the sample kurtosis, you need to be aware of which convention is being followed.

Examples

The following example shows histograms for 10,000 random numbers generated from a normal, a double exponential, a Cauchy, and a Weibull distribution.

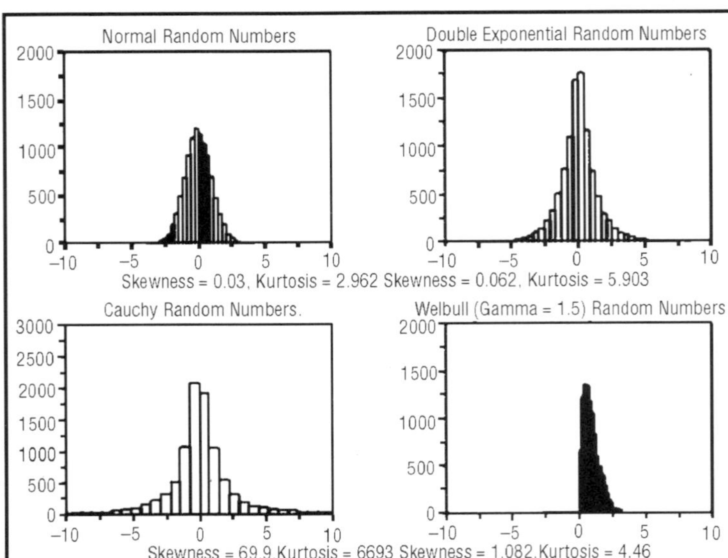

Sample Skewness

For a sample of n values the *sample skewness* is:

$$g_1 = \frac{m_3}{m_2^{3/2}} = \frac{\frac{1}{n}\sum_{i=1}^{n}(x_i - \bar{x})^3}{\left(\frac{1}{n}\sum_{i=1}^{n}(x_i - \bar{x})^2\right)^{3/2}},$$

where x_i is the ith value, $\bar{x}$ is the sample mean, m_3 is the sample third central moment, and m_2 is the sample variance.

Given samples from a population, the equation for the sample skewness g_1 above is a biased estimator of the population skewness.

The usual estimator of skewness is,

$$G_1 = \frac{k_3}{k_2^{3/2}} = \frac{\sqrt{n(n-1)}}{n-2} g_1,$$

where k_3 is the unique symmetric unbiased estimator of the third cumulant and k_2 is the symmetric unbiased estimator of the second cumulant. Unfortunately G_1 is, nevertheless, generally biased. Its expected value can even have the opposite sign from the true skewness; compare unbiased estimation of standard deviation.

Properties

If Y is the sum of n independent random variables, all with the same distribution as X, then it can be shown that Skew[Y] = Skew[X] / $\sqrt{n}$.

Applications

Skewness has benefits in many areas. Many simplistic models assume normal distribution *i.e.* data is symmetric about the mean. The normal distribution has a skewness of zero. But in reality, data points are not perfectly symmetric.

So, an understanding of the skewness of the dataset indicates whether deviations from the mean are going to be positive or negative. D'Agostino's K-squared test is a goodness-of-fit normality test based on sample skewness and sample kurtosis.

Pearson's Skewness Coefficients

Karl Pearson suggested simpler calculations as a measure of skewness: The Pearson mode skewness, defined by,

- (Mean " mode)/ standard deviation,
  Pearson's first skewness coefficient, defined by
- 3 (mean " mode)/ standard deviation,
  as well as Pearson's second skewness coefficient, defined by
- 3 (mean " median)/ standard deviation.

Starting from a standard cumulant expansion around a Normal distribution, one can actually show that skewness = 6 (mean " median)/ standard deviation (1 + kurtosis/8) + O(skewness^2)

There is no guarantee that these will be the same sign as each other or as the ordinary definition of skewness.

Normal Distribution

The first histogram is a sample from a normal distribution. The normal distribution is a symmetric distribution with well-behaved tails.

This is indicated by the skewness of 0.03. The kurtosis of 2.96 is near the expected value of 3. The histogram verifies the symmetry.

Double Exponential Distribution

The second histogram is a sample from a double exponential distribution. The double exponential is a symmetric distribution.

Compared to the normal, it has a stronger peak, more rapid decay, and heavier tails. That is, we would expect a skewness near zero and a kurtosis higher than 3. The skewness is 0.06 and the kurtosis is 5.9.

Cauchy Distribution

The third histogram is a sample from a Cauchy distribution. For better visual comparison with the other data sets, we restricted the histogram of the Cauchy distribution to values between –10 and 10.

The full data set for the Cauchy data in fact has a minimum of approximately -29,000 and a maximum of approximately 89,000.

The Cauchy distribution is a symmetric distribution with heavy tails and a single peak at the centre of the distribution.

Since it is symmetric, we would expect a skewness near zero. Due to the heavier tails, we might expect the kurtosis to be larger than for a normal distribution.

In fact the skewness is 69.99 and the kurtosis is 6,693. These extremely high values can be explained by the heavy tails. Just as the mean and standard deviation can be distorted by extreme values in the tails, so too can the skewness and kurtosis measures.

Weibull Distribution

The fourth histogram is a sample from a Weibull distribution with shape parameter 1.5. The Weibull distribution is a skewed distribution with the amount of skewness depending on the value of the shape parameter. The degree of decay as we move away from the centre also depends on the value of the shape parameter.

For this data set, the skewness is 1.08 and the kurtosis is 4.46, which indicates moderate skewness and kurtosis.

Dealing with Skewness and Kurtosis

Many classical statistical tests and intervals depend on normality assumptions. Significant skewness and kurtosis clearly indicate that data are not normal.

If a data set exhibits significant skewness or kurtosis (as indicated by a histogram or the numerical measures), what can we do about it? One approach is to apply some type of transformation to try to make the data normal, or more nearly normal. The Box-Cox transformation is a useful technique for trying to normalize a data set.

In particular, taking the log or square root of a data set is often useful for data that exhibit moderate right skewness. Another approach is to use techniques based on distributions other than the normal. For example, in reliability studies, the exponential, Weibull, and lognormal distributions are typically used as a basis for modeling rather than using the normal distribution. Theprobability plot correlation coefficient plot and the probability plotare useful tools for determining a good distributional model for the data.

RELATIONSHIP BETWEEN THE TWO VARIABLES

It is important to specify the scale of measurement of each of the two variables when examining the relationship between two variables because these determine the type of analysis and summary to be performed upon the data.

The following table, summarizes some of the important analyses that are often performed to investigate the relationship between two variables.

Type of variables	**X is Interval or Ratio**	**X is Nominal or Ordinal**
Y is Interval or Ratio	Catterplots Running median/spline fit Regression Correlation	Side-by-side dot plot Side-by-side box plot ANOVA (to be covered later)
Y is Nominal or Ordinal	Logistic regression (a topic for graduate level statistics)	Mosaic chart Contingency tables

In JMP these combination of two variables are obtained by the Analyse->Fit Y by X platform or by the Analyse->Correlation-of-Ys platform. When analyzing two variables, a new questions also becomes important. Is the purpose to explore the nature of the relationship, or is the purpose to use one variable to explain variation in another variable? For example, there is a difference between examining the relationship between height and weight to see if there is a strong relationship, as opposed to using height to predict weight. Consequently, you need to distinguish between a:

Response Variable

The Response variable is a local text variable set to the user's response as follows:

- If there is a question at the current Node, the Response variable is set to the user's response as shown in the Flowchart of a Question/ Response Session.
  Example: A user dials in to the Call Tree created In the Quick-Start Tutorial example. The user presses 1 at the Answer_Phone Node's prompt to leave a message for Bill. In this case, at the Answer_Phone Node, the Response variable will equal"1".
- If there is no question at the current Node but the response from the previous Node matches a response on the Responses tab, the Response variable is set to the user's response from the previous Node.
  Example: A user dials in to the Call Tree created In the Quick-Start Tutorial example. The user presses 2 at the Answer_Phone Node's prompt to leave a message for Mary. The Call continues to the Check_Response Node, where there is no question. There are two responses defined on the Responses tab at the Check_Response Node:"1" and"2". Since the user's response from the previous Node (Answer_Phone) matched a response defined at the Check_Response Node, the Response variable will equal"2" (the user's response at the previous Node) at the Check_Response Node during this call.
- If there is no question at the current Node and the response from the previous Node does not match a response on the Responses tab, the Response variable will be blank.
  Example: A user dials in to the Call Tree created In the Quick-Start Tutorial example. The user presses 3 at the Answer_Phone Node's prompt by accident. The Call continues to the Check_Response Node, where there is no question. There are two responses defined on the Responses tab at the Check_Response Node:"1" and"2". Since the user's response from the previous Node (Answer_Phone) does not match a response defined at the Check_Response Node, the Response variable will be blank at the Check_Response Node during this call.

Explanatory Variable

Any variable that explains the response variable. Often called an independent variable or predictor variable. In general identifying these amounts to deciding which variable(s) would be used to predict another. Here follow a few examples.

Example: Consider a study performed by a medical centre to determine which of two heart surgeries is most effective: angioplasty (running rubber tubes through the arteries) or bypass (rerouting arteries). The purpose of either procedure is to prolong the life of the patient. The study will certainly record the survival time of each patient (measured from the time of the surgery). This really is the outcome of the study; survival time is the response variable. Now, each patient will get one of the two types of operations; this is a second variable...let's call it the"procedure" variable; it takes one of two possible values, Angioplasty and Bypass.

The entire purpose of the study is to determine how, if at all, the procedure affects survival time. Type of surgery is an explanatory variable. We would use type of operation (explanatory variable or predictor) to predict survival time (response or predicted variable). Survival time may well depend on procedure; survival time is the dependent variable and procedure is the independent variable. Note that the response is measured after the explanatory. This is often---but not always---the case.

The response variable is quantitative, the explanatory variable is categorical. In a true clinical trial many more explanatory variables would be recorded: gender, age at the time of surgery, state of health pre-surgery (how would this be measured?), numerous physiological indicators and so forth. There would be but one response variable, survival time! (Actually, there would be others. Quality of life after the operation is important, as is an analysis of the side-effects attributable to the two procedures.)

4

Probability

INTRODUCTION TO PROBABILITY

- Compute probability in a situation where there are equally-likely outcomes
- Apply concepts to cards and dice
- Compute the probability of two independent events both occurring
- Compute the probability of either of two independent events occurring
- Do problems that involve conditional probabilities
- Compute the probability that in a room of N people, at least two share a birthday
- Describe the gamblers' fallacy

Probability is an important and complex field of study. The introductory section discusses the definitions of probability. This is not as simple as it may seem. The section on basic concepts covers how to compute probabilities in a variety of simple situations.

The Gambler's Fallacy Simulation provides an opportunity to explore this fallacy by simulation. The Birthday Demonstration illustrates the probability of finding two or more people with the same birthday.

The Binomial Demonstration shows the binomial distribution for different parameters. The section on base rates discusses an important but often-ignored factor in determining probabilities. It also presents Bays' Theorem. The Bays' Theorem Demonstration shows how a tree diagram and Bays' Theorem result in the same answer. Finally, the Monty Hall Demonstration lets you play a game with a very counterintuitive result.

PROBABILITY OF A SINGLE EVENT

If you roll a six-sided die, there are six possible outcomes, and each of these outcomes is equally likely. A six is as likely to come up as a three, and likewise for the other four sides of the die. What, then, is the probability that a one will come up? Since there are six possible outcomes, the probability is 1/6. What is the probability that either a one or a six will come up? The two outcomes about which we are concerned (a one or a six coming up) are called *favorable outcomes*. Given that all outcomes are equally likely, we can compute the probability of a one or a six using the formula:

$$\Pr obaility = \frac{Number\ of\ avorable\ outcomes}{Number\ of\ Possible\ equally - \text{li}\ kely\ outcomes}$$

In this case there are two favorable outcomes and six possible outcomes. So the probability of throwing either a one or six is 1/3. Don't be misled by our use of the term "favorable," by the way. You should understand it in the sense of "favorable to the event in question happening." That event might not be favorable to your well-being. You might be betting on a three, for example.

The above formula applies to many games of chance. For example, what is the probability that a card drawn at random from deck of playing cards will be an ace? Since the deck has four aces, there are four favorable outcomes; since the deck has 52 cards, there are 52 possible outcomes. The probability is therefore 4/52 = 1/13. What about the probability that the card will be a club? Since there are 13 clubs, the probability is 13/52 = 1/4.

Let's say you have a bag with 20 cherries, 14 sweet and 6 sour. If you pick a cherry at random, what is the probability that it will be sweet? There are 20 possible cherries that could be picked, so the number of possible outcomes is 20. Of these 20 possible outcomes, 14 are favorable (sweet), so the probability that the cherry will be sweet is 14/20 =7/10. There is one potential complication to this example, however. It must be assumed that the probability of picking any of the cherries is the same as the probability of picking any other.

This wouldn't be true if (let us imagine) the sweet cherries are smaller than the sour ones. (The sour cherries would come to hand more readily when you sampled from the bag.) Let us keep in mind, therefore, that when we assess probabilities in terms of the ratio of favorable to all potential cases, we rely heavily on the assumption of equal probability for all outcomes.

Here is a more complex example. You throw 2 dice. What is the probability that the sum of the two dice will be 6? To solve this problem, list all the possible outcomes. There are 36 of them since each die can come up one of six ways. The 36 possibilities are shown below.

You can see that 5 of the 36 possibilities total 6. Therefore, the probability is 5/36. If you know the probability of an event occurring, it is easy to compute the probability that the event does not occur. If P(A) is the probability of Event A, then 1 – P(A) is the probability that the event does not occur. For the last example, the probability that the total is 6 is 5/36. Therefore, the probability that the total is not 6 is 1 – 5/36 = 31/36.

Die 1	Die 2	Total	Die 1	Die 2	Total	Die 1	Die 2	Total
1	1	2	3	1	4	5	1	6
1	2	3	3	2	5	5	2	7
1	3	4	3	3	6	5	3	8
1	4	5	3	4	7	5	4	9
1	5	6	3	5	8	5	5	10
1	6	7	3	6	9	5	6	11
2	1	3	4	1	5	6	1	7
2	2	4	4	2	6	6	2	8
2	3	5	4	3	7	6	3	9
2	4	6	4	4	8	6	4	10
2	5	7	4	5	9	6	5	11
2	6	8	4	6	10	6	6	12

PROBABILITY OF TWO (OR MORE) INDEPENDENT EVENTS

Events A and B are *independent events* if the probability of Event B occurring is the same whether or not Event A occurs. Let's take a simple example. A fair coin is tossed two times. The probability that a head comes up on the second toss is 1/2 regardless of whether or not a head came up on the first toss.

The two events are:

- First toss is a head
- Second toss is a head.

So these events are independent. Consider the two events,

- It will rain tomorrow in Houston
- It will rain tomorrow in Galveston (a city near Houston).

These events are not independent because it is more likely that it will rain in Galveston on days it rains in Houston than on days it does not.

Probability of A and B

When two events are independent, the probability of both occurring is the product of the probabilities of the individual events. More formally, if events A and B are independent, then the probability of both A and B occurring is:

$$P(A \text{ and } B) = P(A) \times P(B)$$

where P(A and B) is the probability of events A and B both occurring, P(A) is the probability of event A occurring, and P(B) is the probability of event B occurring. If you flip a coin twice, what is the probability that it will come up heads both times? Event A is that the coin comes up heads on the first flip and Event B is that the coin comes up heads on the second flip.

Since both P(A) and P(B) equal 1/2, the probability that both events occur is:

$$1/2 \times 1/2 = 1/4$$

Lets take another example. If you flip a coin and roll a six-sided die, what is the probability that the coin comes up heads and the die comes up 1? Since the two events are independent, the probability is simply the probability of a head (which is 1/2) times the probability of the die coming up 1 (which is 1/6). Therefore, the probability of both events occurring is:

$$1/2 \times 1/6 = 1/12.$$

One final example: You draw a card from a deck of cards, put it back, and then draw another card. What is the probability that the first card is a heart and the second card is black? Since there are 52 cards in a deck, and 13 of them are hearts, the probability that the first card is a heart is 13/52 = 1/4. Since there are 26 black cards in the deck, the probability that the second card is black is 26/52 = 1/2. The probability of both events occurring is therefore:

$$1/4 \times 1/2 = 1/8.$$

Probability of A or B

If Events A and B are independent, the probability that either Event A or Event B occurs is:

$$P(A \text{ or } B) = P(A) + P(B) - P(A \text{ and } B)$$

In this discussion, when we say "A or B occurs" we include three possibilities:

- A occurs and B does not occur
- B occurs and A does not occur
- Both A and B occur

This use of the word "or" is technically called *inclusive or* because it includes the case in which both A and B occur. If we included only the first two cases, then we would be using an *exclusive or*. We can derive the law for P(A-or-B) from our law about P(A-and-B). The event "A-or-B" can happen in any of the following ways:

- A-and-B happens
- A-and-not-B happens
- Not-A-and-B happens.

The simple event A can happen if either A-and-B happens, or A-and-not-B happens. Similarly, the simple event B happens if either A-and-B happens or not-A-and-B happens. P(A) + P(B) is therefore P(A-and-B) + P(A-and-not-B) + P(A-and-B) + P(not-A-and-B) whereas P(A-or-B) is P(A-and-B) + P(A-and-not-B) + P(not-A-and-B). We can make these two sums equal by subtracting one occurrence of P(A-and-B) from the first. Hence, P(A-or-B) = P(A) + P(B) - P(A-and-B).

Now for some examples. If you flip a coin two times, what is the probability that you will get a head on the first flip or a head on the second flip (or both)? Letting Event A be a head on the first flip and Event B be head on the second flip then P(A) = 1/2, P(B) = 1/2, and P(A and B) = 1/4.

Therefore,

$$P(A \text{ or } B) = 1/2 + 1/2 - 1/4 = 3/4.$$

If you throw a six-sided die and then flip a coin, what is the probability that you will get either a 6 on the die or a head on the coin flip (or both)? Using the formula,

$$\begin{aligned} P(6 \text{ or head}) &= P(6) + P(\text{head}) - P(6 \text{ and head}) \\ &= (1/6) + (1/2) - (1/6)(1/2) \\ &= 7/12 \end{aligned}$$

An alternate approach to computing this value is to start by computing the probability of not getting either a 6 or a head. Then subtract this value from 1 to compute the probability of getting a 6 or a head. Although this is a complicated method, it has the advantage of being applicable to problems with more than two events.

Here is the calculation in the present case. The probability of not getting either a 6 or a head can be recast as the probability of (not getting a 6) AND (not getting a head). This follows because if you did not get a 6 and you did not get a head, then you did not get a 6 or a head. The probability of not getting a six is 1 – 1/6 = 5/6.

The probability of not getting a head is 1 – 1/2 = 1/2. The probability of not getting a six and not getting a head is 5/6 x 1/2 = 5/12. This is therefore the probability of not getting a 6 or a head. The probability of getting a six or a head is therefore (once again) 1 – 5/12 = 7/12.

If you throw a die three times, what is the probability that one or more of your throws will come up with a 1? That is, what is the probability of getting a 1 on the first throw OR a 1 on the second throw OR a 1 on the third throw? The easiest way to approach this problem is to compute the probability of:

NOT getting a 1 on the first throw
AND not getting a 1 on the second throw
AND not getting a 1 on the third throw.

The answer will be 1 minus this probability. The probability of not getting a 1 on any of the three throws is 5/6 x 5/6 x 5/6 = 125/216. Therefore, the probability of getting a 1 on at least one of the throws is 1 – 125/216 = 91/216.

CONDITIONAL PROBABILITY

Conditional probability is the probability of some event *A*, given the occurrence of some other event *B*. Conditional probability is written $P(A|B)$, and is read "the probability of *A*, given *B*".

Joint probability is the probability of two events in conjunction. That is, it is the probability of both events together. The joint probability of *A* and *B* is written:

$$P(A \cap B) \text{ or } P(A, B)$$

Marginal probability is then the unconditional probability *P*(*A*) of the event *A*; that is, the probability of *A*, regardless of whether event *B* did or did not occur. If *B* can be thought of as the event of a random variable *X* having a given outcome, the marginal probability of *A* can be obtained by summing (or integrating, more generally) the joint probabilities over all outcomes for*X*. For example, if there are two possible outcomes for *X* with corresponding events *B* and *B′*, this means that:

$$P(A) = P(A \cap B) + P(A \cap B').$$

this is called marginalization.

In these definitions, note that there need not be a causal or temporal relation between *A* and *B*.*A* may precede *B* or vice versa or they may happen at the same time. *A* may cause *B* or vice versa or they may have no causal relation at all.

Notice, however, that causal and temporal relations are informal notions, not belonging to the probabilistic framework. They may apply in some examples, depending on the interpretation given to events. Conditioning of probabilities, *i.e.* updating them to take account of (possibly new) information, may be achieved through Bayes' theorem. In such conditioning, the probability of A given only initial information I, $P(A \mid I)$, is known as the prior probability. The updated conditional probability of A, given I and the outcome of the event B, is known as the posterior probability, $P(A \mid B, I)$. Consider the simple scenario of rolling two fair six-sided dice, labelled die 1 and die 2. Define the following three events:

- Die 1 lands on 3.
- Die 2 lands on 1.
- The dice sum to 8.

The prior probability of each event describes how likely the outcome is before the dice are rolled, without any knowledge of the roll's outcome. For example, die 1 is equally likely to fall on each of its 6 sides, so P(*A*) = 1/6. Similarly P(*B*) = 1/ 6. Likewise, of the 6 × 6 = 36 possible ways that a pair of dice can land, just 5 result in a sum of 8 (namely 2 and 6, 3 and 5, 4 and 4, 5 and 3, and 6 and 2), so P(*C*) = 5/ 36. Some of these events can both occur at the same time; for example events *A* and *C* can happen at the same time, in the case where die 1 lands on 3 and die 2 lands on 5. This is the only one of the 36 outcomes where both *A* and *C* occur, so its probability is 1/36. The probability of both *A*and *C* occurring is called the *joint probability* of *A* and *C* and is written,

$$P(A \cap C),, \text{ so } P(A \cap C), = 1/136.$$

On the other hand, if die 2 lands on 1, the dice cannot sum to 8, so:

$$P(B \cap C) = 0.$$

Now suppose we roll the dice and cover up die 2, so we can only see die 1, and observe that die 1 landed on 3. Given this partial information, the probability that the dice sum to 8 is no longer 5/36; instead it is 1/6, since die 2 must land on 5 to achieve this result.

This is called the*conditional* probability, because it is the probability of C under the condition that A is observed, and is written $P(C \mid A)$, which is read "the probability of C given A." Similarly, $P(C \mid B) = 0$, since if we observe die 2 landed on 1, we already know the dice can't sum to 8, regardless of what the other die landed on.

On the other hand, if we roll the dice and cover up die 2, and observe die 1, this has no impact on the probability of event B, which only depends on die 2. We say events A and B are*statistically independent* or just *independent* and in this case

$$P(B \mid A) = P(B)$$

In other words, the probability of B occurring after observing that die 1 landed on 3 is the same as before we observed die 1. Intersection events and conditional events are related by the formula:

$$P(C \mid A) = \frac{P(A \cap C)}{P(A)}$$

In this example, we have:

$$1/6 = \frac{1/36}{1/6}$$

As noted above, $P(B \mid A) = P(B)$, so by this formula:

$$P(B) = P(B \mid A) = \frac{P(A \cap B)}{P(A)}$$

On multiplying across by $P(A)$,

$$P(A) = P(B) = P(A \cap B).$$

In other words, if two events are independent, their joint probability is the product of the prior probabilities of each event occurring by itself.

Definition

Given a probability space (Ω, F, P) and two events A, B " F with $P(B) > 0$, the conditional probability of A given B is defined by,

$$P(A \mid B) = \frac{P(A \cap B)}{P(B)}.$$

If $P(B) = 0$ then $P(A \mid B)$ is undefined (see Borel–Kolmogorov paradox for an explanation). However it is possible to define a conditional probability with respect to a ó-algebra of such events (such as those arising from a continuous random variable). For example, if X and Y are non-degenerate and jointly continuous random variables with density $f_{X,Y}(x, y)$ then, if *B* has positive measure,

$$P(X \in A \mid Y \in B) = \frac{\int_{y \in B} \int_{x \in A} \int XY(x, y) dxdy}{\int_{y \in B} \int_{x \in \Omega} fX, Y(x, y) dxdy}.$$

The case where *B* has zero measure can only be dealt with directly in the case that $B=\{y_0\}$, representing a single point, in which case,

$$P(X \in A \mid Y = y_0) = \frac{\int_{x \in A} \int XY(x, y_0) dx}{\int_{x \in \Omega} fX, Y(x, y_0) dx}.$$

It is important to note that if *A* has measure zero the conditional probability is zero. An indication of why the more general case of zero measure cannot be dealt with in a similar way can be seen by noting that that the limit, as all δy_i approach zero, of depends on their relationship as they approach zero.

$$P(X \in A \mid Y \in U_i[y_i, y_i + \delta yi)) \approx \frac{\sum_i f_{XY}, (x, y_i) \delta yi}{\sum_i \int_{x \in \Omega} f_{X,Y}(x, y_i) dx \delta yi}.$$

Derivation

The following derivation is taken from Grinstead and Snell's Introduction to Probability.

Let,

$$\Omega = \{w_1, ... w_n\}$$

be the original sample space, with elementary outcomes or elementary events ω_i, and the probability operation *P* given as,

$$P : \Omega \rightarrow [0,1],$$

for example,

$$P(w_i) \in [0,1]..$$

Suppose event $P : \Omega \rightarrow [0,1]$, has occurred and an altered probability $P(\omega_i \mid E)$ is to be assigned to the elementary events to reflect the fact that *E* has occurred.

For all $w_j \notin E$ we want to make sure that the intuitive result $P(\omega_j \mid E) = 0$ is true.

Also, without further information provided, we can be certain that the relative magnitude of probabilities is conserved:

$$w_i, w_k \in E : P(w_i) \leq P(w_k) \Rightarrow P(w_i \mid E) \leq P(w_k \mid E).$$

This requirement leads us to state:

$$w_i, \in E : P(w_i \mid E) = \alpha \cdot P(w_i)$$

where $\alpha \in \mathbb{R}^+$,, *i.e.* α is a positive constant or scaling factor to reflect the above requirement.

Since we know E has occurred, we can state

$$P(E \mid E) = \sum_{\forall w_i \in E} P(w_i \mid E) = 1$$

which allows us to say:

$$\sum_{\forall w_i \in E} P(w_i \mid E) = \sum_{\forall w_i \in E} \alpha \cdot P(w_i) = \alpha \cdot \sum_{\forall w_i \in E} P(w_i) = 1$$

From the above we obtain:

$$\alpha = \frac{1}{\sum_{\forall wi \in E} P(w_i)} = \frac{1}{P(E)} \Leftrightarrow P(E) > 0$$

This leads us to state the following:

$$\forall w_i \in E : P(w_i \mid E) = \frac{P(w_i)}{P(E)}$$

Now for an event $F \subseteq \Omega$ and since,

$$\forall w_j \notin E : P(w_j \mid E) = 0 :$$

$$P(F \mid E) = \sum_{\forall w_k \in F} P(w_k \mid E) = \sum_{\forall w_i \in F \cap E} P(w_i \mid E) + \sum_{\forall w_j \notin F \cap E} \underbrace{P(w_j \mid E)}_{=0} =$$

$$\sum_{\forall w_{iF} \cap E} P(w_i \mid E) = \sum_{\forall w_i \in F \cap E} \frac{P(w_i)}{P(E)} = \frac{P(F \cap E)}{P(E)}$$

Statistical Independence

Two random events A and B are statistically independent if and only if,

$$P(A \cap B) = P(A)P(B)$$

Thus, if A and B are independent, then their joint probability can be expressed as a simple product of their individual probabilities. Equivalently, for two independent events A and B with non-zero probabilities,

$$P(A \mid B) = P(A)$$

and

$$P(B \mid A) = P(B)$$

In other words, if A and B are independent, then the conditional probability of A, given B is simply the individual probability of A alone; likewise, the probability of B given A is simply the probability of B alone.

Mutual Exclusivity

Two events A and B are mutually exclusive if and only if $A \cap B = \phi$.

Then $P(A \cap B) = 0$. Therefore, if $P(B) > 0$ then $P(A \mid B)$ is defined and equal to 0.

The Conditional Probability Fallacy

The conditional probability fallacy is the assumption that $P(A \mid B)$ is approximately equal to $P(B \mid A)$. The mathematician John Allen Paulos discusses this in his book *Innumeracy* (p. 63 et seq.), where he points out that it is a mistake often made even by doctors, lawyers, and other highly educated non-statisticians. It can be overcome by describing the data in actual numbers rather than probabilities.

The relation between $P(A \mid B)$ and $P(B \mid A)$ is given by Bayes' theorem:

$$P(B \mid A) = P(A \mid B)\frac{P(B)}{P(A)}.$$

In other words, one can only assume that $P(A \mid B)$ is approximately equal to $P(B \mid A)$ if the prior probabilities $P(A)$ and $P(B)$ are also approximately equal.

An Example

In the following constructed but realistic situation, the difference between $P(A \mid B)$ and $P(B \mid A)$ may be surprising, but is at the same time obvious. In order to identify individuals having a serious disease in an early curable form, one may consider screening a large group of people. While the benefits are obvious, an argument against such screenings is the disturbance caused by false positive screening results: If a person not having the disease is incorrectly found to have it by the initial test, they will most likely be quite distressed until a more careful test shows that they do not have the disease. Even after being told they are well, their lives may be affected negatively. The magnitude of this problem is best understood in terms of conditional probabilities.

Suppose 1% of the group suffer from the disease, and the rest are well. Choosing an individual at random,

$$P(\text{ill}) = 1\% = 0.01 \text{ and } P(\text{well}) = 99\% = 0.99.$$

Suppose that when the screening test is applied to a person not having the disease, there is a 1% chance of getting a false positive result, *i.e.*

$P(\text{positive} \mid \text{well}) = 1\%$, and $P(\text{negative} \mid \text{well}) = 99\%$.

Finally, suppose that when the test is applied to a person having the disease, there is a 1% chance of a false negative result, *i.e.*

$P(\text{negative} \mid \text{ill}) = 1\%$ and $P(\text{positive} \mid \text{ill}) = 99\%$.

Now, one may calculate the following:

The fraction of individuals in the whole group who are well and test negative:

$$P(well \cap negative)\, P(well) \times P(negative \mid well)$$

$$= 99\% \times 99\% = 98.01\%.$$

The fraction of individuals in the whole group who are ill and test positive:

$P(ill \cap positive) = P(ill) \times P(positive \mid ill) =$

$1\% \times 99\% = 0.99\%.$

The fraction of individuals in the whole group who have false positive results:

$P(well \cap positive) = P(well) \times P(positive \mid well)$

$= 99\% \times 1\% = 0.99\%.$

The fraction of individuals in the whole group who have false negative results:

$P(ill \cap negative) = P(ill) \times P(negative \mid ill)$

$= 1\% \times 1\% = 0.09\%.$

Furthermore, the fraction of individuals in the whole group who test positive:

$P(positive) = P(well \cap positive) + P(ill \cap positive)$

$= 0.99\% + 0.99\% = 1.98\%.$

Finally, the probability that an individual actually has the disease, given that the test result is positive:

$$P(ill \mid positive) = \frac{P(ill \cap positive)}{P(positive)} = \frac{0.99\%}{1.98\%} = 50\%.$$

In this example, it should be easy to relate to the difference between the conditional probabilities P(positive | ill) (which is 99%) and P(ill | positive) (which is 50%): the first is the probability that an individual who has the disease tests positive; the second is the probability that an individual who tests positive actually has the disease. With the numbers chosen here, the last result is likely to be deemed unacceptable: half the people testing positive are actually false positives.

Second Type of Conditional Probability Fallacy

Another type of fallacy is interpreting conditional probabilities of events (or a series of events) as (unconditional) probabilities, or seeing them as being in the same order of magnitude. A conditional probability of an event and its (total) probability are linked with each other through the formula of total probability, but without additional information one of them says little about the other.

The fallacy to view P(A | B) as P(A) or as being close to P(A) is often related with some forms of statistical bias but it can be subtle. *Here is an example*: One of the conditions for the legendary wild-west hero Wyatt Earp to have become a legend was having survived all the duels he survived. Indeed, it is reported that he was never wounded, not even scratched by a bullet. The probability of this to happen is very small, contributing to his fame because events of very small probabilities attract attention. However, the point is that the degree of attention depends very much on the observer. Somebody impressed by a specific event (here seeing a "hero") is prone to view effects of randomness differently from others which are less impressed. In general makes not much sense to ask after observation of a remarkable series of events "What is the probability of this?", because this is a conditional probability upon observation. The distinction between conditional and unconditional probabilities can be intricate if the observer who asks "What is the probability?" is himself/herself outcome of a random selection. The name "Wyatt Earp effect" was coined in an article "Der Wyatt Earp Effekt" (in German) showing through several examples its subtlety and impact in various scientific domains.

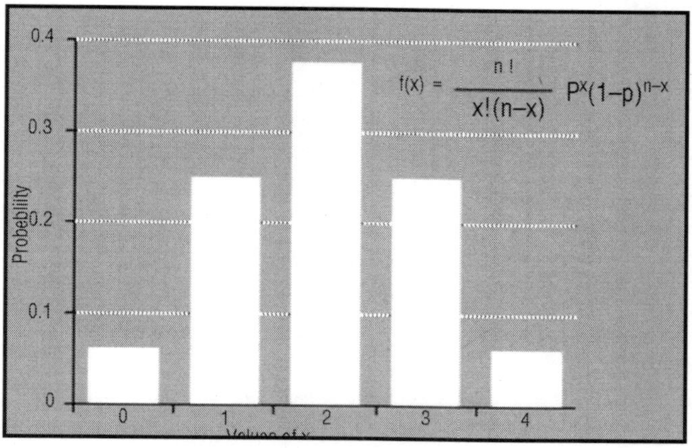

Conditioning on a Random Variable

There is also a concept of the conditional probability of an event given a discrete random variable. Such a conditional probability is a random variable in its own right. Suppose X is a random variable that can be equal either to 0 or to 1. As above, one may speak of the conditional probability of any event A given the event $X = 0$, and also of the conditional probability of A given the event $X = 1$. The former is denoted $P(A \mid X = 0)$ and the latter $P(A \mid X = 1)$. Now define a new random variable Y, whose value is $P(A \mid X = 0)$ if $X = 0$ and $P(A \mid X = 1)$ if $X = 1$. That is

$$Y = \begin{cases} P(A \mid X = 0) & \text{if} \quad X = 0; \\ P(A \mid X = 1) & \text{if} \quad X = 1. \end{cases}$$

This new random variable Y is said to be the conditional probability of the event A given the discrete random variable X:

$$\mathrm{Y} = \mathrm{P}\ (\mathrm{A} \mid \mathrm{X}).$$

According to the "law of total probability", the expected value of Y is just the marginal (or "unconditional") probability of A.

BINOMIAL DISTRIBUTION

In statistics the so-called binomial distribution describes the possible number of times that a particular event will occur in a sequence of observations. The event is coded binary, it may or may not occur. The binomial distribution is used when a researcher is interested in the occurrence of an event, not in its magnitude. For instance, in a clinical trial, a patient may survive or die. The researcher studies the number of survivors, and not how long the patient survives after treatment. Another example is whether a person is ambitious or not. Here, the binomial distribution describes the number of ambitious persons, and not how ambitious they are. The binomial distribution is specified by the number of observations, n, and the probability of occurence, which is denoted by p. A classic example that is used often to illustrate concepts of probability theory, is the tossing of a coin. If a coin is tossed 4 times, then we may obtain 0, 1, 2, 3, or 4 heads. We may also obtain 4, 3, 2, 1, or 0 tails, but these outcomes are equivalent to 0, 1, 2, 3, or 4 heads. The likelihood of obtaining 0, 1, 2, 3, or 4 heads is, respectively, 1/16, 4/16, 6/16, 4/16, and 1/16. In the figure on this page the distribution is shown with p = 1/2 Thus, in the example discussed here, one is likely to obtain 2 heads in 4 tosses, since this outcome has the highest probability. Other situations in which binomial distributions arise are quality control, public opinion surveys, medical research, and insurance problems.

Poisson Limit

If the probability p is small and the number of observations is large the binomial probabilities are hard to calculate. In this instance it is much easier to approximate the binomial probabilities by poisson probabilities. The binomial distribution approaches the poisson distribution for large n and small p. In the movie we increase the number of observations from 6 to 50, where the parameter p in the binomial distribution remains 1/10. The movie shows that the degree of approximations improves as the number of observations increases. For moderate values of p, the binomial distribution approaches the normal distribution if the number of observations is large. This is an example of thecentral limit theorem.

The *binomial distribution* describes the behaviour of a count variable *X* if the following conditions apply:

- *The number of observations n is fixed.*
- Each observation is independent.
- Each observation represents one of two outcomes ("success" or "failure").
- The probability of "success" p is the same for each outcome.

If these conditions are met, then *X* has a binomial distribution with parameters *n* and *p*, abbreviated *B(n,p)*.

Example: Suppose individuals with a certain gene have a 0.70 probability of eventually contracting a certain disease. If 100 individuals with the gene participate in a lifetime study, then the distribution of the random variable describing the number of individuals who will contract the disease is distributed *B(100,0.7)*.

Note: The sampling distribution of a count variable is only well-described by the binomial distribution is cases where the population size is significantly larger than the sample size. As a general rule, the binomial distribution should not be applied to observations from a simple random sample (SRS) unless the population size is at least 10 times larger than the sample size.

To find probabilities from a binomial distribution, one may either calculate them directly, use a binomial table, or use a computer. The number of sixes rolled by a single die in 20 rolls has a *B(20,1/6)*distribution.

The probability of rolling more than 2 sixes in 20 rolls, *P(X>2)*, is equal to 1 – *P(X<2) = 1 – (P(X=0) + P(X=1) + P(X=2))*. Using the MINITAB command "cdf" with subcommand "binomial n=20 p=0.166667" gives the cumulative distribution function as follows:

```
Binomial with n = 20 and p = 0.166667
x       P(X⇐ x)
0       0.0261
1       0.1304
2       0.3287
3       0.5665
4       0.7687
5       0.8982
6       0.9629
7       0.9887
8       0.9972
9       0.9994
```

The corresponding graphs for the probability density function and cumulative distribution function for the *B(20,1/6)* distribution are shown below:

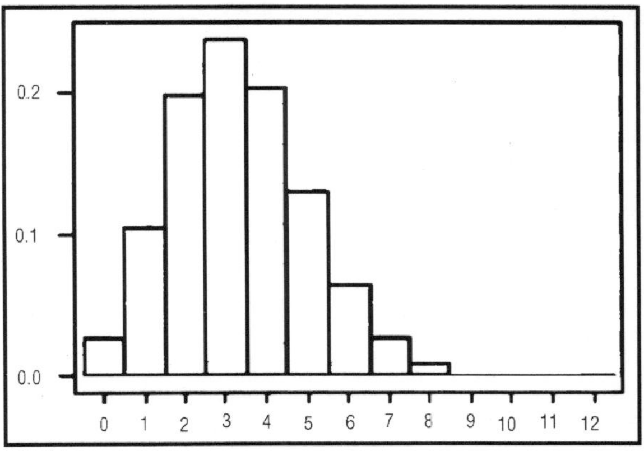

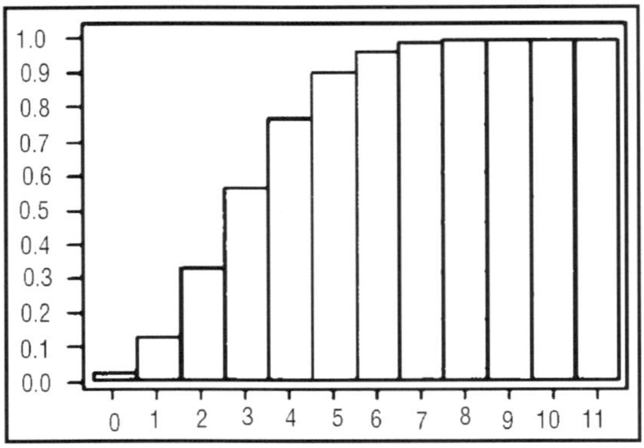

Since the probability of 2 or fewer sixes is equal to 0.3287, the probability of rolling more than 2 sixes = 1 – 0.3287 = 0.6713. The probability that a random variable X with binomial distribution $B(n,p)$ is equal to the value k, where $k = 0, 1....,n$, is given by

$$P(X = k) = \binom{n}{k} P^k (1-p)^{n-k},$$

where,

$$\binom{n}{k} = \frac{n!}{k!(n-k)!}.$$

The latter expression is known as the *binomial coefficient*, stated as "*n choose k*," or the number of possible ways to choose k "successes" from n observations.

For example, the number of ways to achieve 2 heads in a set of four tosses is,

"4 choose 2", or 4!/2!2! = (4 × 3)/(2 × 1) = 6.

The possibilities are {HHTT, HTHT, HTTH, TTHH, THHT, THTH}, where "H" represents a head and "T" represents a tail.

The binomial coefficient multiplies the probability of *one* of these possibilities (which is $(1/2)^2(1/2)^2 = 1/16$ for a fair coin) by the number of ways the outcome may be achieved, for a total probability of 6/16.

Poisson Theorem

The Poisson theorem gives a Poisson approximation to the binomial distribution, under certain conditions.[1] The theorem was named after Siméon-Denis Poisson (1781 – 1840).

$$n \to \infty \to 0, \text{ such that } np \to \lambda$$

then,

$$\frac{n!}{(n-k)!k!} p^k (1-p) n - k \to e - \lambda \frac{\lambda^k}{k!}.$$

Example

Suppose that in an interval of length 1000, 500 points are placed randomly. Now what is the number points that will be placed in a sub-interval of length 10? If we look here, the probability that a random point will be placed in the sub-interval is p = 10/1000 = 0.01. Here n = 500 so that np = 5. The probabilistically precise way of describing the number of points in the sub-interval would be to describe it as a binomial distribution pn(k). That is, the probability that k points lie in the sub-interval is,

$$pn(k) = \frac{n!}{(n-k)!k!} p^k (1-p)^{n-k}.$$

But using the Poisson Theorem we can approximate it as,

$$e - \lambda \frac{\lambda^k}{k!} = e^{-5} \frac{5^k}{k!}.$$

The Proof

Accordingly to factorial's rate of growth, we replace factorials of large numbers with approximations:

$$\frac{n!}{(n-k)!k!} p^k (1-p)^{n-k} \frac{\sqrt{2\pi n}\left(\frac{n}{e}\right)^n}{\sqrt{2\pi(n-k)}\left(\frac{n-k}{e}\right)^{n-k} k!} p^k (1-p)^{n-k}.$$

After simplifying the fraction:

$$\frac{\sqrt{2\pi n}\left(\frac{n}{e}\right)^n}{\sqrt{2\pi(n-k)}\left(\frac{n-k}{e}\right)^{n-k} k!} p^k (1-p)^{n-k} \to \frac{\sqrt{n}\, n^n p^k (1-p)^{n-k}}{\sqrt{n-k}\,(n-k)^{n-k} e^k k!}$$

$$\to \frac{n^n p^k (1-p)^{n-k}}{(n-k)^{n-k} e^k k!}$$

After using the condition $np \to \lambda$:

$$\frac{n^n p^k (1-p)n-k}{(n-k)^{n-k} e^k k!} \to \frac{n^k \left(\frac{\lambda}{n}\right)^k \left(1-\frac{\lambda}{n}\right)^{n-k}}{\left(1-\frac{\lambda}{n}\right)^{n-k} e^k k!}$$

$$= \frac{\lambda^k \left(1-\frac{\lambda}{n}\right)^{n-k}}{\left(1-\frac{\lambda}{n}\right)^{n-k} e^k k!} \to \frac{\lambda^k \left(1-\frac{\lambda}{n}\right)^{n}}{\left(1-\frac{k}{n}\right)^{n} e^k k!}$$

Apply, that due to $n \to \infty$ we get $\left(1-\frac{\lambda}{n}\right)^n \to e$:

$$\frac{\lambda^k\left(1-\frac{\lambda}{n}\right)^n}{\left(1-\frac{\lambda}{n}\right)^{n-k} e^k k!} \to \frac{\lambda^k e^{-\lambda}}{e^{-k} e^k k!} = \frac{\lambda^k e - \lambda}{k!}$$

Mean and Variance of the Binomial Distribution

The binomial distribution for a random variable X with parameters n and p represents the sum of n independent variables Z which may assume the values 0 or 1. If the probability that each Z variable assumes the value 1 is equal to p, then the mean of each variable is equal to $1p + 0(1-p) = p$, and the variance is equal to $p(1-p)$. By the addition properties for independent random variables, the mean and variance of the binomial distribution are equal to the sum of the means and variances of the n independent Z variables,

$$\mu_X = np$$

so

$$\sigma_X^2 np(1-p)$$

These definitions are intuitively logical. Imagine, for example, 8 flips of a coin. If the coin is fair, then $p = 0.5$. One would expect the mean number of heads to be half the flips, or $np = 8 \times 0.5 = 4$. The variance is equal to $np(1-p) = 8 \times 0.5 \times 0.5 = 2$.

Sample Proportions

If we know that the count X of "successes" in a group of n observations with sucess probability p has a binomial distribution with mean np and variance $np(1-p)$, then we are able to derive information about the distribution of the *sample proportion* $\hat{p}$, the count of successes X divided by the number of observations n. By the multiplicative properties of the mean, the mean of the distribution of X/n is equal to the mean of X divided by n, or $np/n = p$. This proves that the sample proportion $\hat{p}$ is an *unbiased estimator* of the population proportion p.

The variance of X/n is equal to the variance of X divided byn^2, or $(np(1-p))/n^2 = (p(1-p))/n$. This formula indicates that as the size of the sample increases, the variance decreases. In the example of rolling a six-sided die 20 times, the probability p of rolling a six on any roll is 1/6, and the count X of sixes has a $B(20, 1/6)$ distribution. The mean of this distribution is 20/6 = 3.33, and the variance is 20 × 1/6 × 5/6 = 100/36 = 2.78. The mean of the *proportion* of sixes in the 20 rolls, $X/20$, is equal to p = 1/6 = 0.167, and the variance of the proportion is equal to (1/6 × 5/6)/20 = 0.007.

Normal Approximations for Counts and Proportions

For large values of *n*, the distributions of the count *X* and the sample proportion $\hat{p}$ are approximately normal. This result follows from the Central Limit Theorem. The mean and variance for the approximately normal distribution of X are *np* and *np(1-p)*, identical to the mean and variance of the binomial(*n*,*p*) distribution. Similarly, the mean and variance for the approximately normal distribution of the sample proportion are *p* and *(p(1-p)/n)*.

Note: Because the normal approximation is not accurate for small values of n, a good rule of thumb is to use the normal approximation only if np>10 and np(1–p)>10. For example, consider a population of voters in a given state. The true proportion of voters who favour candidate A is equal to 0.40. Given a sample of 200 voters, what is the probability that more than half of the voters support candidate A?

The count *X* of voters in the sample of 200 who support candidate A is distributed *B(200,0.4)*. The mean of the distribution is equal to 200 × 0.4 = 80, and the variance is equal to 200 × 0.4 × 0.6 = 48. The standard deviation is the square root of the variance, 6.93.

The probability that more than half of the voters in the sample support candidate A is equal to the probability that *X* is greater than 100, which is equal to 1– *P(X*< 100). To use the normal approximation to calculate this probability, we should first acknowledge that the normal distribution is *continuous* and apply the *continuity correction*. This means that the probability for a single discrete value, such as 100, is extended to the probability of the *interval* (99.5,100.5).

Because we are interested in the probability that X is less than or equal to 100, the normal approximation applies to the upper limit of the interval, 100.5. If we were interested in the probability that X is strictly less than 100, then we would apply the normal approximation to the lower end of the interval, 99.5. So, applying the continuity correction and standardizing the variable X gives the following:

$$1 - P(X \leq 100)$$
$$= 1 - P(X \leq 100.5)$$
$$= 1 - P(Z \leq (100.5 - 80)/6.93)$$
$$= 1 - P(Z \leq 20.5/6.93)$$
$$= 1 - P(Z \leq 2.96) = 1 - (0.9985) = 0.0015.$$

Since the value 100 is nearly three standard deviations away from the mean 80, the probability of observing a count this high is extremely small.

BAYES' THEOREM

However, just for the sake of argument, let's say that you want to know what Bayes' formula is. Let's use the same example, but shorten each event to its one letter initial, ie: A, B, C, and D instead of Aberations, Brochmailians, Chomp-ieliens, and Defective. P(D | B) is not a Bayes problem. This is given in the problem.

Bayes' formula finds the reverse conditional probability P(B | D). It is based that the Given (D) is made of three parts, the part of D in A, the part of D in B, and the part of D in C.

$$P(B|D) = \frac{P(B \text{ and } D)}{P(A \text{ and } D) + P(B \text{ and } D) + P(C \text{ and } D)}$$

Inserting the multiplication rule for each of these joint probabilities gives,

$$P(B|D) = \frac{P(D|B) \times P(B)}{P(D|A) \times P(A) + P(D|B) \times P(B) + P(D|C) \times P(C)}$$

However, hope you agree, it is much easier to take the joint probability divided by the marginal probability. The table does the adding for you and makes the problems doable without having to memorize the formulas. Let A and B be sets. Conditional probability requires that,

$$P(A \cap B_j) = P(A)P(B_j|A), \quad (1)$$

where $\cap$ denotes intersection ("and"), and also that

$$P(A \cap B_j) = P(B_j \cap A) = P(B_j)P(A|B_j). \quad (2)$$

Therefore,

$$P(B_j|A) = \frac{P(B_j)PP(A|B_j)}{P(A)}. \quad (3)$$

Now, let

$$s \equiv \bigcup_{i=1}^{v} A_j, \quad (4)$$

so A_j is an event in s and $Aj \equiv \cap A_j = \phi \text{ for } i \neq j$, then

$$A = A \cap S = A \cap \left(\bigcap_{i=1}^{v} A_j\right) = \bigcap_{i=1}^{v} (A \cap A_i) \quad (5)$$

$$P(A) = P\left(\bigcap_{i=1}^{v} (A \cap A_i)\right) = \sum_{i=1}^{N} P(A \cap A_j). \quad (6)$$

But this can be written,

$$P(A) = \sum_{i=1}^{N} P(A_i)P(A|A_j), \quad (7)$$

So,

$$P\left(A_j|A\right)=\frac{P\left(A_j\right)P\left(A|A_j\right)}{\sum_{j=1}^{N}P\left(A_j\right)P\left(A|A_j\right)} \quad (8)$$

MONTY HALL PROBLEM DEMONSTRATION

The problem we are going to discuss is publicly one of the most well known problems in probability.

Suppose you are in a game show, and you're given the choice of three doors. Behind one door is a new car; behind the others, goats. The car and the goats were placed randomly behind the doors before the show. The rules of the game show are as follows: After you've chosen a door, the door remains closed for the time being.

The game show host, Monty Hall, who knows what is behind the doors, now has to open one of the two remaining doors, and the door he opens must have a goat behind it. If both remaining doors have goats behind them, he chooses one randomly.

After Monty Hall opens a door with a goat, he will ask you to decide whether you want to stay with your first choice or to switch to the last remaining door. Imagine that you choose Door 1 and the host opens Door 3, which has a goat. He then asks you "Do you want to switch to Door 2?" Is it to your advantage to change your choice?

In search of a new Car, the player picks door 1. The game host then opens door 3to reveal a goat offers to let the player pick door 2 instead o door1. Before going through the solution, give the problem a great deal of thought. Will switching change the probability of wining? Or will it not matter because it is equally likely that the car may be behind Door 1 or Door 2 ? O.K., now the solution. We are assuming that the player initially picked Door 1. (However, the player may initially choose any of the three doors). We'll now calculate the probability of winning by switching, by listing out all cases explicitly.

Case 1: The car is behind Door 1. In this case, the game host Monty Hall must open one of the two remaining doors randomly

Case 2: The car is behind Door 2. Then the host must open Door 3

Case 3: The car is behind Door 3. Then the host must open Door 2

If the player chooses to switch, he'll win only if the car is behind either of the two unchosen doors rather than the one that was originally picked. The following diagram visually depicts the various cases and what happens with switching.

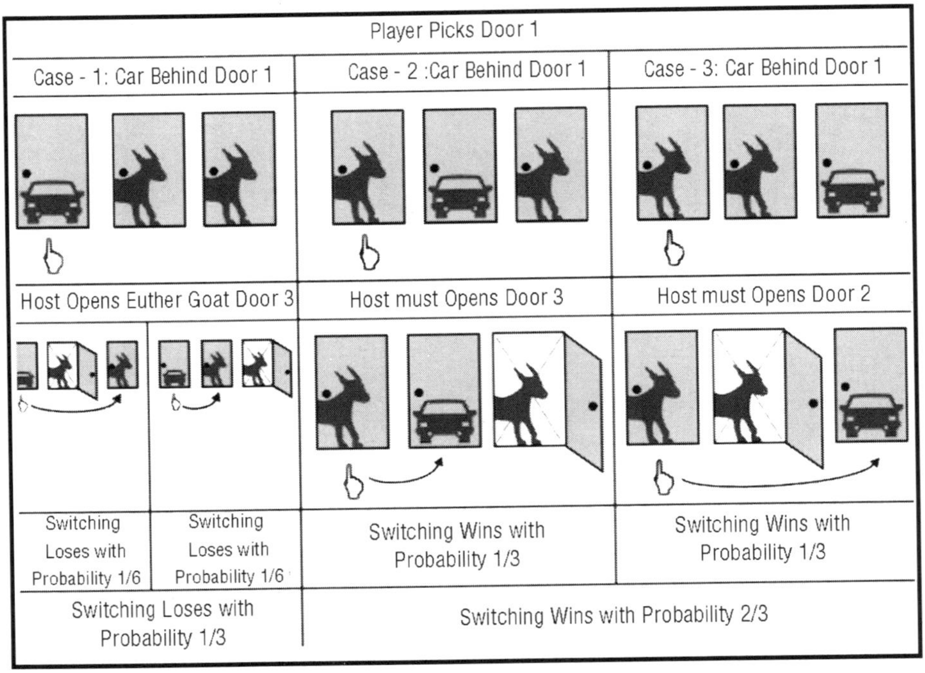

Let us explain how we arrived at the various probabilities using a probability tree. Thus, switching leads to winning with probability 2/3, that is, the player should switch for a higher probability of winning! This result may seem very counter-intuitive to you.

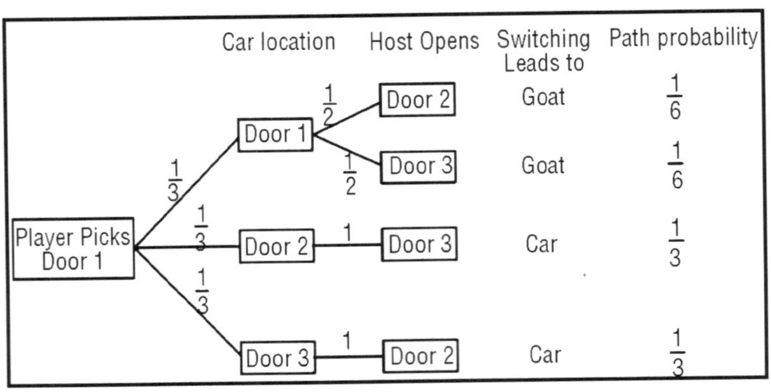

After all, you may say, the remaining two doors must each have a probability 1/2 of containing the car. However, this intuition is wrong. In fact, you are not alone in this intuition. When first presented with this problem, an overwhelming majority of people assume that each door has an equal probability and conclude that switching does not matter.

Even Nobel laureates have been known to have given the wrong answer and to have insisted upon it! For more interesting facts about this problem, you'll find a lot of resources online. Here's a different version of the same problem call "The Prisoner's Dilemma".

5

Discrete Probability Distributions

INTRODUCTION

In lecture number two, we said a Random Variable is a quantity resulting from a random experiment that, by chance, can assume different values. Such as, number of defective light bulbs produced during a week. Also, we said a Discrete Random Variable is a variable which can assume only integer values, such as, 7, 9, and so on. In other words, a discrete random variable cannot take fractions as value. Things such as people, cars, or defectives are things we can count and are discrete items.

Here three types of Discrete Probability Distribution: *Binomial Distribution, Poisson Distribution, and Hypergeometric Distribution.*

PROBABILITY DISTRIBUTION:

A probability distribution is similar to the frequency distribution of a quantitative population because both provide a long-run frequency for outcomes. In other words, a probability distribution is listing of all the possible values that a random variable can take along with their probabilities. for example, suppose we want to find out the probability distribution for the number of heads on three tosses of a coin:

First toss.........T T T T H H H H
Second toss.....T T H H T T H H
Third toss........T H T H T H T H

The probability distribution of the above experiment is as follows (columns 1, and 2 in the following table).

(Column 1)	(Column 2)	(Column 3)
Number of heads	Probability	(1)(2)
X	P(X)	(X)P(X)
0	1/8	0.0
1	3/8	0.375
2	3/8	0.75
3	1/8	0.375
Total		1.5 = E(X)

MEAN, AND VARIANCE OF DISCRETE RANDOM VARIABLES

The equation for computing the mean, or expected value of discrete random variables is as follows:

Mean = E(X) = Summation[X.P(X)]

where: E(X) = expected value, X = an event, and P(X) = probability of the event

Note that in the above equation, the probability of each event is used as the weight. For example, going back to the problem of tossing a coin three times, the expected value is: E(X) = [0(1/8) + 1(3/8) + 2(3/8) + 3(1/8) = 1.5 (column 3 in the above table). Thus, on the average, the number of heads showing face up in a large number of tossing a coin is 1.5. The expected value has many uses in gambling, for example, it tells us what our long-run average losses per play will be. The equations for computing the expected value, varance, and standard deviation of discrete random variables are as follows:

Mean (Expected) Value of a Discrere Distribution:

$$\mu = E(X) = \sum [X \cdot P(X)]$$

Variance of a Discrete Distribution:

$$\sigma' = \sum [X - \mu)^2 \cdot P(X)]$$

Standard Deiation of a Discrete Distribution:

$$\sigma = \sqrt{\sum [X - \mu)^2 \cdot P(X)]}$$

Example: Suppose a charity organization is mailing printed return-address stickers to over one million homes in the U.S. Each recipient is asked to donate either \$1, \$2, \$5, \$10, \$15, or \$20. Based on past experience, the amount a person donates is believed to follow the following probability distribution:

X:..... \$1......\$2........\$5......\$10.........\$15......\$20
P(X)....0.1.....0.2.......0.3.......0.2..........0.15.....0.05

The question is, what is expected that an average donor to contribute, and what is the standard devation. The solution is as follows.

(1)	(2)	(3)	(4)	(5)	(6)
X	P(X)	X.P(X)	X – mean	[(X – mean)] squared	(5)x(2)
1	0.1	0.1	–6.25	39.06	3.906
2	0.2	0.4	– 5.25	27.56	5.512
5	0.3	1.5	– 2.25	5.06	1.518
10	0.2	2.0	2.75	7.56	1.512
15	0.15	2.25	7.75	60.06	9.009
20	0.05	1.0	12.75	162.56	8.125
Total		7.25 = E(X)			29.585

Thus, the expected value is \$7.25, and standard deviation is the square root of \$29.585, which is equal to \$5.55. In other words, an average donor is expected to donate \$7.25 with a standard deviation of \$5.55.

Binomial Distribution

One of the most widely known of all discrete probability distributions is the binomial distribution. Several characteristics underlie the use of the binomial distribution.

Characteristics of the Binomial Distribution

- The experiment consists of n identical trials.
- Each trial has only one of the two possible mutually exclusive outcomes, success or a failure.
- The probability of each outcome does not change from trial to trial, and
- The trials are independent, thus we must sample with replacement.

Note that if the sample size, n, is less than 5% of the population, the independence assumption is not of great concern. Therefore the acceptable sample size for using the binomial distribution with samples taken without replacement is [n<5% n] where n is equal to the sample size, and N stands for the size of the population. The birth of children (male or female), true-false or multiple-choice questions (correct or incorrect answers) are some examples of the binomial distribution.

Binomial Equation

When using the binomial formula to solve problems, all that is necessary is that we be able to identify three things: the number of trials (n), the probability of a success on any one trial (p), and the number of successes desired (X). The formulas used to compute the probability, the mean, and the standard deviation of a binomial distribution are as follows.

Binomial Formula,

$$ {}_nC_x \cdot P^x \cdot q^{n-x} = \frac{n!}{X!(n-X)!} \cdot P^x \cdot q^{n-x} $$

Meab of a Binomial Distribution,

$$ \mu = n \cdot p $$

Standard Deviation of a Binomial Distribution,

$$ \sigma = \sqrt{n \cdot p \cdot q} $$

where: n = the sample size or the number of trials, X = the number of successes desired, p = probability of getting a success in one trial, and q = (1 – p) = the probability of getting a failure in one trial.

Example: Let's go back to lecture number four and solve the probability problem of defective TVs by applying the binomial equation once again. We said, suppose that 4% of all TVs made by W&B Company in 1995 are defective. If eight of these TVs are randomly selected from across the country and tested, what is the probability that *exactly* three of them are defective? Assume that each TV is made independently of the others. In this problem, n = 8, X = 3, p = 0.04, and q = (1 – p) = 0.96. Plugging these numbers into the binomial formula (see the above equation) we get: P(X) = P(3) = 0.0003 or 0.03% which is the same answer as in lecture number four. The mean is equal to (n) x (p) = (8)(0.04)=0.32, the variance is equal to np (1 – p) = (0.32) (0.96) = 0.31, and the standard deviation is the square root of 0.31, which is equal to 0.6.

The Binomial Table

Occasionally we can avoid the binomial formula. Our text has probability distributions for the binomial distribution already worked out. The values of n range from 1 to 20, and the values of p that are included are 0.05, 0.1, 0.2, 0.3, 0.4, 0.5, 0.6, 0.7, 0.8, 0.9 and 0.95. So, if the value of n is less than or equal to 20 and the value of p is one of the 12 values listed above, you should use the tables. The calculations are done for you, and all you have to be able to do is read a table. You should only resort to the formula if you can not use the tables. Ex. The probability that a student that received a C in a math class goes on to receive a C or better in their next math class is 0.1. If 5 students in a class receive C's, find the probability that 3 of them go on to receive a C or better in their next math class. n = 5 and p = 0.1, so we can use the table. Here's what it looks like.

***n* = 5**

X	.05	.1	.2	.3	.4	.5	.6	.7	.8	.9	.95
0	.774	.590	.328	.168	.078	.031	.010	.002	.000	.000	.000
1	.204	.328	.410	.360	.259	.156	.077	.028	.006	.000	.000
2	.021	.073	.205	.309	.346	.312	.230	.132	.051	.008	.001
3	.001	.008	.051	.132	.230	.312	.346	.309	.205	.073	.021
4	.000	.000	.006	.028	.077	.156	.259	.360	.410	.328	.204
5	.000	.000	.000	.002	.010	.031	.078	.168	.328	.590	.774

Once you've identified the proper table for your value of n, go down to the row that corresponds to the correct value of x.

***n* = 5**

	X	.05	.1	.2	.3	.4	.5	.6	.7	.8	.9 .95
0	.774	.590	.328	.168	.078	.031	.010	.002	.000	.000	.000
1	.204	.328	.410	.360	.259	.156	.077	.028	.006	.000	.000
2	.021	.073	.205	.309	.346	.312	.230	.132	.051	.008	.001
3	.001	.008	.051	.132	.230	.312	.346	.309	.205	.073	.021
4	.000	.000	.006	.028	.077	.156	.259	.360	.410	.328	.204
5	.000	.000	.000	.002	.010	.031	.078	.168	.328	.590	.774

Then go across to the column that corresponds to the value of p. Where this column crosses the row for x, you'll find the probability. The tables tell us the probability is 0.008, we calculated it to be 0.0081. Which do you find to be easier? If you still prefer the formula, consider the following problem. Ex. The probability that a student that received a C in a math class goes on to receive a C or better in their next math class is 0.1. If 5 students in a class receive C's, find the probability that at least 1 of them go on to receive a C or better in their next math class.

$$\begin{aligned} P(\text{at least } 1) &= P(x = 1, 2, 3, 4, \text{or } 5) \\ &= 0.328 + 0.073 + 0.008 + 0.000 + 0.000 (\text{from the table}) \\ &= 0.409 \end{aligned}$$

Much easier that using the formula 5 different times. Of course, we could have used the following strategy as well.

$$\begin{aligned} P(\text{at least } 1) &= P(x = 1, 2, 3, 4, \text{or } 5) \\ &= 1 - P(x = 0) \\ &= 1 - (0.590)(\text{from the table}) \\ &= 0.410 \end{aligned}$$

Mathematicians constructed a set of binomial tables containing presolved probabilities. Binomial distributions are a family of distributions. In other words, every different value of n and/or every different value of p gives a different binomial distribution. Tables are available for different combinations of n and p values. For the tables, refer to the text. Each table is headed by a value of n, and values of p are presented in the top row of each table of size n.

In the column below each value of p is the binomial distribution for that value of n and p. The binomial tables are easy to use. Simply look up n and p, then find X (located in the first column of each table), and read the corresponding probability. The following table is the binomial probabilities for n = 6. Note that the probabilities in each column of the binomial table must add up to 1.0.

Binomial Probability Distribution Table

(n = 6)

— —

Probability

X.....0.1........0.2.....0.3.....0.4.....0.5.....0.6.....0.7.....0.8.....0.9

— —

0.....0.531............0.118..0.000
1.....0.354............0.303..0.000
2.....0.098............0.324..0.001
3.....0.015............0.185..0.015
4.....0.001............0.060..0.098
5.....0.000............0.010..0.354
6.....0.000............0.001..0.531

Example: Suppose that an examination consists of six true and false questions, and assume that a student has no knowledge of the subject matter. The probability that the student will guess the correct answer to the first question is 30%. Likewise, the probability of guessing each of the remaining questions correctly is also 30%. What is the probability of getting more than three correct answers?

For the above problem, n = 6, p = 0.30, and X >3. In the above table, search along the row of p values for 0.30. The problem is to locate the P(X > 3). Thus, the answer involves summing the probabilities for X = 4, 5, and 6. These values appear in the X column at the intersection of each X value and p = 0.30, as follows:

P (X > 3) = Summation of {P (X=4) + P(X=5) +P(X=6)} = (0.060)+(0.010)+(0.001) = 0.071 or 7.1%

Thus, we may conclude that if 30% of the exam questions are answered by guessing, the probability is 0.071 (or 7.1%) that more than four of the questions are answered correctly by the student.

Graphing the Binomial Distribution

The graph of a binomial distribution can be constructed by using all the possible X values of a distribution and their associated probabilities. The X values are graphed along the X axis, and the probabilities are graphed along the Y axis.

Note that the graph of the binomial distribution has three shapes: If p<0.5, the graph is positively skewed, if p>0.5, the graph is negatively skewed, and if p=0.5, the graph is symmetrical. The skewness is eliminated as n gets large. In other words, if n remains constant but p becomes larger and larger up to 0.50, the shape of the binomial probability distribution becomes more symmetrical.

If p remains the same but n becomes larger and larger, the shape of the binomial probability distribution becomes more symmetrical.

The Poisson Distribution

The poisson distribution is another discrete probability distribution. It is named after Simeon-Denis Poisson (1781-1840), a French mathematician. The poisson distribution depends *only* on the average number of occurrences per unit time of space. There is no n, and no p. The poisson probability distribution provides a close approximation to the binomial probability distribution when n is large and p is quite small or quite large. In other words, if n>20 and np<=5 [or n(1-p)<="5]," then we may use poisson distribution as an approximation to binomial distribution. for detail discussion of the poisson probability distribution, refer to the text.

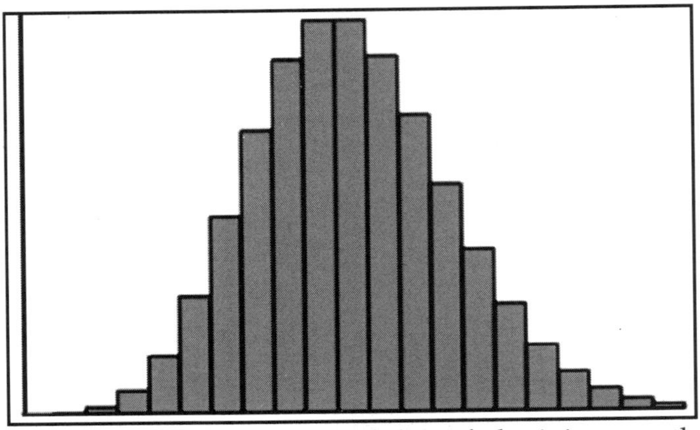

Given a Poisson process, the probability of obtaining exactly ^{n}successes in ^{N} trials is given by the limit of a binomial distribution,

$$Pp(n|N) = \frac{N!}{n!(N-n)!} p^{n} (1-p)^{N-n} \quad (1)$$

Viewing the distribution as a function of the expected number of successes,

$$\nu \equiv Np \ (2)$$

instead of the sample size ^{N}for fixed^{n}, equation (2) then becomes,

$$P\nu / N(n|N) = \frac{N!}{n!(N-n)!} \left(\frac{\nu}{N}\right)^{n} \left(1-\frac{\nu}{N}\right)^{N-n} \quad (3)$$

Letting the sample size become large, the distribution then approaches

$$P_{\nu}(n) = P\nu(n) = \lim_{x \to \infty} P_{p}(n|N) \quad (4)$$

$$= \lim_{x \to \infty} \frac{N(n-1)\cdots(N-n+1)}{n!} \frac{\nu^{n}}{N^{n}} \left(1-\frac{\nu}{N}\right)^{N} \left(1-\frac{\nu}{N}\right)^{-n} \quad (5)$$

$$= \lim_{x \to \infty} \frac{N(n-1)\cdots(N-n+1)}{N^{n}} \frac{\nu^{n}}{n!} \left(1-\frac{\nu}{N}\right)^{N} \left(1-\frac{\nu}{N}\right)^{-n} \quad (6)$$

$$= 1 \cdot \frac{\nu^{n}}{n!} \cdot e^{-\nu} \cdot 1 \quad (7)$$

$$= \frac{\nu^n e^{-\nu}}{n!}, \quad (8)$$

which is known as the Poisson distribution (Papoulis 1984, pp. 101 and 554; Pfeiffer and Schum 1973, p. 200). Note that the sample size N has completely dropped out of the probability function, which has the same functional form for all values of ν. The Poisson distribution is implemented in Mathematica as PoissonDistribution [mu].

As expected, the Poisson distribution is normalized so that the sum of probabilities equals 1, since

$$\sum_{n=0}^{\infty} P_\nu(n) = e^{-\nu} \sum_{n=0}^{\infty} \frac{\nu^n}{n!} = e^{-\nu} e^{\nu} = 1. \quad (9)$$

The ratio of probabilities is given by,

$$\frac{P_\nu(n=i+1)}{P(n=i)} = \frac{\dfrac{\nu^{2+1} e^{-\nu}}{(i+1)!}}{\dfrac{e^{-\nu}\nu^i}{1!}} = \frac{\nu}{i+1}. \quad (10)$$

The Poisson distribution reaches a maximum when,

$$\frac{d P\nu(n)}{dn} = \frac{e^{-\nu}(\gamma - H_n + \ln \nu)}{n!} = 0 \quad (11)$$

where γ is the Euler-Mascheroni constant and H_n is a harmonic number, leading to the transcendental equation $\gamma - Hn + \ln \nu = 0$, (12) which cannot be solved exactly for n.

The moment-generating function of the Poisson distribution is given by,

$$M(t) = e^{-\nu} e^{\nu e2} = e^{\nu(e^2-1)} \quad (13)$$

$$M'(t) = \nu e^1 e^{\nu(e^2-1)} \quad (14)$$

$$M''(t) = (\nu e^1)^2 e^{\nu(e^2-1)} + \nu e^1 e^{\nu(e^2-1)} \quad (15)$$

$$R(t) = \nu(e^2-1) \quad (16)$$

$$R'(t) = \nu e^1 \quad (17)$$

$$R''(t) = \nu e^1 \quad (18)$$

So,

$$\mu = R'(0) = \nu \quad (19)$$

$$\sigma^2 = R''(0) = \nu \quad (20)$$

The raw moments can also be computed directly by summation, which yields an unexpected connection with the exponential polynomial $\phi_n(x)$ and Stirling numbers of the second kind,

$$\phi_n(x) = \sum_{k=0}^{\infty} \frac{e^{-x}x^k}{k!} k^n = \sum_{k=0}^{\infty} x^k S(n,k) \qquad (21)$$

known as Dobinski's formula.

Therefore,

$$\mu_2' = \nu\,(1 + \nu) \qquad (22)$$

$$\mu_3' = \nu\,(1 + 3\nu + \nu^2) \qquad (23)$$

$$\mu_4' = \nu\,(1 + 7\nu + 6\nu^2 + \nu^3) \qquad (24)$$

The central moments can then be computed as,

$$\mu_2' = \nu \qquad (25)$$

$$\mu_3' = \nu \qquad (26)$$

$$\mu_4' = \nu\,(1 + 3\nu), \qquad (27)$$

so the mean, variance, skewness, and kurtosis are

$$\mu = \nu \qquad (28)$$

$$\sigma^2 = \nu \qquad (29)$$

$$\gamma_1 = \frac{\mu_3}{\sigma^3} = \frac{\nu}{\nu^{3/2}} = \nu^{-1/2} \qquad (30)$$

$$\gamma_2 = \nu = \bar{N} \qquad (31)$$

$$= \frac{\nu + 3\nu^2 - 3\nu^2}{\nu^2} = \nu^{-1} \qquad (32)$$

The characteristic function for the Poisson distribution is,

$$\phi(t) = e^{\nu\left(e^{it}-1\right)} \qquad (33)$$

and the cumulant-generating function is,

$$K(h) = \nu\left(e^h - 1\right) = \nu\left(h + \frac{1}{21}h^2 + \frac{1}{31}h^3 + \ldots\right). \qquad (34)$$

So,

$$K_r = \nu. \qquad (35)$$

The mean deviation of the Poisson distribution is given by,

$$MD = \frac{2e^{-\nu}\nu^{\lfloor \nu \rfloor + 1}}{\lfloor \nu \rfloor !}. \qquad (36)$$

The Poisson distribution can also be expressed in terms of,

$$\gamma \equiv \frac{\nu}{x}, \qquad (37)$$

the rate of changes, so that,

$$P\nu(n) = \frac{(\gamma x)^n\, e^{-\gamma x}}{n!} > \qquad (38)$$

The moment-generating function of a Poisson distribution in two variables is given by,

$$M(t)=e^{(v_1+v_2)(e^2-1)} \tag{39}$$

If the independent variables $x_1, x_2, \ldots, x_N$ have Poisson distributions with parameters $\mu_1, \mu_2, \ldots, \mu_N$, then,

$$X=\sum_{j=1}^{N} xj \tag{40}$$

has a Poisson distribution with parameter,

$$\mu=\sum_{j=1}^{N} \mu j. \tag{41}$$

This can be seen since the cumulant-generating function is,

$$Kj(h)=\mu_j\left(e^h-1\right) \tag{42}$$

$$K \equiv \sum_j Kj(h)=\left(e^h-1\right)\sum_j \mu j=\mu\left(e^h-1\right). \tag{43}$$

A generalization of the Poisson distribution has been used by Saslaw (1989) to model the observed clustering of galaxies in the universe. The form of this distribution is given by

$$f_b(N)=\frac{\bar{N}(1-b)}{N!}\left[\bar{N}(1-b)+Nb\right]^{N-1} e^{\bar{N}(1-b)-Nb}, \tag{44}$$

where N is the number of galaxies in a volume $V, \bar{N}=\bar{n}V, \bar{n}$ is the average density of galaxies, and

$$b=-W/(2K)\approx 0.70\pm 0.05,$$

with is the ratio of gravitational energy to the kinetic energy of peculiar motions, Letting b = 0 gives

$$f_0(N)=\frac{e^{-\bar{N}}\bar{N}^N}{N!}, \tag{45}$$

which is indeed a Poisson distribution with $v=\bar{N}$. Similarly, letting $b=1$ gives $f_1(N) = 0$.

The Hypergeometric Distribution

Another discrete probability distribution is the hypergeometric distribution. The binomial probability distribution assumes that the population from which the sample is selected is very large. For this reason, the probability of success does not change with each trial

The hypergeometric distribution is used to determine the probability of a specified number of successes and/or failures when (1) a sample is selected from a finite population without replacement and/or (2) when the sample size, n, is greater than or equal to 5% of the population size, N, *i.e.*, [n>=5% N].

Note that by *finite population we mean a population which consist of a fixed number of known individuals, objects, or measurments*. For example, there were 489 applications for the nursing school at Clayton State College in 1994. For detail discussion of the hypergeometric probability distribution, refer to the text.

An urn contains N balls, of which:

- W are white,
- R are red,

with W+R = N.

n balls are drawn from the urn, without replacement. That is, n balls (the sample) are randomly selected and taken out of the urn. The number of white balls in the sample is a random variable Y, whose distribution is known as the hypergeometric distribution.

It depends on the three parameters N, W and n and will be denoted HG(N, W, n).

Probability Mass function of the Hypergeometric Distribution

We denote P{Y = w} the probability for the sample to contain exactly w white balls.

$$P\{Y = \omega\} = \frac{\binom{W}{\omega}\binom{R}{n-\omega}}{\binom{N}{n}}$$

with max(0, n-R) ≤ w ≤ min(B, n).

Mean of the Hypergeoemtric Distribution

$$\mu = n\frac{W}{N}$$

If p denotes the initial proportion of white balls in the urn, this can also be written:

$$\mu = np$$

Variance of the Hypergeometric Distribution

$$\sigma^2 = n.\frac{WR}{N^2}\left(1 - \frac{n-1}{N-1}\right)$$

If p denotes the initial proportion of white balls in the urn, this can also be written:

$$\sigma^2 = np\ (1 - p)(1 - (n - 1)/(N - 1))$$

Note that, for a given value of p, the value of σ^2 converges to np(1 – p), that is, the variance of the binomial distribution with parameters (n, p), when N grows without limit.

6

Continuous Probability Distributions

CONTINUOUS PROBABILITY DISTRIBUTION

Continuous variables are measured, not counted. Items such as height, weight and time are continuous and can take on fractional values. For example, a basketball player may be 6.8432 feet tall. There are many continuous probability distributions, such as, uniform distribution, normal distribution, the t distrib-ution, the chi-square distribution, exponential distribution, and F distribution. In this lecture note, we will concentrate on the uniform distribution, and normal distribution.

Uniform (or Rectangular) Distribution

Among the continuous probability distribution, the uniform distribution is the simplest one of all. The following figure shows an example of a uniform distribution. In a uniform distribution, the area under the curve is equal to the product of the length and the height of the rectangle and equals to one.

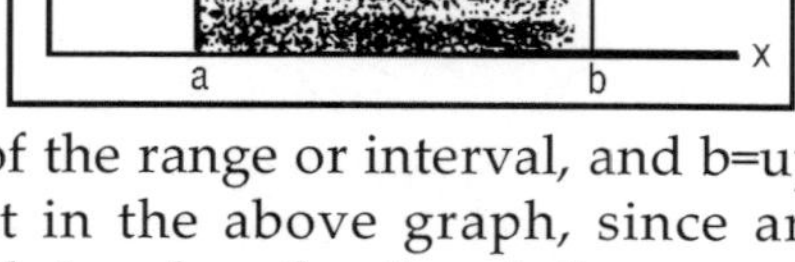

where: a=lower limit of the range or interval, and b=upper limit of the range or interval. Note that in the above graph, since area of the rectangle = (length)(height) =1, and since length = (b – a), thus we can write: (b – a)(height) = 1 or height = f(X) = 1/(b – a).

The following equations are used to find the mean and standard deviation of a uniform distribution:

Mean =

$$\mu = \frac{a+b}{2}$$

Standard deviation =

$$\sigma = \frac{b-a}{\sqrt{12}}$$

$$f(X) = Heights = \frac{1}{(b-a)}$$

Example: There are many cases in which we may be able to apply the uniform distribution. As an example, suppose that the research department of a steel factory believes that one of the company's rolling machines is producing sheets of steel of different thickness. The thickness is a uniform random variable with values between 150 and 200 millimeters. Any sheets less than 160 millimeters thick must be scrapped because they are unacceptable to the buyers.

We want to calculate the mean and the standard deviation of the X (the tickness of the sheet produced by this machine), and the fraction of steel sheet produced by this machine that have to be scrapped. The following figure displays the uniform distribution for this example.

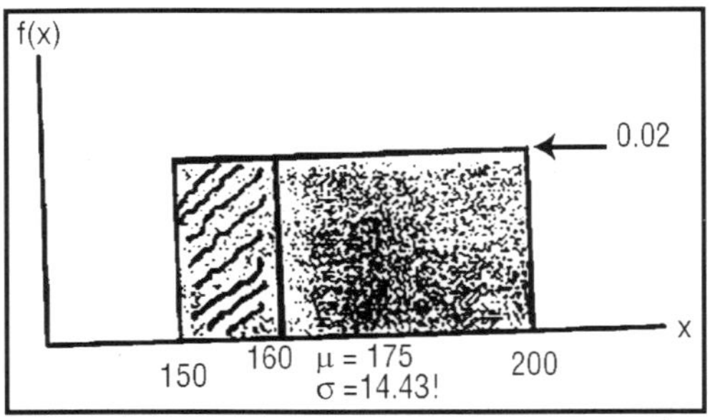

Note that for continuous distribution, probability is calculated by finding the area under the function over a specific interval. In other words, for continuous distributions, there is no probability at any one point. The probability of X>= b or of X ⇐ a is zero because there is no area above b or below a, and area between a and b is equal to one. The probability of the variables falling between any two points, such as c and d in figure are calculated as follows:

P (c ⇐ x ⇐"d)" c)/(b a))=?

In this example c=a=150, d=160, and b=200, therefore:

Mean = (a + b)/2 = (150 + 200)/2 = 175 millimeters, standard deviation is the square root of 208.3, which is equal to 14.43 millimeters, and P(c ⇐ x ⇐"d)" 150)/(200 150)="1/5" thus, of all the sheets made by this machine, 20% of the production must be scrapped.)

Normal Distribution or Normal Curve

Normal distribution is probably one of the most important and widely used continuous distribution. It is known as a normal random variable, and its probability distribution is called a normal distribution. The following are the characteristics of the normal distribution:

Characteristics of the Normal Distribution

- It is bell shaped and is symmetrical about its mean.
- It is asymptotic to the axis, *i.e.*, it extends indefinitely in either direction from the mean.
- It is a continuous distribution.
- It is a family of curves, *i.e.*, every unique pair of mean and standard deviation defines a different normal distribution. Thus, the normal distribution is completely described by two parameters: mean and standard deviation.
- Total area under the curve sums to 1, *i.e.*, the area of the distribution on each side of the mean is 0.5.
- It is unimodal, *i.e.*, values mound up only in the centre of the curve.
- The probability that a random variable will have a value between any two points is equal to the area under the curve between those points.

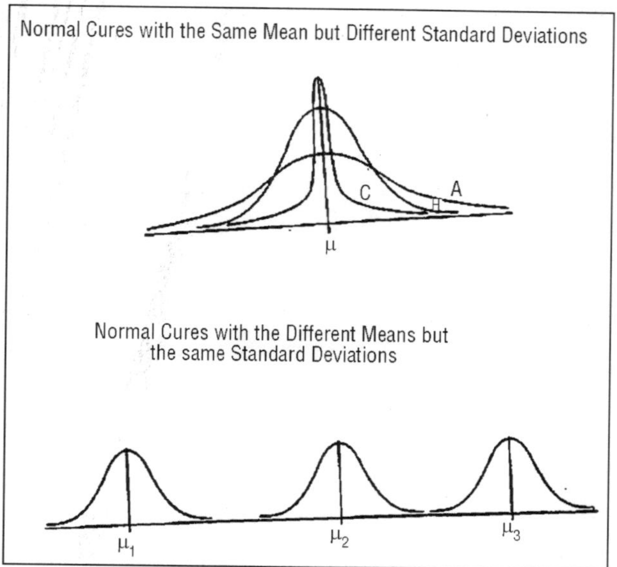

Note that the integral calculus is used to find the area under the normal distribution curve. However, this can be avoided by transforming all normal distribution to fit the standard normal distribution.

This conversion is done by rescalling the normal distribution axis from its true units (time, weight, dollars, and...) to a standard measure called Z score or Z value. A Z score is the number of standard deviations that a value, X, is away from the mean. If the value of X is greater than the mean, the Z score is positive; if the value of X is less than the mean, the Z score is negative.

The Z score or equation is as follows:

$$Z = (X - \text{Mean})/\text{Standard deviation}$$

A standard Z table can be used to find probabilities for any normal curve problem that has been converted to Z scores. For the table, refer to the text. The Z distribution is a normal distribution with a mean of 0 and a standard deviation of 1.

The following steps are helpfull when working with the normal curve problems:

- Graph the normal distribution, and shade the area related to the probability you want to find.
- Convert the boundaries of the shaded area from X values to the standard normal random variable Z values using the Z formula above.
- Use the standard Z table to find the probabilities or the areas related to the Z values in step 2.

Example one: Graduate Management Aptitude Test (GMAT) scores are widely used by graduate schools of business as an entrance requirement.

Suppose that in one particular year, the mean score for the GMAT was 476, with a standard deviation of 107. Assuming that the GMAT scores are normally distributed, answer the following questions: Question 1. What is the probability that a randomly selected score from this GMAT falls between 476 and 650? <= x ⇐"650)" the following figure shows a graphic representation of this problem.

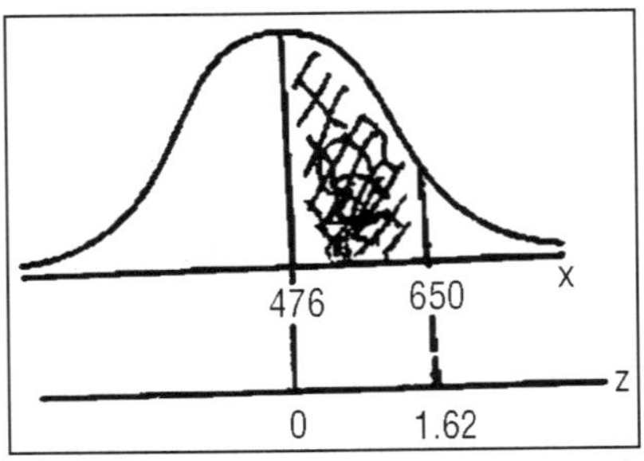

Applying the Z equation, we get: Z = (650 - 476)/107 = 1.62. The Z value of 1.62 indicates that the GMAT score of 650 is 1.62 standard deviation above the mean. The standard normal table gives the probability of value falling between 650 and the mean.

The whole number and tenths place portion of the Z score appear in the first column of the table. Across the top of the table are the values of the hundredths place portion of the Z score. Thus the answer is that 0.4474 or 44.74% of the scores on the GMAT fall between a score of 650 and 476. Question 2. What is the probability of receiving a score greater than 750 on a GMAT test that has a mean of 476 and a standard deviation of 107? *i.e.*, P(X > = 750) = ?. This problem is asking for determining the area of the upper tail of the distribution. The Z score is: Z = (750 – 476)/107 = 2.56. From the table, the probability for this Z score is 0.4948. This is the probability of a GMAT with a score between 476 and 750.

The rule is that when we want to find the probability in either tail, we must substract the table value from 0.50. Thus, the answer to this problem is: 0.5 – 0.4948 = 0.0052 or 0.52%. Note that P(X >= 750) is the same as P(X >750), because, in continuous distribution, the area under an exact number such as X=750 is zero. The following figure shows a graphic representation of this problem.

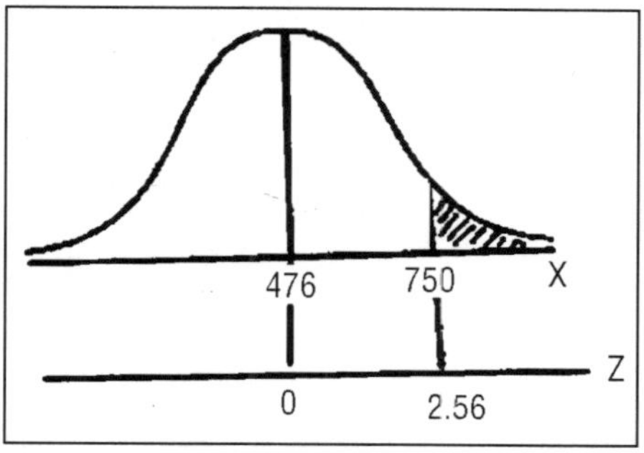

Question 3. What is the probability of receiving a score of 540 or less on a GMAT test that has a mean of 476 and a standard deviation of 107? *i.e.,* P(X <= 540)="?."

we are asked to determine the area under the curve for all values less than or equal to 540. the z score is: z="(540" 476)/107="0.6." from the table, the probability for this z score is 0.2257 which is the probability of getting a score between the mean (476) and 540. the rule is that when we want to find the probability between two values of x on*either side of the mean, we just add the two areas together.*

Thus, the answer to this problem is: 0.5 + 0.2257 = 0.73 or 73%. The following figure shows a graphic representation of this problem.

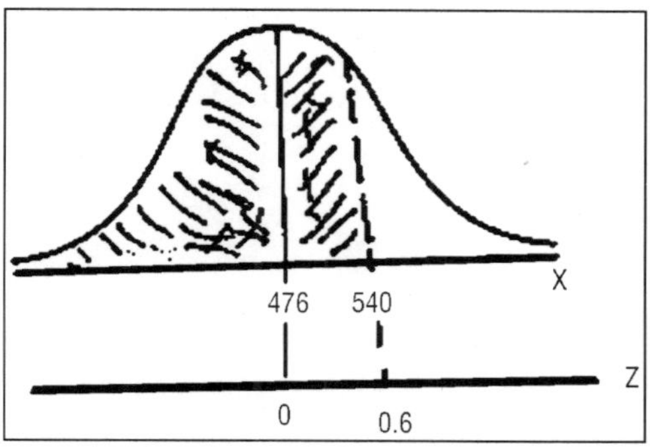

Question 4. What is the probability of receiving a score between 440 and 330 on a GMAT test that has a mean of 476 and a standard deviation of 107?

i.e., P(330 < 440)="?." the solution to this problem involves determining the area of the shaded slice in the lower half of the curve in the following figure.

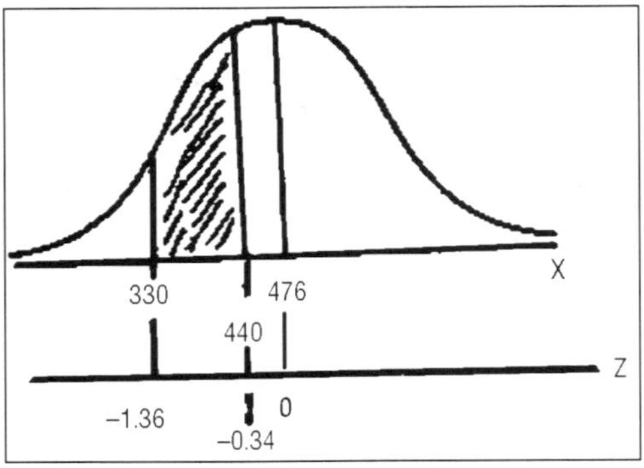

In this problem, the two values fall on the same side of the mean. The Z scores are: Z1 = (330 – 476)/107 = –1.36, and Z2 = (440 – 476)/107 = – 0.34. The probability associated with Z = –1.36 is 0.4131, and the probability associated with Z = –0.34 is 0.1331.

The rule is that when we want to find the probability between two values of X on one side of the mean, we just subtract the smaller area from the larger area to get the probability between the two values. Thus, the answer to this problem is: 0.4131 – 0.1331 = 0.28 or 28%.

Example two: Suppose that a tire factory wants to set a mileage guarantee on its new model called LA 50 tire. Life tests indicated that the mean mileage is 47,900, and standard deviation of the normally distributed distribution of mileage is 2,050 miles.

The factory wants to set the guaranteed mileage so that no more than 5% of the tires will have to be replaced. What guaranteed mileage should the factory announce? *i.e.,* P(X ⇐ ?)="5%.<br"> In this problem, the mean and standard deviation are given, but X and Z are unknown. The problem is to solve for an X value that has 5% or 0.05 of the X values less than that value.

If 0.05 of the values are less than X, then 0.45 lie between X and the mean (0.5 - 0.05), see the following graph.

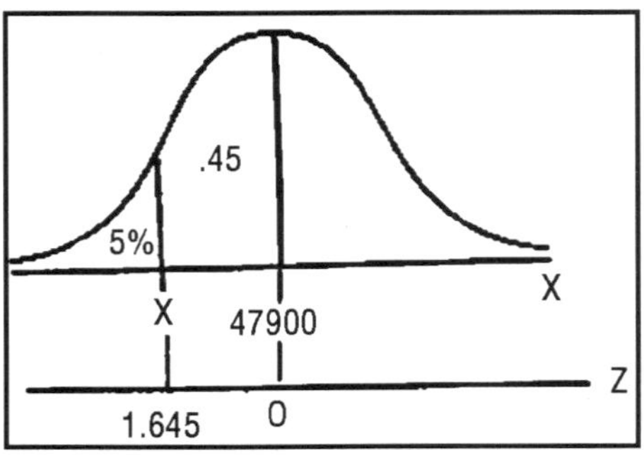

Refer to the standard normal distribution table and search the body of the table for 0.45. Since the exact number is not found in the table, search for the closest number to 0.45. There are two values equidistant from 0.45— 0.4505 and 0.4495. Move to the left from these values, and read the Z scores in the margin, which are: 1.65 and 1.64. Take the average of these two Z scores, *i.e.*, (1.65 + 1.64)/2 = 1.645. Plug this number and the values of the mean and the standard deviation into the Z equation, you get:

Z =(X – mean)/standard deviation or –1.645 =(X – 47,900)/2,050 = 44,528 miles.

Thus, the factory should set the guaranteed mileage at 44,528 miles if the objective is not to replace more than 5% of the tires.

The Normal Approximation to the Binomial Distribution

The binomial probability distribution is a discrete distribution. You remember that we said as sample sizes get larger, binomial distribution approach the normal distribution in shape regardless of the value of p (probability of success). For large sample values, the binomial distribution is cumbersome to analyse without a computer.

Fortunately, the normal distribution is a good approximation for binomial distribution problems for large values of n. The commonly accepted guidelines for using the normal approximation to the binomial probability distribution is when (n x p) and [n(1 – p)] are both greater than 5.

Example: Suppose that the management of a restaurant claimed that 70% of their customers returned for another meal. In a week in which 80 new (first-time) customers dined at the restaurant, what is the probability that 60 or more of the customers will return for another meal?, ie., P(X >= 60) =?.

The solution to this problem can be illustrated as follows: First, the two guidelines that (n x p) and [n(1 - p)] should be greater than 5 are satisfied:

$$(n \times p) = (80 \times 0.70) = 56 > 5,$$

and

$$[n(1 - p)] = 80(1 - 0.70) = 24 > 5.$$

Second, we need to find the mean and the standard deviation of the binomial distribution. The mean is equal to (n x p) = (80 x 0.70) = 56 and standard deviation is square root of [(n x p)(1 - p)], *i.e.*, square root of 16.8, which is equal to 4.0988.

Using the Z equation we get, Z = (X - mean)/standard deviation = (59.5 - 56)/4.0988 = 0.85. From the table, the probability for this Z score is 0.3023 which is the probability between the mean (56) and 60. We must substract this table value 0.3023 from 0.5 in order to get the answer, *i.e.*, P(X >= 60) = 0.5 – 0.3023 = 0.1977. Therefore, the probability is 19.77% that 60 or more of the 80 first-time customers will return to the restaurant for another meal.

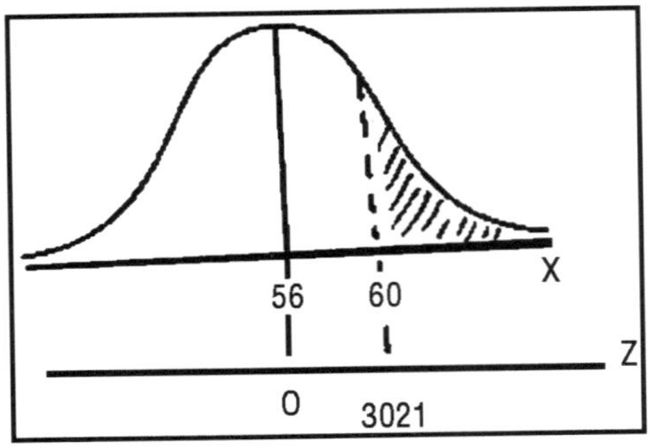

Correction Factor

The value 0.5 is added or subtracted, depending on the problem, to the value of X when a binomial probability distribution is being approximated by a normal distribution. This correction ensures that most of the binomial problem's information is correctly transferred to the normal curve analysis. This correction is called the correction for continuity. The decision as to how to correct for continuity depends on the equality sign and the direction of the desired outcomes of the binomial distribution.

The following table shows some rules of thumb that can help in the application of the correction for continuity.

Value Being Determined ....Correction
X >...+0.50
X > =..-0.50
X <...-0.50
X <=..+0.50
<= X <=”....................................-0.50" & +0.50
<..+0.50 & 0.50
X =...*-0.50 & +0.50*

7

Database Management Systems

BACKGROUND OF DBMSS

DBMSs come in many shapes and sizes. For a few hundred dollars, you can purchase a DBMS for your desktop computer. For larger computer systems, much more expensive DBMSs are required. Many mainframe-based DBMSs are leased by organisations. DBMSs of this scale are highly sophisticated and would be extremely expensive to develop from scratch. Therefore, it is cheaper for an organisation to lease such a DBMS programme than to develop it.

HISTORY

Databases have been in use since, the earliest days of electronic computing. Unlike modern systems, which can be applied to widely different databases and needs, the vast majority of older systems were tightly linked to the custom databases in order to gain speed at the expense of flexibility. Originally DBMSs were found only in large organisations with the computer hardware needed to support large data sets.

1960s Navigational DBMS

As computers grew in speed and capability, a number of general-purpose database systems emerged; by the mid-1960s there were a number of such systems in commercial use. Interest in a standard began to grow, and Charles Bachman, author of one such product, the Integrated Data Store (IDS), founded the "Database Task Group" within CODASYL, the group responsible for the creation and standardisation of COBOL. In 1971 they delivered their standard, which generally became known as the "Codasyl approach", and soon a number of commercial products based on this approach were made available. The Codasyl approach was based on the "manual" navigation of a linked data set which was formed into a large network. When the database was first opened, the programme was handed back a link to the first record in the database, which also contained pointers to other pieces of data. To find any particular record the programmer had to step through these pointers one at a time until the required record was returned. Simple queries like "find all the people in

India" required the programme to walk the entire data set and collect the matching results one by one. There was, essentially, no concept of "find" or "search".

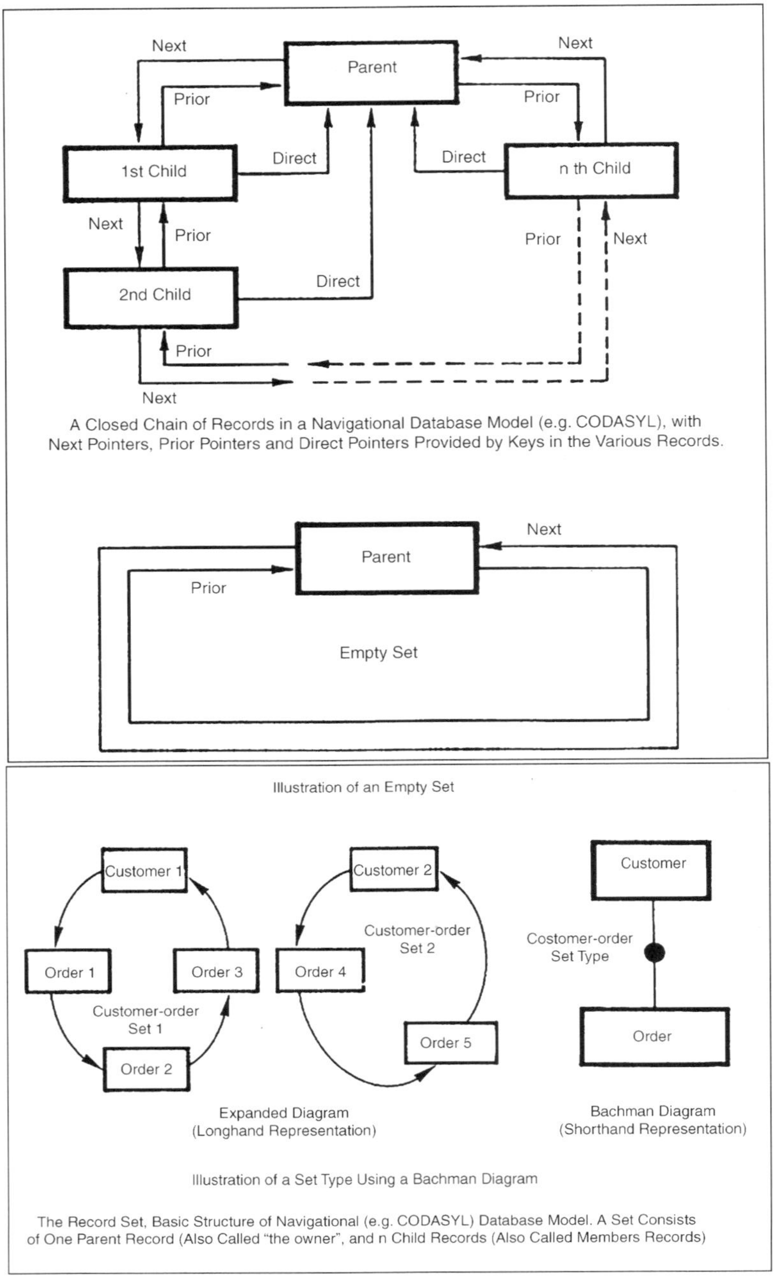

Fig. Basic Structure of Navigational CODASYL Database Model.

This may sound like a serious limitation today, but in an era when most data was stored on magnetic tape such operations were too expensive to contemplate anyway. Solutions were found to many of these problems. Prime Computer created a CODASYL compliant DBMS based entirely on B-Trees that circumvented the record by record problem by providing alternate access paths. They also added a query language that was very straightforward. Further, there is no reason that relational normalisation concepts cannot be applied to CODASYL databases however, in the final tally, CODASYL was very complex and required significant training and effort to produce useful applications.

IBM also had their own DBMS system in 1968, known as IMS. IMS was a development of software written for the Apollo programme on the System/ 360. IMS was generally similar in concept to Codasyl, but used a strict hierarchy for its model of data navigation instead of Codasyl's network model. Both concepts later became known as navigational databases due to the way data was accessed, and Bachman's 1973 Turing Award presentation was The Programmer as Navigator. IMS is classified as a hierarchical database. IDMS and CINCOM's TOTAL database are classified as network databases.

1970s Relational DBMS

Edgar Codd worked at IBM in San Jose, California, in one of their offshoot offices that was primarily involved in the development of hard disk systems. He was unhappy with the navigational model of the Codasyl approach, notably the lack of a "search" facility. In 1970, he wrote a number of papers that outlined a new approach to database construction that eventually culminated in the groundbreaking A Relational Model of Data for Large Shared Data Banks.

In this paper, he described a new system for storing and working with large databases. Instead of records being stored in some sort of linked list of free-form records as in Codasyl, Codd's idea was to use a "table" of fixed-length records. A linked-list system would be very inefficient when storing "sparse" databases where some of the data for any one record could be left empty. The relational model solved this by splitting the data into a series of normalised tables (or relations), with optional elements being moved out of the main table to where they would take up room only if needed.

For instance, a common use of a database system is to track information about users, their name, login information, various addresses and phone numbers. In the navigational approach all of these data would be placed in a single record, and unused items would simply not be placed in the database. In the relational approach, the data would be normalised into a user table, an address table and a phone number table (for instance). Records would be created in these optional tables only if the address or phone numbers were actually provided.

Linking the information back together is the key to this system. In the relational model, some bit of information was used as a "key", uniquely defining a particular record. When information was being collected about a user, information stored in the optional tables would be found by searching for this key.

For instance, if the login name of a user is unique, addresses and phone numbers for that user would be recorded with the login name as its key. This "re-linking" of related data back into a single collection is something that traditional computer languages are not designed for.

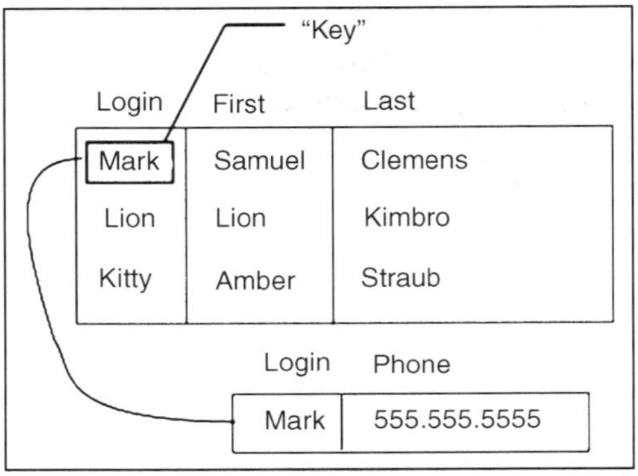

Fig. In the Relational Model, Related Records are Linked Together with a "Key"

Just as the navigational approach would require programmes to loop in order to collect records, the relational approach would require loops to collect information about any one record. Codd's solution to the necessary looping was a set-oriented language, a suggestion that would later spawn the ubiquitous SQL. Using a branch of mathematics known as tuple calculus, he demonstrated that such a system could support all the operations of normal databases (inserting, updating, etc.) as well as providing a simple system for finding and returning sets of data in a single operation.

Codd's paper was picked up by two people at Berkeley, Eugene Wong and Michael Stonebraker. They started a project known as INGRES using funding that had already been allocated for a geographical database project, using student programmers to produce code. Beginning in 1973, INGRES delivered its first test products which were generally ready for widespread use in 1979. During this time, a number of people had moved "through" the group - perhaps as many as 30 people worked on the project, about five at a time. INGRES was similar to System R in a number of ways, including the use of a "language" for data access, known as QUEL - QUEL was in fact relational, having been based on Codd's own Alpha language, but has since, been corrupted to follow SQL, thus violating much the same concepts of the relational model as SQL itself. IBM itself did one test implementation of the relational model, PRTV, and a production one, Business System 12, both now discontinued. Honeywell did MRDS for Multics, and now there are two new implementations: Alphora Dataphor and Rel. All other DBMS implementations usually called relational are actually SQL DBMSs. In 1970, the University of Michigan began development of the MICRO Information Management System based on D.L.

Childs' Set-Theoretic Data model. Micro was used to manage very large data sets by the US Department of Labour, the U.S. Environmental Protection Agency, and researchers from the University of Alberta, the University of Michigan, and Wayne State University. It ran on IBM mainframe computers using the Michigan Terminal System. The system remained in production until 1998.

Late-1970s SQL DBMS

IBM started working on a prototype system loosely based on Codd's concepts as System R in the early 1970s. The first version was ready in 1974/5, and work then started on multi-table systems in which the data could be split so that all of the data for a record (some of which is optional) did not have to be stored in a single large "chunk". Subsequent multi-user versions were tested by customers in 1978 and 1979, by which time a standardised query language - SQL - had been added. Codd's ideas were establishing themselves as both workable and superior to Codasyl, pushing IBM to develop a true production version of System R, known as SQL/DS, and, later, Database 2 (DB2).

Many of the people involved with INGRES became convinced of the future commercial success of such systems, and formed their own companies to commercialise the work but with an SQL interface. Sybase, Informix, NonStop SQL and eventually Ingres itself were all being sold as offshoots to the original INGRES product in the 1980s. Even Microsoft SQL Server is actually a re-built version of Sybase, and thus, INGRES. Only Larry Ellison's Oracle started from a different chain, based on IBM's papers on System R, and beat IBM to market when the first version was released in 1978.

Stonebraker went on to apply the lessons from INGRES to develop a new database, Postgres, which is now known as PostgreSQL. PostgreSQL is often used for global mission critical applications (the.org and.info domain name registries use it as their primary data store, as do many large companies and financial institutions). In Sweden, Codd's paper was also read and Mimer SQL was developed from the mid-70s at Uppsala University. In 1984, this project was consolidated into an independent enterprise. In the early 1980s, Mimer introduced transaction handling for high robustness in applications, an idea that was subsequently implemented on most other DBMS.

1980s Object-oriented Databases

The 1980s, along with a rise in object oriented programming, saw a growth in how data in various databases were handled. Programmers and designers began to treat the data in their databases as objects. That is to say that if a person's data were in a database, that person's attributes, such as their address, phone number, and age, were now considered to belong to that person instead of being extraneous data. This allows for relations between data to be relations to objects and their attributes and not to individual fields.

Another big game changer for databases in the 1980s was the focus on increasing reliability and access speeds. In 1989, two professors from the University of Wisconsin at Madison published an article at an ACM associated conference outlining their methods on increasing database performance. The idea was to replicate specific important, and often queried information, and store it in a smaller temporary database that linked these key features back to the main database.

This meant that a query could search the smaller database much quicker, rather than search the entire dataset. This eventually leads to the practice of indexing, which is used by almost every operating system from Windows to the system that operates Apple iPod devices.

21st Century NoSQL Databases

In the 21st century a new trend of NoSQL databases was started. Those non-relational databases are significantly different from the classic relational databases. They often do not require fixed table schemas, avoid join operations by storing denormalised data, and are designed to scale horizontally. Most of them can be classified as either key-value stores or document-oriented databases.

In recent years there was a high demand for massively distributed databases with high partition tolerance but according to the CAP theorem it is impossible for a distributed system to simultaneously provide consistency, availability and partition tolerance guarantees. A distributed system can satisfy any two of these guarantees at the same time, but not all three. For that reason many NoSQL databases are using what is called eventual consistency to provide both availability and partition tolerance guarantees with a maximum level of data consistency. The most popular software in that category include: MongoDB, memcached, Redis, CouchDB, Apache Cassandra and HBase, that all are open-source software products.

XML DATABASES

A subset of NoSQL databases are XML databases. They all use industry standard XML data storage format. XML is open, machine-readable and cross-platform data format widely used for interoperability among different IT systems.

Software in this category include: BaseX, eXist, MarkLogic Server, MonetDB/XQuery, Sedna. All XML databases can be attributed to document-oriented databases.

AN INTRODUCTION TO DATABASE MANAGEMENT SYSTEMS

A database is a collection of related files that are usually integrated, linked or cross-referenced to one another. The advantage of a database is that data and records contained in different files can be easily organised and retrieved using specialised database management software called a database management system (DBMS) or database manager.

DBMS FUNDAMENTALS

A database management system is a set of software programmes that allows users to create, edit and update data in database files, and store and retrieve data from those database files. Data in a database can be added, deleted, changed, sorted or searched all using a DBMS. If you were an employee in a large organisation, the information about you would likely be stored in different files that are linked together.

One file about you would pertain to your skills and abilities, another file to your income tax status, another to your home and office address and telephone number, and another to your annual performance ratings. By cross-referencing these files, someone could change a person's address in one file and it would automatically be reflected in all the other files. DBMSs are commonly used to manage:

DBMSs and File Management Systems

Computerised file management systems (sometimes called file managers) are not considered true database management systems because files cannot be easily linked to each other.

However, they can serve as useful data management functions by providing a system for storing information in files. For example, a file management system might be used to store a mailing list or a personal address book. When files need to be linked, a relational database should be created using database application software such as Oracle, Microsoft Access, IBM DB2, or FileMaker Pro.

The Advantages of a DBMS

Improved availability: One of the principle advantages of a DBMS is that the same information can be made available to different users.

Minimized redundancy: The data in a DBMS is more concise because, as a general rule, the information in it appears just once. This reduces data redundancy, or in other words, the need to repeat the same data over and over again. Minimizing redundancy can therefore significantly reduce the cost of storing information on hard drives and other storage devices. In contrast, data fields are commonly repeated in multiple files when a file management system is used.

Accuracy: Accurate, consistent, and up-to-date data is a sign of data integrity. DBMSs foster data integrity because updates and changes to the data only have to be made in one place. The chances of making a mistake are higher if you are required to change the same data in several different places than if you only have to make the change in one place.

Programme and file consistency: Using a database management system, file formats and system programmes are standardised. This makes the data files easier to maintain because the same rules and guidelines apply across all types of data. The level of consistency across files and programmes also makes it easier to manage data when multiple programmers are involved.

User-friendly: Data is easier to access and manipulate with a DBMS than without it. In most cases, DBMSs also reduce the reliance of individual users on computer specialists to meet their data needs.

Improved security: As stated earlier, DBMSs allow multiple users to access the same data resources. This capability is generally viewed as a benefit, but there are potential risks for the organisation. Some sources of information should be protected or secured and only viewed by select individuals. Through the use of passwords, database management systems can be used to restrict data access to only those who should see it.

The Disadvantages of a DBMS

There are basically two major downsides to using DBMSs. One of these is cost, and the other the threat to data security.

Cost: Implementing a DBMS system can be expensive and time-consuming, especially in large organisations. Training requirements alone can be quite costly.

Security: Even with safeguards in place, it may be possible for some unauthorised users to access the database. In general, database access is an all or nothing proposition. Once an unauthorised user gets into the database, they have access to all the files, not just a few. Depending on the nature of the data involved, these breaches in security can also pose a threat to individual privacy. Steps should also be taken to regularly make backup copies of the database files and store them because of the possibility of fires and earthquakes that might destroy the system.

TYPES OF DBMS: HIERARCHICAL DATABASES

There are four structural types of database management systems: hierarchical, network, relational, and object-oriented.

Hierarchical Databases (DBMS), commonly used on mainframe computers, have been around for a long time. It is one of the oldest methods of organising and storing data, and it is still used by some organisations for making travel reservations. A hierarchical database is organised in pyramid fashion, like the branches of a tree extending downwards. Related fields or records are grouped together so that there are higher-level records and lower-level records, just like the parents in a family tree sit above the subordinated children.

Based on this analogy, the parent record at the top of the pyramid is called the root record. A child record always has only one parent record to which it is linked, just like in a normal family tree. In contrast, a parent record may have more than one child record linked to it. Hierarchical databases work by moving from the top down. A record search is conducted by starting at the top of the pyramid and working down through the tree from parent to child until the appropriate child record is found. Furthermore, each child can also be a parent with children underneath it.

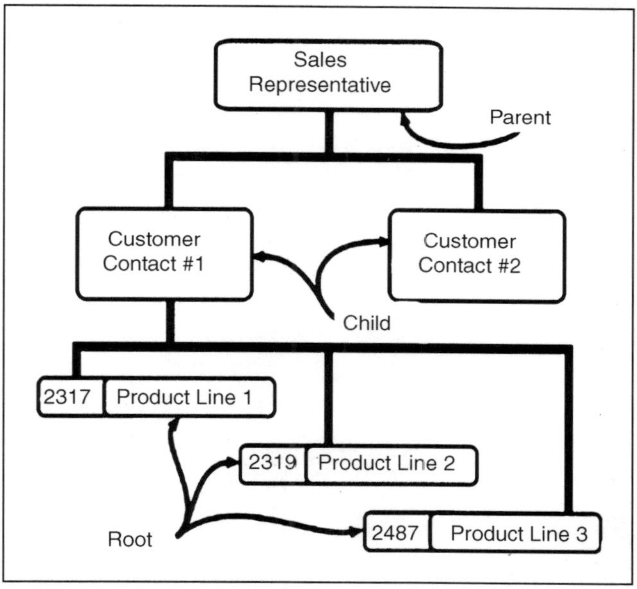

Fig. Hierarchical Databases

The advantage of hierarchical databases is that they can be accessed and updated rapidly because the tree-like structure and the relationships between records are defined in advance. However, this feature is a two-edged sword. The disadvantage of this type of database structure is that each child in the tree may have only one parent, and relationships or linkages between children are not permitted, even if they make sense from a logical standpoint. Hierarchical databases are so rigid in their design that adding a new field or record requires that the entire database be redefined.

THE HIERARCHICAL STRUCTURE

The hierarchical structure was used in early mainframe DBMS. Records' relationships form a treelike model. This structure is simple but nonflexible because the relationship is confined to a one-to-many relationship. IBM's IMS system and the RDM Mobile are examples of a hierarchical database system with multiple hierarchies over the same data. RDM Mobile is a newly designed embedded database for a mobile computer system. The hierarchical structure is used primarily today for storing geographic information and file systems.

A hierarchical database model is a data model in which the data is organised into a tree-like structure. The structure allows representing information using parent/child relationships: each parent can have many children, but each child has only one parent (also known as a 1-to-many relationship). All attributes of a specific record are listed under an entity type.

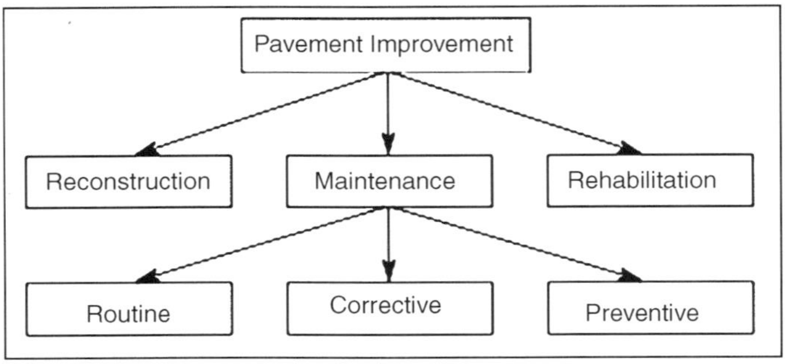

Fig. Hierarchical Model.

In a database an entity type is the equivalent of a table. Each individual record is represented as a row, and each attribute as a column. Entity types are related to each other using 1:N mappings, also known as one-to-many relationships. This model is recognised as the first database model created by IBM in the 1960s. Currently the most widely used hierarchical databases are IMS developed by IBM and Windows Registry by Microsoft.

The Network Structure

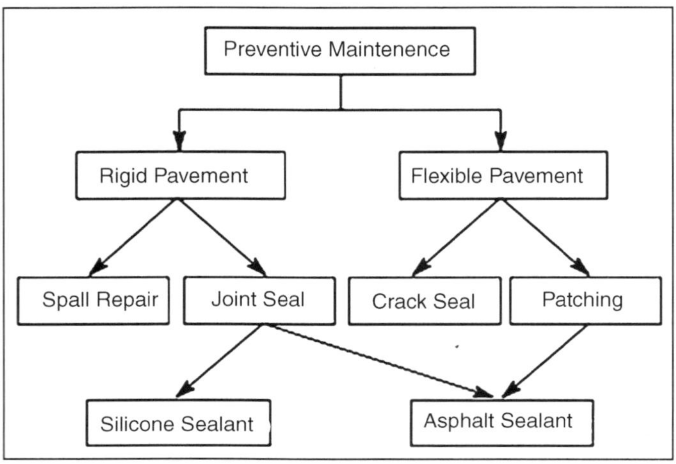

Fig. Network Model.

The network structure consists of more complex relationships. Unlike the hierarchical structure, it can relate to many records and accesses them by following one of several paths. In other words, this structure allows for many-to-many relationships. For computer network models, see network topology, packet generation model and channel model. The network model is a database model conceived as a flexible way of representing objects and their relationships. Its distinguishing feature is that the schema, viewed as a graph in which object types are nodes and relationship types are arcs, is not restricted to being a hierarchy or lattice.

The network model's original inventor was Charles Bachman, and it was developed into a standard specification published in 1969 by the CODASYL Consortium.

The Relational Structure

The relational structure is the most commonly used today. It is used by mainframe, midrange and microcomputer systems. It uses two-dimensional rows and columns to store data. The tables of records can be connected by common key values. While working for IBM, E.F. Codd designed this structure in 1970. The model is not easy for the end user to run queries with because it may require a complex combination of many tables.

The Multidimensional Structure

The multidimensional structure is similar to the relational model. The dimensions of the cube-like model have data relating to elements in each cell. This structure gives a spreadsheet-like view of data. This structure is easy to maintain because records are stored as fundamental attributes-in the same way they are viewed-and the structure is easy to understand. Its high performance has made it the most popular database structure when it comes to enabling online analytical processing (OLAP).

The Object-oriented Structure

The object-oriented structure has the ability to handle graphics, pictures, voice and text, types of data, without difficulty unlike the other database structures. This structure is popular for multimedia Web-based applications. It was designed to work with object-oriented programming languages such as Java.

The dominant model in use today is the ad hoc one embedded in SQL, despite the objections of purists who believe this model is a corruption of the relational model since, it violates several fundamental principles for the sake of practicality and performance. Many DBMSs also support the Open Database Connectivity API that supports a standard way for programmers to access the DBMS. Before the database management approach, organisations relied on file processing systems to organise, store, and process data files. End users criticised file processing because the data is stored in many different files and each organised in a different way. Each file was specialised to be used with a specific application.

File processing was bulky, costly and inflexible when it came to supplying needed data accurately and promptly. Data redundancy is an issue with the file processing system because the independent data files produce duplicate data so when updates were needed each separate file would need to be updated. Another issue is the lack of data integration. The data is dependent on other data to organise and store it. Lastly, there was not any consistency or standardisation of the data in a file processing system which makes maintenance difficult. For these reasons, the database management approach was produced.

TYPES OF DBMS: NETWORK DATABASES

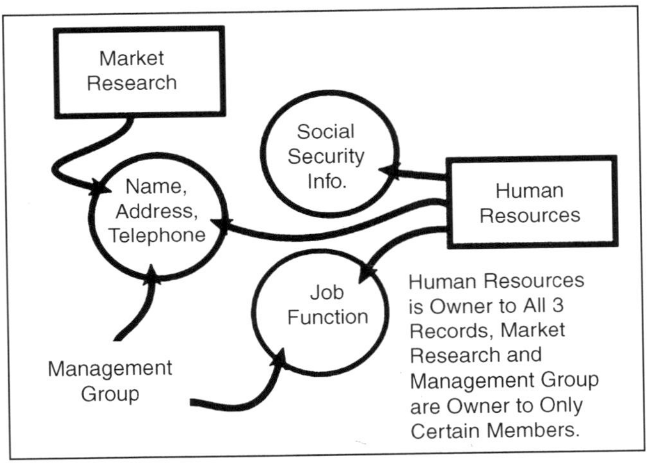

Fig. Network Databases.

Network databases are similar to hierarchical databases by also having a hierarchical structure. There are a few key differences, however. Instead of looking like an upside-down tree, a network database looks more like a cobweb or interconnected network of records. In network databases, children are called members and parents are called owners. The most important difference is that each child or member can have more than one parent (or owner).

Like hierarchical databases, network databases are principally used on mainframe computers. Since, more connections can be made between different types of data, network databases are considered more flexible. However, two limitations must be considered when using this kind of database. Similar to hierarchical databases, network databases must be defined in advance. There is also a limit to the number of connections that can be made between records.

TYPES OF DBMS: RELATIONAL DATABASES

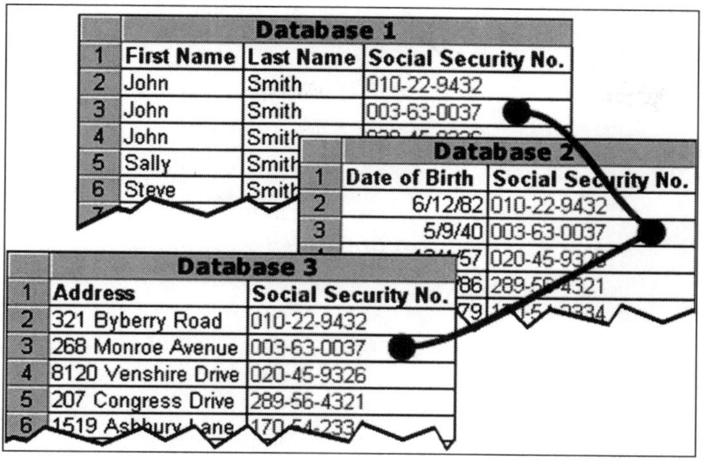

Fig. Relational Databases.

In relational databases, the relationship between data files is relational, not hierarchical. Hierarchical and network databases require the user to pass down through a hierarchy in order to access needed data. Relational databases connect data in different files by using common data elements or a key field. Data in relational databases is stored in different tables, each having a key field that uniquely identifies each row. Relational databases are more flexible than either the hierarchical or network database structures. In relational databases, tables or files filled with data are called relations, tuples designates a row or record, and columns are referred to as attributes or fields.

Relational databases work on the principle that each table has a key field that uniquely identifies each row, and that these key fields can be used to connect one table of data to another. Thus, one table might have a row consisting of a customer account number as the key field along with address and telephone number. The customer account number in this table could be linked to another table of data that also includes customer account number (a key field), but in this case, contains information about product returns, including an item number (another key field). This key field can be linked to another table that contains item numbers and other product information such as production location, colour, quality control person, and other data. Therefore, using this database, customer information can be linked to specific product information.

The relational database has become quite popular for two major reasons. First, relational databases can be used with little or no training. Second, database entries can be modified without redefining the entire structure. The downside of using a relational database is that searching for data can take more time than if other methods are used.

TYPES OF DBMS: OBJECT-ORIENTED DATABASES (OODBMS)

Able to handle many new data types, including graphics, photographs, audio, and video, object-oriented databases represent a significant advance over their other database cousins. Hierarchical and network databases are all designed to handle structured data; that is, data that fits nicely into fields, rows, and columns.

They are useful for handling small snippets of information such as names, addresses, zip codes, product numbers, and any kind of statistic or number you can think of. On the other hand, an object-oriented database can be used to store data from a variety of media sources, such as photographs and text, and produce work, as output, in a multimedia format.

Object-oriented databases use small, reusable chunks of software called objects. The objects themselves are stored in the object-oriented database. Each object consists of two elements: 1) a piece of data (*e.g.*, sound, video, text, or graphics), and 2) the instructions, or software programmes called methods, for what to do with the data. Part two of this definition requires a little more explanation.

The instructions contained within the object are used to do something with the data in the object. For example, test scores would be within the object as would the instructions for calculating average test score. Object-oriented databases have two disadvantages. First, they are more costly to develop. Second, most organisations are reluctant to abandon or convert from those databases that they have already invested money in developing and implementing. However, the benefits to object-oriented databases are compelling. The ability to mix and match reusable objects provides incredible multimedia capability. Health care organisations, for example, can store, track, and recall CAT scans, X-rays, electrocardiograms and many other forms of crucial data.

THE VALUE OF DATA AND DATABASES

Many of the actions you make during the day become data for organisations to use for their own profit and learning. Using an automated teller machine, filling out a form for a driver's license, ordering a book on the Internet, booking a flight on an airline - all become digitised data to be sorted, managed, and used by others. In each of these cases, someone at some time has decided how the data from these users will be received, stored, processed, and made available to others.

DATA AND ORGANISATIONS

For financial and/or legal reasons, organisations collect and store vast amounts of data about employees, customers, finances, vendors, inventory, competitors, and markets, to name only a few. The amount of data needed is important because people generally make better decisions if they have more data available to them. For example, a car dealership, bank, or crédit union will make better decisions about who to give car loans by looking at a person's credit report information than if they simply based their decision on the word of the customer.

Looking at your credit report, a bank representative would see a listing of your payment history on loans and credit cards, including your mortgage. She would also see information about outstanding loans, debt repayment and credit limits. The report may also contain information about jobs you have held and public record information (birth date and address). Likewise, a factory will improve its ability to manufacture products by tracking and managing data about inventory (name, identification number, location, and quantity), production schedule, quality control measures, and much more. You can begin to see why collecting data is important. However, the true value of data cannot be realised until it is appropriately organised, stored, analysed, and eventually used for a specific purpose.

Extracting Meaning from Data

Raw data is not very useful. Suppose a human resources manager of a local hospital sends out a survey consisting of 25 multiple-choice questions to assess the level of employee satisfaction of its 150 nurses. Let's assume for a moment that 114 surveys are completed and returned to the manager. This is the raw data and basically has no meaning.

As a next step, the responses of each nurse to each question on the survey are entered and stored in a computer. The data is still raw and meaningless. It becomes more organised if it is entered into a computer with a plan and purpose in mind. If the manager is smart, he will assign each a nurse an ID number and enter all of his or her responses, not at random, but in the order in which they appear in the survey.

Ultimately, the data cannot be understood until it is analysed. This can be accomplished by calculating the average score for each nurse, the average score for all the nurses at the hospital, the average score for the nurses in each department, and so on. As the manager begins to process and analyse the data, it eventually begins to tell a story. Hopefully, the story will increase understanding in a way that enables the manager to improve the level of satisfaction of the group of employees.

COMPUTERISED OF DATABASES

A computerised database refers to a collection of related files that are digitised. More often than not, this kind of database is more useful than manila folders and filing cabinets. For one, it provides an efficient method of pulling facts together. It allows the slicing, dicing, mixing, and matching of information for a myriad of purposes and needs.

TYPES OF DATABASES

Some databases are small enough to be created and contained on your desktop computer while others are so large that they are stored on network servers or powerful mainframe computers. Popular database management software applications such as Paradox, Access, and dBASE 5 are utilised to manage databases small enough to be stored on a desktop computer. Individuals use these programmes to perform specific tasks, such as to keep track of customers and manage data for small research projects. Some databases are so large that they must be stored on a server or mainframe computer and accessed by going online. Some large, public databases can be accessed online for a fee. These are referred to as information utilities or online services. You may have heard of or used some of the more popular online services including America Online, CompuServe, and Microsoft Network. These online services provide access to a myriad of information sources concerning weather, news, travel, shopping, and a great deal more. Even specialised public databases can be accessed online. Lexis, which gives lawyers access to local, state, and federal laws, is just one example. There are many other types of large databases. Many museums have put artwork online, creating virtual art museums. Most university libraries have created electronic databases to compliment or substitute for their card catalogues.

Database Access

Database access is a sticky issue, as you will see. The following example illustrates some of the difficulties that data administrators, organisations, and society in general now face. A decade ago, Congress created a medical practitioner database to keep physicians disciplined by the medical board of one state from avoiding detection if they moved to another state and applied for a medical license. Should doctor databases be opened to the public? If given access to the database, patients could look up information about a specific doctor and find out if other patents have lodged complaints against them. In one case, a women whose obstetrician left unsightly scars on her abdomen after delivering her baby said if she had been allowed access to the database, she would have learned of other patients' complaints and chosen another doctor. On the other hand, many physicians complain that by making such data available, they are less likely to perform high-risk procedures, even when it might be beneficial to the patient. Those doctors performing high-risk procedures are more likely to receive complaints and could potentially face disciplinary action. You can begin to see the challenges associated with determining who should have access to certain types of information.

Database Attributes for Effective Use

It is important to keep some database files separate, even though they contain closely related information. For example, it's usually a good idea to keep employee files containing home address, telephone number, job title, and work location separate from files containing an employee's tax and salary information.

There are at least two reasons for maintaining these records in separate files:

- It is generally more efficient and effective to search for and extract information from smaller sets of data. In other words, users can access data more rapidly by using smaller files than by trying to access the same data in a large composite file containing vast amounts and types of data. The more types of data contained in a database, the more complex the database becomes and the more difficult it is for database management systems to manipulate it accurately and efficiently.
- Different types of data should be accessible to different groups of people. For example, all employees may be given access to employee information such as work location, job title, and home telephone number. Tax deduction and salary information might only be made available to human resource personnel and the accounting department in an organisation. Different functional groups in an organisation require access to different types of data. This makes sense when you consider the need to maintain some degree of security and personal privacy.

Multiple Sources

A database is more useful if there is little redundancy between the files it contains. In other words, it would be inefficient and a waste of human and computer resources to have the same information repeated over and over again in different files. Some companies maintain databases with very similar information. Sometimes there are good reasons for this; *e.g.,* for security purposes. However, it's simply more costly to maintain accurate information in multiple locations. In addition, there would also be a need to resolve discrepancies occurring between the same information in multiple files. One of the beauties of databases is the ability to link together data from multiple sources to accomplish a specific task. For example, I might store the file containing a mailing list for Pennsylvania with similar lists compiled for individuals in the other fifty states. If a political action group in Pennsylvania decides to develop a campaign for the northeast region, they can extract the names of potential supporters for the states of New York, Connecticut, Maine, and other northeastern states.

DATA SECURITY AND RECOVERY

Who to give access to data, how to protect data, and how to recover lost data are important considerations for those responsible for designing and managing electronic databases.

DATABASE SECURITY

Fig. Database Security.

It is usually the responsibility of a database administrator to determine the different access privileges for different users of the system. Most users will be allowed to view and retrieve some types of data and not others. Some users are only allowed to view data in a database, while others who are qualified will be allowed to view and make changes to data in a database. The purpose of determining who has access, as well as the degree of access, is to protect the data from unauthorised use and sabotage. Databases must also be protected physically from harm or accident. Some organisations have opted to store database files in a vault and limit employee access to the actual computer system using security devices that verify personal identity.

DATA RECOVERY

As with almost all complex forms of computer hardware and software, there is always the possibility of failure. Therefore, it becomes crucial for data administrators to have system recovery features in place to be able to recover database contents that are damaged or lost when problems occur. Performing an actual recovery can be a difficult task. In all likelihood, it may not be possible to completely and seamlessly restore data once an interruption has taken place. The volatility of computer memory and timing and complexity of computer processing inhibit the ability of data administrators to recreate data accurately.

Solutions Scenario

At all times, there are threats to data security, especially when a database fails. These threats include accidental losses attributable to human error, software failure, hardware failure, theft and fraud, improper data access, loss of privacy (personal data), loss of confidentiality (corporate data), loss of data integrity, loss of customers, loss of corporate integrity, loss of availability (through sabotage, for example), exposure through com links, aborted transactions, incorrect data, system failure (database intact), loss of transfers and backups, loss of money, loss of time, and database destruction.

To prevent some of these issues, most corporations and companies using databases have backup and recovery systems. They include, but are not limited to, backup facilities, journalising facilities, transaction logs (time, records, and input values), database change logs (before & after images), checkpoint facilities, recovery managers, and a restart point after a failure. It is safe to say that, even in this age of technology, it does not hurt to back up data in paper format as well!

Strategies for Data Recovery

However, a variety of strategies may be used to facilitate system recovery when problems occur.

Two of the more common approaches include mirroring and reprocessing.

- Mirroring involves making frequent simultaneous copies of a database to ensure that two or more copies are maintained in different locations at all times. This approach is expensive, but is most suitable when rapid recovery is needed. Travel agencies and airline reservation system databases often rely on this method of recovery
- Reprocessing involves going back to a known point of database activity before the problem occurred and reprocessing work from that point forward. However, periodic database saves must be performed so that the data administrator can go back and begin again at a clean starting point. In addition, records must be kept of all transactions made since, the last save. These records are used to reenter and reprocess transactions that were lost as a result of the failure. This strategy is more time-consuming than mirroring, and all other transactions are delayed until the recovery process is complete.

DATABASE DEVELOPMENT PROCESS

Anyone with a desktop computer and the right software package can develop a small database. As we move to the development of large databases, such as those used by many business organisations, the task becomes much more complex. The primary responsibility for planning and developing large databases usually falls to a data administrator and database design analysts in an organisation.

Before a new house can be built, architects must first develop a blueprint. A blueprint provides a symbolic representation of the house and its characteristics before it is actually created. In a similar manner, the process of developing an electronic database also depends on blueprints and advanced planning. Before a database can be created, developers must decide what data should be included and how the database should be structured.

DATABASE DEVELOPMENT PROCESS: STEP ONE

Database development is a systematic process that moves from concept to design to implementation. It also takes into account the needs of potential users and the operational and/or business processes in the organisation.

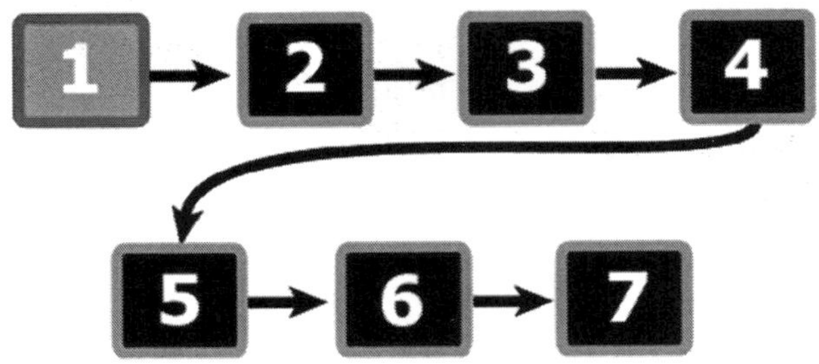

1. Define business processes

1. *Define business processes*: Many database development efforts begin by defining the key business and/or operational processes within the organisation. Developers first create high-level models showing the major activity steps associated with marketing, sales, production, human resource management, public relations, research and development, and so on. Taken together, these process maps represent an enterprise-wide model of the organisation and its core processes.

DATABASE DEVELOPMENT PROCESS: STEP TWO

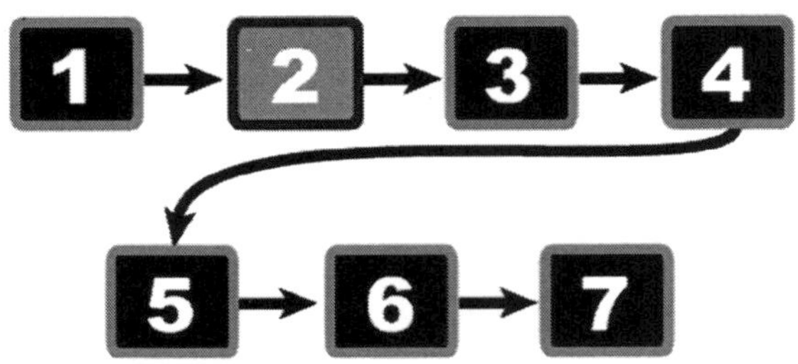

2. Determine the Scope of the Database Development Effort

2. *Determine scope of database development effort*: The next step in the database development effort is to select one process or a set of related processes for further analysis and improvement.

DATABASE DEVELOPMENT PROCESS: STEP THREE

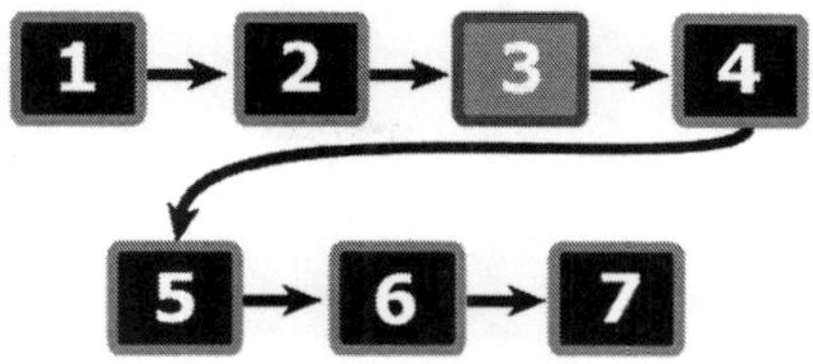

3. Define the Information Needs

3. Define the information needs: Once a business process (or set of processes) has been selected, the next step is to define the information needs of users involved in or affected by the business process.

DATABASE DEVELOPMENT PROCESS: STEP FOUR

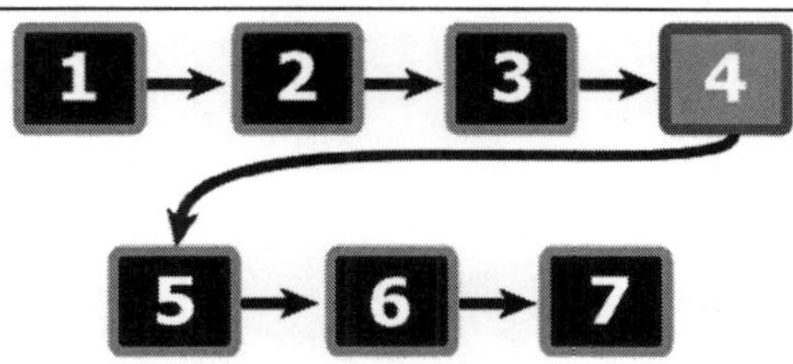

4. Develop Conceptual Design

4. *Develop conceptual design*: A basic understanding of these needs is used to create a conceptual design for the database. At this stage, a conceptual data model is created that illustrates relationships between information sources, users, and business process steps.

DATABASE DEVELOPMENT PROCESS: STEP FIVE

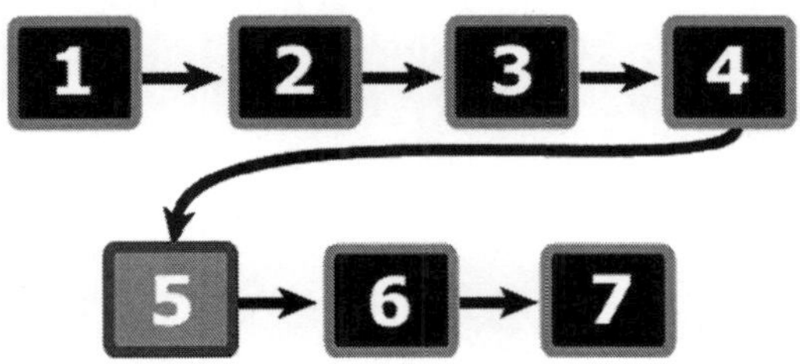

5. Develop Logical Data Model

5. *Develop logical data model*: The conceptual data model is used to develop a logical data model based on one of the primary DBMS types: relational, hierarchical, network, or object-oriented approaches.

DATABASE DEVELOPMENT PROCESS: STEP SIX

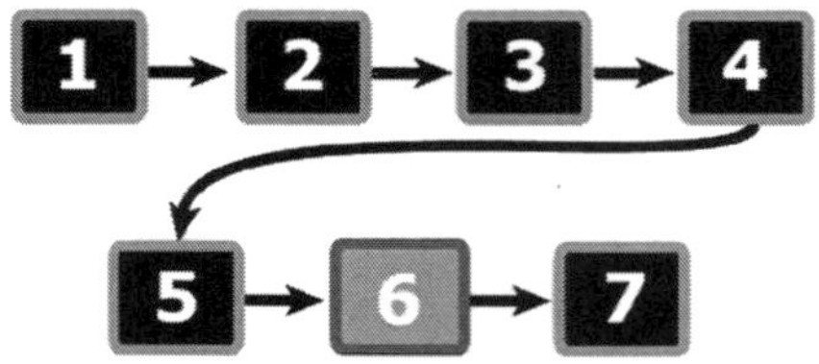

6. Develop Physical Design

6. *Develop physical design*: With the logical data model in hand, developers move to the physical design, which involves determining the specific storage and access methods and structures.

DATABASE DEVELOPMENT PROCESS: STEP SEVEN

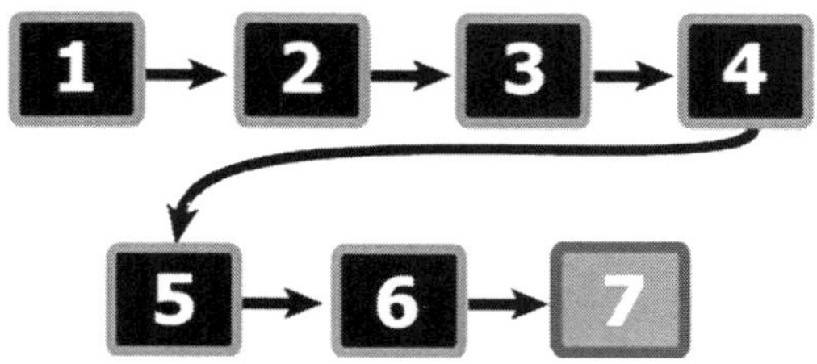

7. Create and Test Database

7. *Create and test database*: Once this step is complete, developers can go ahead and create the database using whatever DBMS has been selected. Small amounts of data can be entered into the database for testing purposes. This is also the time to start developing sample screens and reports to determine if the database design will meet the predefined requirements. It is much easier to revise and change the database during this testing phase, before all of the data have been entered. The term prototyping refers to the iterative process used to try different report formats and input screens to determine their suitability and effectiveness.

8

The Management of Distributed Transactions

Transaction processing includes mechanisms for concurrency control and recovery, as well as transaction management that maintains the necessary overall context information of transactions and conducts the concurrency control and recovery activities.

However, transaction processing suffers from two scalability problems for large transactions.

- Concurrency control for transactions that access large amount of data and last for long period. This will cause large amount of data to be locked for long period and thus hinder concurrent access of them. Moreover, the more data each transaction accesses, the higher chances of deadlocks among transactions.
- Management of distributed transactions that involve many server sites. The most noticeable tasks for transaction management are transaction enlistment and commitment processing. These tasks may involve extra remote invocations and eventually also disk accesses, which are the main causes to poor performance.

Most applications therefore choose to adopt a less stringent approach such as TP-lite, low isolation levels or other limited scopes of distributed transactions.

In this chapter we focus on scalability issues of distributed transaction management, *i.e.,* transaction enlistment and commitment processing. There has not been much research on these issues though, mainly because it is widely believed that transactions should be kept small and should involve as few sites as possible. However we think it is now time to face these issues, given, for instance, that large-scale enterprise systems and application integration are expected to be one of the most important directions in IT industry, and that global computational grid for large-scale resource sharing is regarded as a promising research field. Furthermore, given the huge data space, transactions accessing many sites may not necessarily lead to high deadlock rates. As a matter of fact, compared to transactions involving human interactions (such as transactions for software engineering), those involving many sites may not necessarily last long (though many remote invocations do take longer time than a few local procedure calls).

Furthermore, it is often the size of data relative to the overall data space that is the real problem for concurrency control. The current distributed transaction management approaches and propose an architecture that is particularly aimed at distributed transactions accessing many sites and combines the advantages of current approaches. We will show that this architecture does not require much reengineering efforts.

REQUIREMENTS FOR MANAGEMENT OF LARGE DISTRIBUTED TRANSACTIONS

INTEROPERABILITY

In a large distributed environment, the many systems or sites involved are inevitably heterogeneous and autonomous with respect to various aspects including transaction management. Mechanisms must be provided to resolve heterogeneity and to some extend release autonomy. The overhead of this, however, should not increase significantly with the number of sites involved. Furthermore, the scope for administration and configuration should be kept as local as possible.

Security

When a distributed transaction proceeds, there are two kinds of interactions among sites happening at the same time:

- Remote method invocations, among application programmes and/ or resource managers,
- Management of transactions, among transaction management subsystems at each site.

Both these interactions have particular requirements on security. Regarding the latter, the coordinators and participants must be trusted principals. Otherwise a non-trusted coordinator may hold locked resources arbitrarily long or a non-trusted participant may repeatedly cause transactions to abort.

Note that this kind of interactions is typically invisible to the application. Again, the security overhead should not grow significantly with the number of sites and much of the security checking efforts should be able to be reused beyond transactions' lifetimes.

Performance and Optimisations

During the last three decades, enormous efforts have been made to enhance performance of transaction processing. Optimisations are critical aspects of TP products. When involved in larger environments, these somewhat localised optimisations should continue contributing to the overall performance of transactional applications.

Management of Resources

One important resource in transactional applications is sessions between sites, such as remote database connections. A session may include, among other things, a network connection between the sites, options and attributes of various settings, application specific context or state like database cursor positions, etc. Sometimes sessions are also used for transaction management purposes.

A session is typically not durable, but still managed within a transaction scope, such that associated resources are released upon transaction termination. Establishment of a session may involve for instance security checking as mentioned before and is thus expensive. Management mechanisms such as pooling can be used to avoid unnecessary overhead of session establishment.

Reengineering

Management of very large transactions is a new challenge. New mechanisms might be introduced or existing ones extended. One important requirement is that reengineering should be enforced under limited scope and should not affect considerably the existing mechanisms.

CURRENT TRANSACTION MANAGEMENT ALTERNATIVES

Basically, the sites involved in a transaction form a tree. The difference of the transaction management mechanisms lies in the shape of the trees.

Trees of Transaction Sites

This approach is used in almost all TP products. The tree of sites that a transaction accesses parallels the invocation patterns in the application. Usually, the root of the tree is the first site that the transaction accesses. There is an edge from *a* to *b* if *b* is first invoked from a on behalf of the transaction. Enlistment of a site to the transaction is done the first time that site is accessed by the transaction. Typically, the transaction manager (TM) of a site maintains information of TM of its parent site and the TMs of it immediate child sites.

Two-phase commitment is proceeded recursively from the root down to the leaves of the tree. Voting results are collected in the opposite direction. There is usually a session maintained for neighbour sites (often in form of a database connection) that must be managed by the transaction. Remote invocations go through the sessions. Sessions can also be pooled and need not be released after termination of transactions. Because transaction management shares the same tree structure as remote invocations, sessions can be used for both purposes. Interactions between the TMs may happen through the sessions with the help of communication managers at both sites. Or a direct connection between TMs is set up for transaction management purposes. Optimisations that piggyback TM messages and make use of synchronous nature of remote invocations like "implicit yes-vote" can be relatively easily enforced. In a large distributed environment, it is generally not known in advance how invocations will occur. Therefore, heterogeneity and autonomy should be resolved at potentially every site pairs upon (first) invocations, so is security checking. This may imply reengineering everywhere.

When the tree gets deep, the daisy chain of communication for commitment processing becomes a severe source of latency. A useful optimisation is flattening of the tree. After flattening, the coordinator site maintains an extra connection to all sites a transaction involves for commitment processing. Since, potentially every site can be a coordinator or a participant, the number of extra connections can be considerably large. The dilemma here is, these connections, if not released, may not be reused often, while establishing one for every invocation is prohibitively expensive.

Flat Collections of Transaction Sites

Unlike the tree-of-site approach in which a TM is enlisted at the TM of the immediate invoker, in this approach, every TM is enlisted at the single TM called the superior coordinator. OMG OTS, when no interposition is used to generate subordinate coordinators, is such an example. For every remote invocation, the global reference to the superior coordinator is included in the transaction context. Upon first invocation of the transaction on a site, the TM of the site enlists itself to the superior coordinator.

The superior coordinator can be either the TM where the transaction starts or configured as one of a few well-known sites. The former is similar to tree flattening mentioned before. In the latter case, interoperability and stringent security checking for transaction management purposes only happen between the superior coordinator and TMs at sites that transactions access, rather than between potentially every pair of sites. However, sessions for remote invocations are not used for transaction management purposes. This will result in extra messages, since, messages for transaction enlistment could otherwise be piggybacked in invocation messages.

DISTRIBUTED TRANSACTION

A distributed transaction is an operations bundle, in which two or more network hosts are involved. Usually, hosts provide transactional resources, while the transaction manager is responsible for creating and managing a global transaction that encompasses all operations against such resources. Distributed transactions, as any other transactions, must have all four ACID properties, where atomicity guarantees all-or-nothing outcomes for the unit of work (operations bundle). Open Group, a vendor consortium, proposed the X/Open Distributed Transaction Processing (DTP) Model (X/Open XA), which became a de-facto standard for behaviour of transaction model components.

Databases are common transactional resources and, often, transactions span a couple of such databases. In this case, a distributed transaction can be seen as a database transaction that must be synchronised (or provide ACID properties) among multiple participating databases which are distributed among different physical locations. The isolation property (the I of ACID) poses a special challenge for multi database transactions, since, the (global) serializability property could be violated, even if each database provides it. In practice most commercial database systems use strong strict two phase locking (SS2PL) for concurrency control, which ensures global serializability, if all the participating databases employ it.

A common algorithm for ensuring correct completion of a distributed transaction is the two-phase commit (2PC). This algorithm is usually applied for updates able to commit in a short period of time, ranging from couple of milliseconds to couple of minutes. There are also long-lived distributed transactions, for example a transaction to book a trip, which consists of booking a flight, a rental car and a hotel. Since, booking the flight might take up to a day to get a confirmation, two-phase commit is not applicable here, it will lock the resources for this long. In this case more sophisticated techniques that involve multiple undo levels are used. The way you can undo the hotel booking by calling a desk and cancelling the reservation, a system can be designed to undo certain operations (unless they are irreversibly finished).

In practice, long-lived distributed transactions are implemented in systems based on Web Services. Usually these transactions utilise principles of Compensating transactions, Optimism and Isolation Without Locking. X/Open standard does not cover long-lived DTP. Several modern technologies, including Enterprise Java Beans (EJBs) and Microsoft Transaction Server (MTS) fully support distributed transaction standards.

BASIC CONCEPTS OF TRANSACTION MANAGEMENT

Transaction management in a database system deals with the problems of maintaining consistency of data in spite of system failures and concurrent accesses to data. A transaction consists of a set of operations that perform a single logical unit of work in a database environment. It may be an entire programme, or a part of a programme, or a single command (SQL command), and it may involve any number of operations on the database. If a transaction is completed successfully, then the database moves from one consistent state to another. This consistency must be ensured irrespective of whether transactions are successfully executed simultaneously or there are failures during execution. Thus, a transaction is a unit of consistency and reliability.

Reliability refers to both the resilience of a system to various types of failures and its capability to recover from them. A resilient system continues its normal execution even when failures occur. A recoverable DBMS always keeps the database in a consistent state either by moving back to a previous consistent state or by moving forward to a new consistent state following various types of failures.

The basic difference between a query and a transaction is the fundamental properties of a transaction: atomicity and durability. A transaction ensures the consistency of the database irrespective of the facts that several transactions are executed concurrently and that failures may occur during their execution. A transaction can be considered to be made up of a sequence of read and write operations on the database, together with some computational steps. In that sense, a transaction may be thought of as a programme with embedded database access queries.

OBJECTIVES OF DISTRIBUTED TRANSACTION MANAGEMENT

The objectives of a transaction management subsystem of a distributed DBMS. The responsibilities of the transaction manager in a distributed DBMS is same as those of a corresponding subsystem in a centralised database system, but its task is complicated owing to fragmentation, replication and the overall distributed nature of the database.

The consistency of the database should not be violated because of transaction executions. Therefore, the primary objective of a transaction manger is to execute transactions in an efficient way in order to preserve the ACID properties of transactions (local as well as global transactions) irrespective of concurrent execution of transactions and system failures. At the same time, the efficiency of transaction executions should be improved to meet the performance criteria.

In addition, a good transaction management scheme must consider the following issues.

- CPU and main memory utilisation should be improved Most of the typical database applications spend much of their time waiting for I/O operations rather than on computations. In a large system, the concurrent execution of these I/O bound applications can turn into a bottleneck in main memory or in CPU time utilisation. To alleviate this problem, that is, to improve CPU and main memory utilisation, a transaction manager should adopt specialised techniques to deal with specific database applications. This aspect is common to both centralised and distributed DBMSs.
- Response time should be minimized To improve the performance of transaction executions, the response time of each individual transaction must be considered and should be minimized. In the

case of distributed applications, it is very difficult to achieve an acceptable response time owing to the additional time required to communicate between different sites.

- Availability should be maximized Although the availability in a distributed system is better than that in a centralised system, it must be maximised for transaction recovery and concurrency control in distributed databases. The algorithms implemented by the distributed transaction manager must not block the execution of those transactions that do not strictly need to access a site that is not operational.
- Communication cost should be minimized In a distributed system an additional communication cost is incurred for each distributed or global application, because a number of message transfers are required between sites to control the execution of a global application. These messages are not only used to transfer data, but are required to control the execution of the application. Preventative measures should be adopted by the transaction manager to minimize the communication cost.

A MODEL FOR TRANSACTION MANAGEMENT IN A DISTRIBUTED SYSTEM

An abstract model for transaction management in a distributed database environment. In a distributed system, transactions are classified into two different categories: local transactions and global transactions (or distributed transactions). If the data requirement of a transaction can be fulfilled from the local site, it is called a local transaction. Local transactions access data only from local sites.

On the other hand, global transactions access data from remote sites or multiple sites. It is obvious that the transaction management in a distributed DBMS is more complicated than in a centralized DBMS, as the distributed DBMS must ensure the atomicity of the global transaction as well as of each component subtransaction executed at the local sites. This complicated task is performed by four high-level interconnected modules of the DBMS. These are transaction manager, concurrency control manager, recovery manager and buffer manager.

The transaction manager coordinates transactions on behalf of application programmes by communicating with the scheduler and implements a particular strategy for concurrency control. The responsibility of the concurrency control manager is to maximize concurrency, without allowing concurrently executing transactions to interfere with one another, and thereby maintain the consistency of the database as well as the isolation property of the transactions. The recovery manager preserves the database in a consistent state in case of failures. The buffer manager manages the efficient transfer of data between disk storage and main memory. In a distributed DBMS, all these modules exist in each local DBMS. In addition, a global transaction manager or transaction coordinator is required at each site to control the execution of global transactions as well as of local transactions initiated at that site. Therefore, an abstract model of transaction management at each site of a distributed system consists of two different submodules: the transaction manager and the transaction coordinator.

Classification of Transactions

These classifications have been defined based on various criteria such as the lifetime of the transaction, organisation of read and write operations within the transaction and the structure of the transaction. Depending on their lifetime or duration, transactions can be classified into two broad categories: short-duration transactions and long-duration transactions.

A short-duration transaction (also called online transaction) requires a very short execution/response time and accesses a relatively small portion of the database. On the other hand, a long-duration transaction (also called a batch transaction) requires a longer execution/response time and generally accesses a larger portion of the database. Most of the statistical applications - report generation, complex queries, image processing - are characterised by long-duration transactions, whereas most of the current normal database applications including railway reservation, banking system, project management require the short-duration category transactions. Another way to divide transactions into different classes is based on the organisation of the read and the write operations within the transaction. In some transactions, read and write operations are organised in a mixed manner; they do not appear in any specific order.

These are called general transactions. Some transactions restrict the organisation of read and write operations in such a way that all the read operations within the transaction are performed before the execution of any write operation.

These transactions are called two-step transactions. Similarly, some transactions may restrict that a data item has to be read before it can be written (updated) within the transaction operation. These transactions are known as restricted (or read-before-write) transactions. If a transaction is characterised by features of both two-step and restricted transactions, then it is called a restricted two-step transaction.

SPECIFYING THE COMMIT POINT STRENGTH OF A NODE

The database with the highest commit point strength determines which node commits first in a distributed transaction. When specifying a commit point strength for each node, ensure that the most critical server will be non-blocking if a failure occurs during a prepare or commit phase. The COMMIT_POINT_STRENGTH initialisation parameter determines the commit point strength of a node. The default value is operating system-dependent.

The range of values is any integer from 0 to 255. For example, to set the commit point strength of a database to 200, include the following line in the database initialisation parameter file:

```
COMMIT_POINT_STRENGTH = 200
```

The commit point strength is only used to determine the commit point site in a distributed transaction.

When setting the commit point strength for a database, note the following considerations:

- Because the commit point site stores information about the status of the transaction, the commit point site should not be a node that is frequently unreliable or unavailable in case other nodes need information about transaction status.
- Set the commit point strength for a database relative to the amount of critical shared data in the database. For example, a database on a mainframe computer usually shares more data among users than a database on a PC. Therefore, set the commit point strength of the mainframe to a higher value than the PC.

NAMING TRANSACTIONS

You can name a transaction. This is useful for identifying a specific distributed transaction and replaces the use of the COMMIT COMMENT statement for this purpose.

To name a transaction, use the SET TRANSACTION...NAME statement. For example:

```
SET TRANSACTION ISOLATION LEVEL SERIALISABLE
      NAME 'update inventory checkpoint 0';
```

This example shows that the user started a new transaction with isolation level equal to SERIALISABLE and named it 'update inventory checkpoint 0'. For distributed transactions, the name is sent to participating sites when a transaction is committed. If a COMMIT COMMENT exists, it is ignored when a transaction name exists. The transaction name is displayed in the NAME column of the V$TRANSACTION view, and in the TRAN_COMMENT field of the DBA_2PC_PENDING view when the transaction is committed.

DISTRIBUTED TRANSACTIONS AND DATABASE

A distributed transaction includes one or more statements that, individually or as a group, update data on two or more distinct nodes of a distributed database. For example, assume the database configuration depicted:

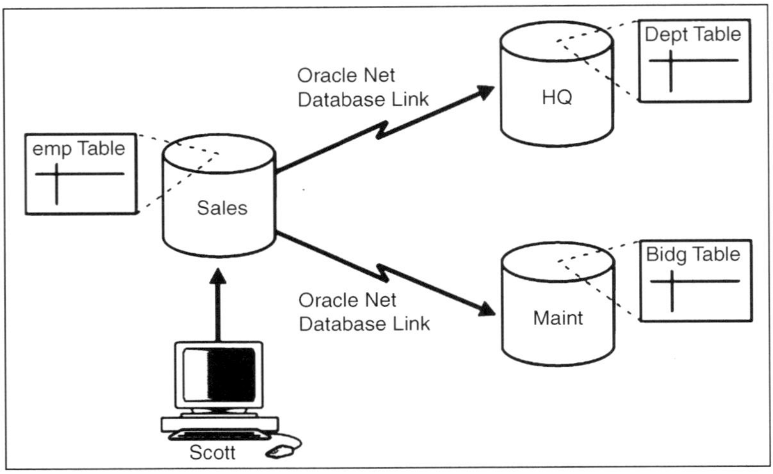

Fig. Distributed System.

The following distributed transaction executed by scott updates the local sales database, the remote hq database, and the remote maint database:

```
UPDATE scott.dept@hq.us.acme.com
    SET loc = 'REDWOOD SHORES'
    WHERE deptno = 10;
UPDATE scott.emp
    SET deptno = 11
    WHERE deptno = 10;
UPDATE scott.bldg@maint.us.acme.com
    SET room = 1225
    WHERE room = 1163;
COMMIT;
```

Note: If all statements of a transaction reference only a single remote node, then the transaction is remote, not distributed.

There are two types of permissible operations in distributed transactions:

- DML and DDL Transactions
- Transaction Control Statements.

DML AND DDL TRANSACTIONS

The following are the DML and DDL operations supported in a distributed transaction:

- CREATE TABLE AS SELECT
- DELETE
- INSERT (default and direct load)
- LOCK TABLE
- SELECT
- SELECT FOR UPDATE.

You can execute DML and DDL statements in parallel, and INSERT direct load statements serially, but note the following restrictions:

- All remote operations must be SELECT statements.
- These statements must not be clauses in another distributed transaction.
- If the table referenced in the table_expression_clause of an INSERT, UPDATE, or DELETE statement is remote, then execution is serial rather than parallel.
- You cannot perform remote operations after issuing parallel DML/ DDL or direct load INSERT.
- If the transaction begins using XA or OCI, it executes serially.
- No loopback operations can be performed on the transaction originating the parallel operation. For example, you cannot reference a remote object that is actually a synonym for a local object.
- If you perform a distributed operation other than a SELECT in the transaction, no DML is parallelised.

Transaction Control Statements

The following are the supported transaction control statements:

- COMMIT
- ROLLBACK
- SAVEPOINT.

SESSION TREES FOR DISTRIBUTED TRANSACTIONS

As the statements in a distributed transaction are issued, the database defines a session tree of all nodes participating in the transaction. A session tree is a hierarchical model that describes the relationships among sessions and their roles.

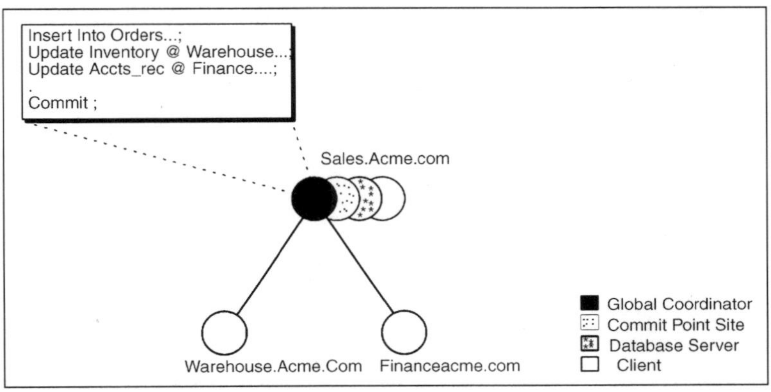

Fig. Example of a Session Tree.

All nodes participating in the session tree of a distributed transaction assume one or more of the following roles:

Role	Description
Client	A node that references information in a database belonging to a different node.
Database server	A node that receives a request for information from another node.
Global coordinator	The node that originates the distributed transaction.
Local coordinator	A node that is forced to reference data on other nodes to complete its part of the transaction.
Commit point site	The node that commits or rolls back the transaction as instructed by the global coordinator.

The role a node plays in a distributed transaction is determined by:

- Whether the transaction is local or remote
- The commit point strength of the node ("Commit Point Site")
- Whether all requested data is available at a node, or whether other nodes need to be referenced to complete the transaction
- Whether the node is read-only.

Clients

A node acts as a client when it references information from a database on another node. The referenced node is a database server. The node sales is a client of the nodes that host the warehouse and finance databases.

Database Servers

A database server is a node that hosts a database from which a client requests data. An application at the sales node initiates a distributed transaction that accesses data from the warehouse and finance nodes. Therefore, sales.acme.com has the role of client node, and warehouse and finance are both database servers. In this example, sales is a database server and a client because the application also modifies data in the sales database.

Local Coordinators

A node that must reference data on other nodes to complete its part in the distributed transaction is called a local coordinator. The sales is a local coordinator because it coordinates the nodes it directly references: warehouse and finance. The node sales also happens to be the global coordinator because it coordinates all the nodes involved in the transaction.

A local coordinator is responsible for coordinating the transaction among the nodes it communicates directly with by:

- Receiving and relaying transaction status information to and from those nodes
- Passing queries to those nodes
- Receiving queries from those nodes and passing them on to other nodes
- Returning the results of queries to the nodes that initiated them.

Global Coordinator

The node where the distributed transaction originates is called the global coordinator. The database application issuing the distributed transaction is directly connected to the node acting as the global coordinator. The transaction issued at the node sales references information from the database servers warehouse and finance. Therefore, sales.acme.com is the global coordinator of this distributed transaction. The global coordinator becomes the parent or root of the session tree.

The global coordinator performs the following operations during a distributed transaction:

- Sends all of the distributed transaction SQL statements, remote procedure calls, and so forth to the directly referenced nodes, thus forming the session tree
- Instructs all directly referenced nodes other than the commit point site to prepare the transaction
- Instructs the commit point site to initiate the global commit of the transaction if all nodes prepare successfully
- Instructs all nodes to initiate a global rollback of the transaction if there is an abort response.

Commit Point Site

The job of the commit point site is to initiate a commit or roll back operation as instructed by the global coordinator. The system administrator always designates one node to be the commit point site in the session tree by assigning all nodes a commit point strength.

The node selected as commit point site should be the node that stores the most critical data.

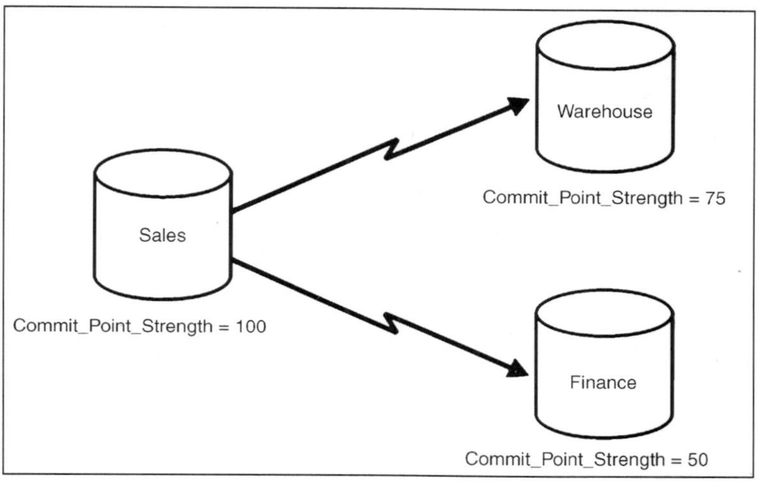

Fig. Commit Point Site.

The commit point site is distinct from all other nodes involved in a distributed transaction in these ways:

- The commit point site never enters the prepared state. Consequently, if the commit point site stores the most critical data, this data never remains in-doubt, even if a failure occurs. In failure situations, failed nodes remain in a prepared state, holding necessary locks on data until in-doubt transactions are resolved.
- The commit point site commits before the other nodes involved in the transaction. In effect, the outcome of a distributed transaction at the commit point site determines whether the transaction at all nodes is committed or rolled back: the other nodes follow the lead of the commit point site. The global coordinator ensures that all nodes complete the transaction in the same manner as the commit point site.

How a Distributed Transaction Commits

A distributed transaction is considered committed after all non-commit-point sites are prepared, and the transaction has been actually committed at the commit point site. The redo log at the commit point site is updated as soon as the distributed transaction is committed at this node. Because the commit point log contains a record of the commit, the transaction is considered committed even though some participating nodes may still be only in the prepared state and the transaction not yet actually committed at these nodes. In the same way, a distributed transaction is considered not committed if the commit has not been logged at the commit point site.

Commit Point Strength

Every database server must be assigned a commit point strength. If a database server is referenced in a distributed transaction, the value of its commit point strength determines which role it plays in the two-phase commit. Specifically, the commit point strength determines whether a given node is the commit point site in the distributed transaction and thus commits before all of the other nodes. This value is specified using the initialisation parameter COMMIT_POINT_STRENGTH. The database determines the commit point site. The commit point site, which is determined at the beginning of the prepare phase, is selected only from the nodes participating in the transaction.

The following sequence of events occurs:

- Of the nodes directly referenced by the global coordinator, the database selects the node with the highest commit point strength as the commit point site.
- The initially-selected node determines if any of the nodes from which it has to obtain information for this transaction has a higher commit point strength.

- Either the node with the highest commit point strength directly referenced in the transaction or one of its servers with a higher commit point strength becomes the commit point site.
- After the final commit point site has been determined, the global coordinator sends prepare responses to all nodes participating in the transaction.

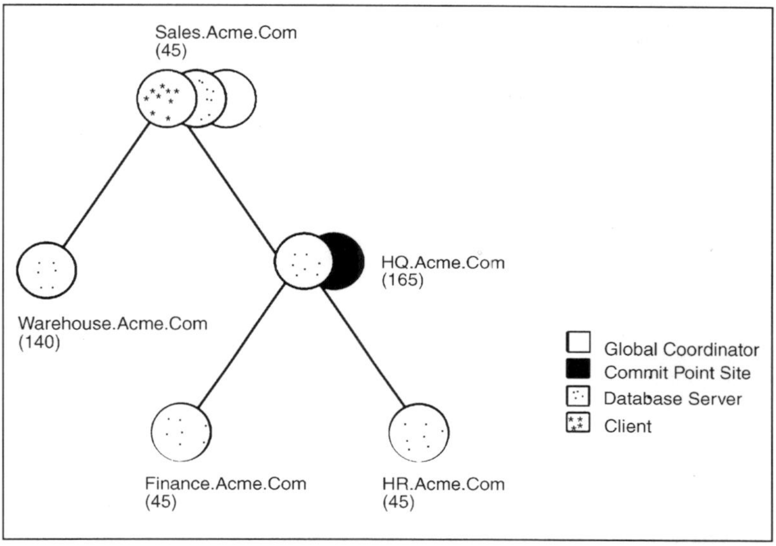

Fig. Commit Point Strengths and Determination of the Commit Point Site.

The following conditions apply when determining the commit point site:

- A read-only node cannot be the commit point site.
- If multiple nodes directly referenced by the global coordinator have the same commit point strength, then the database designates one of these as the commit point site.
- If a distributed transaction ends with a rollback, then the prepare and commit phases are not needed. Consequently, the database never determines a commit point site. Instead, the global coordinator sends a ROLLBACK statement to all nodes and ends the processing of the distributed transaction.

The commit point site and the global coordinator can be different nodes of the session tree.

The commit point strength of each node is communicated to the coordinators when the initial connections are made.

The coordinators retain the commit point strengths of each node they are in direct communication with so that commit point sites can be efficiently selected during two-phase commits. Therefore, it is not necessary for the commit point strength to be exchanged between a coordinator and a node each time a commit occurs.

TWO-PHASE COMMIT MECHANISM

Unlike a transaction on a local database, a distributed transaction involves altering data on multiple databases. Consequently, distributed transaction processing is more complicated, because the database must coordinate the committing or rolling back of the changes in a transaction as a self-contained unit. In other words, the entire transaction commits, or the entire transaction rolls back.

The database ensures the integrity of data in a distributed transaction using the two-phase commit mechanism. In the prepare phase, the initiating node in the transaction asks the other participating nodes to promise to commit or roll back the transaction. During the commit phase, the initiating node asks all participating nodes to commit the transaction. If this outcome is not possible, then all nodes are asked to roll back.

All participating nodes in a distributed transaction should perform the same action: they should either all commit or all perform a rollback of the transaction. The database automatically controls and monitors the commit or rollback of a distributed transaction and maintains the integrity of the global database (the collection of databases participating in the transaction) using the two-phase commit mechanism. This mechanism is completely transparent, requiring no programming on the part of the user or application developer. The commit mechanism has the following distinct phases, which the database performs automatically whenever a user commits a distributed transaction:

Phase	Description
Prepare phase	The initiating node, called the global coordinator, asks participating nodes other than the commit point site to promise to commit or roll back the transaction, even if there is a failure. If any node cannot prepare, the transaction is rolled back.
Commit phase	If all participants respond to the coordinator that they are prepared, then the coordinator asks the commit point site to commit. After it commits, the coordinator asks all other nodes to commit the transaction.
Forget phase	The global coordinator forgets about the transaction.

Prepare Phase

The first phase in committing a distributed transaction is the prepare phase. In this phase, the database does not actually commit or roll back the transaction. Instead, all nodes referenced in a distributed transaction (except the commit point site, described in the "Commit Point Site") are told to prepare to commit.

By preparing, a node:

- Records information in the redo logs so that it can subsequently either commit or roll back the transaction, regardless of intervening failures

- Places a distributed lock on modified tables, which prevents reads.

When a node responds to the global coordinator that it is prepared to commit, the prepared node promises to either commit or roll back the transaction later, but does not make a unilateral decision on whether to commit or roll back the transaction.

The promise means that if an instance failure occurs at this point, the node can use the redo records in the online log to recover the database back to the prepare phase.

Types of Responses in the Prepare Phase

When a node is told to prepare, it can respond in the following ways:

Response	Meaning
Prepared	Data on the node has been modified by a statement in the distributed transaction, and the node has successfully prepared.
Read-only	No data on the node has been, or can be, modified (only queried), so no preparation is necessary.
Abort	The node cannot successfully prepare.

Prepared Response

When a node has successfully prepared, it issues a prepared message. The message indicates that the node has records of the changes in the online log, so it is prepared either to commit or perform a rollback. The message also guarantees that locks held for the transaction can survive a failure.

Read-Only Response

When a node is asked to prepare, and the SQL statements affecting the database do not change any data on the node, the node responds with a read-only message. The message indicates that the node will not participate in the commit phase.

There are three cases in which all or part of a distributed transaction is read-only:

Case	*Conditions*	*Consequence*
Partially read-only	Any of the following occurs: • Only queries are issued at one or more nodes. • No data is changed. • Changes rolled back due to triggers firing or constraint violations.	The read-only nodes recognise their status when asked to prepare. They give their local coordinators a read-only response. Thus, the commit phase completes faster because the database eliminates read-only nodes from subsequent processing.

Completely read-only with prepare phase	All of following occur: • No data changes. • Transaction is not started with SET TRANSACTION READ ONLY statement.	All nodes recognise that they are read-only during prepare phase, so no commit phase is required. he global coordinator, not knowing whether all nodes are read-only, must still perform the prepare phase.
Completely read-only without two-phase commit	All of following occur: • No data changes. • Transaction is started with SET TRANSACTION READ ONLY statement.	Only queries are allowed in the transaction, so global coordinator does not have to perform two-phase commit. Changes by other transactions do not degrade global transaction-level read consistency because of global SCN coordination among nodes. The transaction does not use undo segments.

Note that if a distributed transaction is set to read-only, then it does not use undo segments. If many users connect to the database and their transactions are not set to READ ONLY, then they allocate undo space even if they are only performing queries.

Abort Response

When a node cannot successfully prepare, it performs the following actions:

- Releases resources currently held by the transaction and rolls back the local portion of the transaction.
- Responds to the node that referenced it in the distributed transaction with an abort message.

These actions then propagate to the other nodes involved in the distributed transaction so that they can roll back the transaction and guarantee the integrity of the data in the global database.

This response enforces the primary rule of a distributed transaction: all nodes involved in the transaction either all commit or all roll back the transaction at the same logical time.

Steps in the Prepare Phase

To complete the prepare phase, each node excluding the commit point site performs the following steps:

- The node requests that its descendants, that is, the nodes subsequently referenced, prepare to commit.
- The node checks to see whether the transaction changes data on itself or its descendants. If there is no change to the data, then the node skips the remaining steps and returns a read-only response.

- The node allocates the resources it needs to commit the transaction if data is changed.
- The node saves redo records corresponding to changes made by the transaction to its redo log.
- The node guarantees that locks held for the transaction are able to survive a failure.
- The node responds to the initiating node with a prepared response or, if its attempt or the attempt of one of its descendents to prepare was unsuccessful, with an abort response.

These actions guarantee that the node can subsequently commit or roll back the transaction on the node. The prepared nodes then wait until a COMMIT or ROLLBACK request is received from the global coordinator. After the nodes are prepared, the distributed transaction is said to be in-doubt. It retains in-doubt status until all changes are either committed or rolled back.

Commit Phase

The second phase in committing a distributed transaction is the commit phase. Before this phase occurs, all nodes other than the commit point site referenced in the distributed transaction have guaranteed that they are prepared, that is, they have the necessary resources to commit the transaction.

Steps in the Commit Phase

The commit phase consists of the following steps:

- The global coordinator instructs the commit point site to commit.
- The commit point site commits.
- The commit point site informs the global coordinator that it has committed.
- The global and local coordinators send a message to all nodes instructing them to commit the transaction.
- At each node, the database commits the local portion of the distributed transaction and releases locks.
- At each node, the database records an additional redo entry in the local redo log, indicating that the transaction has committed.
- The participating nodes notify the global coordinator that they have committed.

When the commit phase is complete, the data on all nodes of the distributed system is consistent.

Guaranteeing Global Database Consistency

Each committed transaction has an associated system change number (SCN) to uniquely identify the changes made by the SQL statements within that transaction. The SCN functions as an internal timestamp that uniquely identifies a committed version of the database.

In a distributed system, the SCNs of communicating nodes are coordinated when all of the following actions occur:

- A connection occurs using the path described by one or more database links
- A distributed SQL statement executes
- A distributed transaction commits.

Among other benefits, the coordination of SCNs among the nodes of a distributed system ensures global read-consistency at both the statement and transaction level. If necessary, global time-based recovery can also be completed. During the prepare phase, the database determines the highest SCN at all nodes involved in the transaction. The transaction then commits with the high SCN at the commit point site. The commit SCN is then sent to all prepared nodes with the commit decision.

Forget Phase

After the participating nodes notify the commit point site that they have committed, the commit point site can forget about the transaction.

The following steps occur:

- After receiving notice from the global coordinator that all nodes have committed, the commit point site erases status information about this transaction.
- The commit point site informs the global coordinator that it has erased the status information.
- The global coordinator erases its own information about the transaction.

MANUAL RESOLUTION OF IN-DOUBT TRANSACTIONS

You should only need to resolve an in-doubt transaction in the following cases:

- The in-doubt transaction has locks on critical data or undo segments.
- The cause of the machine, network, or software failure cannot be repaired quickly.

Resolution of in-doubt transactions can be complicated. The procedure requires that you do the following:

- Identify the transaction identification number for the in-doubt transaction.
- Query the DBA_2PC_PENDING and DBA_2PC_NEIGHBORS views to determine whether the databases involved in the transaction have committed.
- If necessary, force a commit using the COMMIT FORCE statement or a rollback using the ROLLBACK FORCE statement.

Relevance of System Change Numbers

A system change number (SCN) is an internal timestamp for a committed version of the database. The Oracle Database server uses the SCN clock value to guarantee transaction consistency. For example, when a user commits a transaction, the database records an SCN for this commit in the redo log. The database uses SCNs to coordinate distributed transactions among different databases.

For example, the database uses SCNs in the following way:

- An application establishes a connection using a database link.
- The distributed transaction commits with the highest global SCN among all the databases involved.
- The commit global SCN is sent to all databases involved in the transaction.

SCNs are important for distributed transactions because they function as a synchronised commit timestamp of a transaction, even if the transaction fails. If a transaction becomes in-doubt, an administrator can use this SCN to coordinate changes made to the global database. The global SCN for the transaction commit can also be used to identify the transaction later, for example, in distributed recovery.

DISTRIBUTED TRANSACTION PROCESSING

In this scenario, a company has separate Oracle Database servers, sales.acme.com and warehouse.acme.com. As users insert sales records into the sales database, associated records are being updated at the warehouse database.

This case study of distributed processing illustrates:

- The definition of a session tree
- How a commit point site is determined
- When prepare messages are sent
- When a transaction actually commits
- What information is stored locally about the transaction.

VIEWING INFORMATION ABOUT DISTRIBUTED TRANSACTIONS

The data dictionary of each database stores information about all open distributed transactions. You can use data dictionary tables and views to gain information about the transactions.

DETERMINING THE ID NUMBER AND STATUS OF PREPARED TRANSACTIONS

The following view shows the database links that have been defined at the local database and stored in the data dictionary:

View	*Purpose*
DBA_2PC_PENDING	Lists all in-doubt distributed transactions. The view is empty until populated by an in-doubt transaction. After the transaction is resolved, the view is purged.

Use this view to determine the global commit number for a particular transaction ID. You can use this global commit number when manually resolving an in-doubt transaction.

The following table shows the most relevant columns:

Table. DBA_2PC_PENDING

Column	Description
LOCAL_TRAN_ID	Local transaction identifier in the format integer.integer.integer. Note: When the LOCAL_TRAN_ID and the GLOBAL_TRAN_ID for a connection are the same, the node is the global coordinator of the transaction.
GLOBAL_TRAN_ID	Global database identifier in the format global_db_name.db_hex_id.local_tran_id, where db_hex_id is an eight-character hexadecimal value used to uniquely identify the database. This common transaction ID is the same on every node for a distributed transaction. Note: When the LOCAL_TRAN_ID and the GLOBAL_TRAN_ID for a connection are the same, the node is the global coordinator of the transaction.
STATE	STATE can have the following values: • *Collecting* This category normally applies only to the global coordinator or local coordinators. The node is currently collecting information from other database servers before it can decide whether it can prepare. • *Prepared* The node has prepared and may or may not have acknowledged this to its local coordinator with a prepared message. However, no commit request has been received. The node remains prepared, holding any local resource locks necessary for the transaction to commit. • *Committed* The node (any type) has committed the transaction, but other nodes involved in the transaction may not have done the same. That is, the transaction is still pending at one or more nodes. • *Forced Commit* A pending transaction can be forced to commit at the discretion of a database administrator. This entry occurs if a transaction is manually committed at a local node. • *Forced termination (rollback)*

	A pending transaction can be forced to roll back at the discretion of a database administrator. This entry occurs if this transaction is manually rolled back at a local node.
MIXED	YES means that part of the transaction was committed on one node and rolled back on another node.
TRAN_COMMENT	Transaction comment or, if using transaction naming, the transaction name is placed here when the transaction is committed.
HOST	Name of the host machine.
COMMIT#	Global commit number for committed transactions.

TRACING THE SESSION TREE OF IN-DOUBT TRANSACTIONS

The following view shows which in-doubt transactions are incoming from a remote client and which are outgoing to a remote server:

View	Purpose
DBA_2PC_NEIGHBORS	Lists all incoming (from remote client) and outgoing (to remote server) in-doubt distributed transactions. It also indicates whether the local node is the commit point site in the transaction. The view is empty until populated by an in-doubt transaction. After the transaction is resolved, the view is purged.

When a transaction is in-doubt, you may need to determine which nodes performed which roles in the session tree.

Use to this view to determine:

- All the incoming and outgoing connections for a given transaction
- Whether the node is the commit point site in a given transaction
- Whether the node is a global coordinator in a given transaction (because its local transaction ID and global transaction ID are the same).

The following table shows the most relevant columns:

Table. DBA_2PC_NEIGHBORS

Column	Description
LOCAL_TRAN_ID	Local transaction identifier with the format integer.integer.integer. Note: When LOCAL_TRAN_ID and GLOBAL_TRAN_ID. DBA_2PC_PENDING for a connection are the same, the node is the global coordina-tor of the transaction.
IN_OUT	IN for incoming transactions; OUT for outgoing transac-tions.

DATABASE	For incoming transactions, the name of the client database that requested information from this local node; for outgoing transactions, the name of the database link used to access information on a remote server.
DBUSER_OWNER	For incoming transactions, the local account used to connect by the remote database link; for outgoing transactions, the owner of the database link.
INTERFACE	C is a commit message; N is either a message indicating a prepared state or a request for a read-only commit. When IN_OUT is OUT, C means that the child at the remote end of the connection is the commit point site and knows whether to commit or terminate. N means that the local node is informing the remote node that it is prepared.©139 When IN_OUT is IN, C means that the local node or a database at the remote end of an outgoing connection is the commit point site. N means that the remote node is informing the local node that it is prepared.

Execute the following script, named neighbors_script, to query pertinent information in DBA_2PC_PENDING (sample output included):

```
COL LOCAL_TRAN_ID FORMAT A13
COL IN_OUT FORMAT A6
COL DATABASE FORMAT A25
COL DBUSER_OWNER FORMAT A15
COL INTERFACE FORMAT A3
SELECT LOCAL_TRAN_ID, IN_OUT, DATABASE, DBUSER_OWNER,
INTERFACE
  FROM DBA_2PC_NEIGHBORS
/
SQL> CONNECT SYS/password@hq.acme.com
SQL> @neighbors_script
LOCAL_TRAN_ID IN_OUT DATABASE   DBUSER_OWNER   INT
------------- ------ ------------------------- -----
1.15.870     out              SALES.ACME.COM SYS          C
```

This output indicates that the local node sent an outgoing request to remote server sales to commit transaction 1.15.870. If sales committed the transaction but no other node did, then you know that sales is the commit point site, because the commit point site always commits first.

DECIDING HOW TO HANDLE IN-DOUBT TRANSACTIONS

A transaction is in-doubt when there is a failure during any aspect of the two-phase commit.

Distributed transactions become in-doubt in the following ways:

- A server machine running Oracle Database software crashes
- A network connection between two or more Oracle Databases involved in distributed processing is disconnected
- An unhandled software error occurs.

Discovering Problems with a Two-Phase Commit

The user application that commits a distributed transaction is informed of a problem by one of the following error messages:

```
ORA-02050: transaction ID rolled back,
               some remote dbs may be in-doubt
ORA-02053: transaction ID committed,
               some remote dbs may be in-doubt
ORA-02054: transaction ID in-doubt
```

A robust application should save information about a transaction if it receives any of the preceding errors. This information can be used later if manual distributed transaction recovery is desired. No action is required by the administrator of any node that has one or more in-doubt distributed transactions due to a network or system failure. The automatic recovery features of the database transparently complete any in-doubt transaction so that the same outcome occurs on all nodes of a session tree (that is, all commit or all roll back) after the network or system failure is resolved. In extended outages, however, you can force the commit or rollback of a transaction to release any locked data. Applications must account for such possibilities.

Determining Whether to Perform a Manual Override

Override a specific in-doubt transaction manually only when one of the following conditions exists:

- The in-doubt transaction locks data that is required by other transactions. This situation occurs when the ORA-01591 error message interferes with user transactions.
- An in-doubt transaction prevents the extents of a undo segment from being used by other transactions. The first portion of the local transaction ID of an in-doubt distributed transaction corresponds to the ID of the undo segment, as listed by the data dictionary view DBA_2PC_PENDING.
- The failure preventing the two-phase commit phases to complete cannot be corrected in an acceptable time period. Examples of such cases include a telecommunication network that has been damaged or a damaged database that requires a long recovery time.

Normally, you should make a decision to locally force an in-doubt distributed transaction in consultation with administrators at other locations. A wrong decision can lead to database inconsistencies that can be difficult to trace and that you must manually correct. If none of these conditions apply, always allow the automatic recovery features of the database to complete the transaction. If any of these conditions are met, however, consider a local override of the in-doubt transaction.

Analysing the Transaction Data

If you decide to force the transaction to complete, analyse available information with the following goals in mind.

Find a Node that Committed or Rolled Back

Use the DBA_2PC_PENDING view to find a node that has either committed or rolled back the transaction. If you can find a node that has already resolved the transaction, then you can follow the action taken at that node.

Look for Transaction Comments

The TRAN_COMMENT column of DBA_2PC_PENDING for the distributed transaction. Comments are included in the COMMENT clause of the COMMIT statement, or if transaction naming is used, the transaction name is placed in the TRAN_COMMENT field when the transaction is committed. For example, the comment of an in-doubt distributed transaction can indicate the origin of the transaction and what type of transaction it is:

```
COMMIT COMMENT 'Finance/Accts_pay/Trans_type 10B';
```

The SET TRANSACTION...NAME statement could also have been used (and is preferable) to provide this information in a transaction name.

Look for Transaction Advice

The ADVICE column of DBA_2PC_PENDING for the distributed transaction. An application can prescribe advice about whether to force the commit or force the rollback of separate parts of a distributed transaction with the ADVISE clause of the ALTER SESSION statement. The advice sent during the prepare phase to each node is the advice in effect at the time the most recent DML statement executed at that database in the current transaction. For example, consider a distributed transaction that moves an employee record from the emp table at one node to the emp table at another node. The transaction can protect the record--even when administrators independently force the in-doubt transaction at each node--by including the following sequence of SQL statements:

```
ALTER SESSION ADVISE COMMIT;
INSERT INTO emp@hq...;/*advice to commit at HQ */
ALTER SESSION ADVISE ROLLBACK;
DELETE FROM emp@sales...;/*advice to roll back at SALES*/
ALTER SESSION ADVISE NOTHING;
```

If you manually force the in-doubt transaction following the given advice, the worst that can happen is that each node has a copy of the employee record; the record cannot disappear.

MANUALLY OVERRIDING IN-DOUBT TRANSACTIONS

Use the COMMIT or ROLLBACK statement with the FORCE option and a text string that indicates either the local or global transaction ID of the in-doubt transaction to commit.

Note: In all examples, the transaction is committed or rolled back on the local node, and the local pending transaction table records a value of forced commit or forced termination for the STATE column the row for this transaction.

Manually Committing an In-Doubt Transaction

Before attempting to commit the transaction, ensure that you have the proper privileges. Note the following requirements:

User Committing the Transaction	Privilege Required
You	FORCE TRANSACTION
Another user	FORCE ANY TRANSACTION

Committing Using Only the Transaction ID

The following SQL statement commits an in-doubt transaction:

```
COMMIT FORCE 'transaction_id';
```

The variable transaction_id is the identifier of the transaction as specified in either the LOCAL_TRAN_ID or GLOBAL_TRAN_ID columns of the DBA_2PC_PENDING data dictionary view.

For example, assume that you query DBA_2PC_PENDING and determine that LOCAL_TRAN_ID for a distributed transaction is 1:45.13.

You then issue the following SQL statement to force the commit of this in-doubt transaction:

```
COMMIT FORCE '1.45.13';
```

Committing Using an SCN

Optionally, you can specify the SCN for the transaction when forcing a transaction to commit. This feature lets you commit an in-doubt transaction with the SCN assigned when it was committed at other nodes. Consequently, you maintain the synchronised commit time of the distributed transaction even if there is a failure. Specify an SCN only when you can determine the SCN of the same transaction already committed at another node. For example, assume you want to manually commit a transaction with the following global transaction ID:

```
SALES.ACME.COM.55d1c563.1.93.29
```

First, query the DBA_2PC_PENDING view of a remote database also involved with the transaction in question. Note the SCN used for the commit of the transaction at that node. Specify the SCN when committing the transaction at the local node. For example, if the SCN is 829381993, issue:

```
COMMIT FORCE 'SALES.ACME.COM.55d1c563.1.93.29', 829381993;
```

Manually Rolling Back an In-Doubt Transaction

Before attempting to roll back the in-doubt distributed transaction, ensure that you have the proper privileges. Note the following requirements:

User Committing the Transaction	Privilege Required
You	FORCE TRANSACTION
Another user	FORCE ANY TRANSACTION

The following SQL statement rolls back an in-doubt transaction:

```
ROLLBACK FORCE 'transaction_id';
```

The variable transaction_id is the identifier of the transaction as specified in either the LOCAL_TRAN_ID or GLOBAL_TRAN_ID columns of the DBA_2PC_PENDING data dictionary view. For example, to roll back the in-doubt transaction with the local transaction ID of 2.9.4, use the following statement:

```
ROLLBACK FORCE '2.9.4';
```

PURGING PENDING ROWS FROM THE DATA DICTIONARY

Before RECO recovers an in-doubt transaction, the transaction appears in DBA_2PC_PENDING.STATE as COLLECTING, COMMITTED, or PREPARED. If you force an in-doubt transaction using COMMIT FORCE or ROLLBACK FORCE, then the states FORCED COMMIT or FORCED ROLLBACK may appear. Automatic recovery normally deletes entries in these states. The only exception is when recovery discovers a forced transaction that is in a state inconsistent with other sites in the transaction. In this case, the entry can be left in the table and the MIXED column in DBA_2PC_PENDING has a value of YES. These entries can be cleaned up with the DBMS_TRANSACTION. PURGE_MIXED procedure.

If automatic recovery is not possible because a remote database has been permanently lost, then recovery cannot identify the re-created database because it receives a new database ID when it is re-created. In this case, you must use the PURGE_LOST_DB_ENTRY procedure in the DBMS_ TRANSACTION package to clean up the entries. The entries do not hold up database resources, so there is no urgency in cleaning them up.

Executing the PURGE_LOST_DB_ENTRY Procedure

To manually remove an entry from the data dictionary, use the following syntax (where trans_id is the identifier for the transaction):

```
DBMS_TRANSACTION.PURGE_LOST_DB_ENTRY('trans_id');
```

For example, to purge pending distributed transaction 1.44.99, enter the following statement in SQL*Plus:

```
EXECUTE DBMS_TRANSACTION.PURGE_LOST_DB_ENTRY('1.4.99');
```

Execute this procedure only if significant reconfiguration has occurred so that automatic recovery cannot resolve the transaction.

Examples include:

- Total loss of the remote database
- Reconfiguration in software resulting in loss of two-phase commit capability
- Loss of information from an external transaction coordinator such as a TPMonitor.

Determining When to Use DBMS_TRANSACTION

The following tables indicates what the various states indicate about the distributed transaction what the administrator's action should be:

State Column	State of Global Transaction	State of Local Transaction	Normal Action	Alternative Action
Collecting	Rolled back	Rolled back	None	PURGE_LOST_DB_ENTRY (only if autorecovery cannot resolve transaction)
Committed	Committed	Committed	None	PURGE_LOST_DB_ENTRY (only if autorecovery cannot resolve transaction)
Prepared	Unknown	Prepared	None	Force commit or rollback
Forced commit	Unknown	Committed	None	PURGE_LOST_DB_ENTRY (only if autorecovery cannot resolve transaction)
Forced rollback	Unknown	Rolled back	None	PURGE_LOST_DB_ENTRY (only if autorecovery cannot resolve transaction)
Forced commit	Mixed	Committed	Manually remove inconsistencies then use PURGE_MIXED	–
Forced rollback	Mixed	Rolled back	Manually remove inconsistencies then use PURGE_MIXED	–

MANUALLY COMMITTING AN IN-DOUBT TRANSACTION: EXAMPLE

The commit of a distributed transaction. In this failure case, the prepare phase completes. During the commit phase, however, the commit confirmation of the commit point site never reaches the global coordinator, even though the commit point site committed the transaction. Inventory data is locked and cannot be accessed because the in-doubt transaction is critical to other transactions. Further, the locks must be held until the in-doubt transaction either commits or rolls back.

DATA ACCESS FAILURES DUE TO LOCKS

When you issue a SQL statement, the database attempts to lock the resources needed to successfully execute the statement. If the requested data is currently held by statements of other uncommitted transactions, however, and remains locked for a long time, a timeout occurs.

Transaction Timeouts

A DML statement that requires locks on a remote database can be blocked if another transaction own locks on the requested data.

If these locks continue to block the requesting SQL statement, then the following sequence of events occurs:

- A timeout occurs.
- The database rolls back the statement.
- The database returns this error message to the user:
- ORA-02049: time-out: distributed transaction waiting for lock.

Because the transaction did not modify data, no actions are necessary as a result of the timeout. Applications should proceed as if a deadlock has been encountered. The user who executed the statement can try to re-execute the statement later. If the lock persists, then the user should contact an administrator to report the problem.

Locks from In-Doubt Transactions

A query or DML statement that requires locks on a local database can be blocked indefinitely due to the locked resources of an in-doubt distributed transaction. In this case, the database issues the following error message:

```
ORA-01591: lock held by in-doubt distributed transaction identifier
```

In this case, the database rolls back the SQL statement immediately. The user who executed the statement can try to re-execute the statement later. If the lock persists, the user should contact an administrator to report the problem, including the ID of the in-doubt distributed transaction. The chances of these situations occurring are rare considering the low probability of failures during the critical portions of the two-phase commit. Even if such a failure occurs, and assuming quick recovery from a network or system failure, problems are automatically resolved without manual intervention. Thus, problems usually resolve before they can be detected by users or database administrators.

SIMULATING DISTRIBUTED TRANSACTION FAILURE

You can force the failure of a distributed transaction for the following reasons.

- To observe RECO automatically resolving the local portion of the transaction
- To practice manually resolving in-doubt distributed transactions and observing the results.

The features available and the steps necessary to perform such operations.

Forcing a Distributed Transaction to Fail

You can include comments in the COMMENT parameter of the COMMIT statement. To intentionally induce a failure during the two-phase commit phases of a distributed transaction, include the following comment in the COMMENT parameter:

```
COMMIT COMMENT 'ORA-2PC-CRASH-TEST-n';
```

where n is one of the following integers:

n	Effect
1	Crash commit point after collect
2	Crash non-commit-point site after collect
3	Crash before prepare (non-commit-point site)
4	Crash after prepare (non-commit-point site)
5	Crash commit point site before commit
6	Crash commit point site after commit
7	Crash non-commit-point site before commit
8	Crash non-commit-point site after commit
9	Crash commit point site before forget
10	Crash non-commit-point site before forget

For example, the following statement returns the following messages if the local commit point strength is greater than the remote commit point strength and both nodes are updated:

```
COMMIT COMMENT 'ORA-2PC-CRASH-TEST-7';
ORA-02054: transaction 1.93.29 in-doubt
ORA-02059: ORA_CRASH_TERST_7 in commit comment
```

At this point, the in-doubt distributed transaction appears in the DBA_2PC_PENDING view. If enabled, RECO automatically resolves the transaction.

Disabling and Enabling RECO

The RECO background process of an Oracle Database instance automatically resolves failures involving distributed transactions. At exponentially growing time intervals, the RECO background process of a node attempts to recover the local portion of an in-doubt distributed transaction. RECO can use an existing connection or establish a new connection to other nodes involved in the failed transaction. When a connection is established, RECO automatically resolves all in-doubt transactions. Rows corresponding to any resolved in-doubt transactions are automatically removed from the pending transaction table of each database. You can enable and disable RECO using the ALTER SYSTEM statement with the ENABLE/DISABLE DISTRIBUTED RECOVERY options. For example, you can temporarily disable RECO to force the failure of a two-phase commit and manually resolve the in-doubt transaction. The following statement disables RECO:

```
ALTER SYSTEM DISABLE DISTRIBUTED RECOVERY;
```

Alternatively, the following statement enables RECO so that in-doubt transactions are automatically resolved:

```
ALTER SYSTEM ENABLE DISTRIBUTED RECOVERY.
```

MANAGING READ CONSISTENCY

An important restriction exists in the Oracle Database implementation of distributed read consistency. The problem arises because each system has its own SCN, which you can view as the database internal timestamp. The Oracle Database server uses the SCN to decide which version of data is returned from a query. The SCNs in a distributed transaction are synchronised at the end of each remote SQL statement and at the start and end of each transaction.

Between two nodes that have heavy traffic and especially distributed updates, the synchronisation is frequent. Nevertheless, no practical way exists to keep SCNs in a distributed system absolutely synchronised: a window always exists in which one node may have an SCN that is somewhat in the past with respect to the SCN of another node.

Because of the SCN gap, you can execute a query that uses a slightly old snapshot, so that the most recent changes to the remote database are not seen. In accordance with read consistency, a query can therefore retrieve consistent, but out-of-date data. Note that all data retrieved by the query will be from the old SCN, so that if a locally executed update transaction updates two tables at a remote node, then data selected from both tables in the next remote access contain data prior to the update.

One consequence of the SCN gap is that two consecutive SELECT statements can retrieve different data even though no DML has been executed between the two statements. For example, you can issue an update statement and then commit the update on the remote database. When you issue a SELECT statement on a view based on this remote table, the view does not show the update to the row. The next time that you issue the SELECT statement, the update is present.

You can use the following techniques to ensure that the SCNs of the two machines are synchronised just before a query:

- Because SCNs are synchronised at the end of a remote query, precede each remote query with a dummy remote query to the same site, for example, SELECT * FROM DUAL@REMOTE.

- Because SCNs are synchronised at the start of every remote transaction, commit or roll back the current transaction before issuing the remote query.

DEVELOPING APPLICATIONS FOR A DISTRIBUTED DATABASE SYSTEM

MANAGING THE DISTRIBUTION OF APPLICATION DATA

In a distributed database environment, coordinate with the database administrator to determine the best location for the data.

Some issues to consider are:

* Number of transactions posted from each location
* Amount of data (portion of table) used by each node
* Performance characteristics and reliability of the network
* Speed of various nodes, capacities of disks
* Importance of a node or link when it is unavailable
* Need for referential integrity among tables.

CONTROLLING CONNECTIONS ESTABLISHED BY DATABASE LINKS

When a global object name is referenced in a SQL statement or remote procedure call, database links establish a connection to a session in the remote database on behalf of the local user. The remote connection and session are only created if the connection has not already been established previously for the local user session. The connections and sessions established to remote databases persist for the duration of the local user's session, unless the application or user explicitly terminates them. Note that when you issue a SELECT statement across a database link, a transaction lock is placed on the undo segments. To release the segment, you must issue a COMMIT or ROLLBACK statement. Terminating remote connections established using database links is useful for disconnecting high cost connections that are no longer required by the application. You can terminate a remote connection and session using the ALTER SESSION statement with the CLOSE DATABASE LINK clause. For example, assume you issue the following transactions:

```
SELECT * FROM emp@sales;
COMMIT;
```

The following statement terminates the session in the remote database pointed to by the sales database link:

```
ALTER SESSION CLOSE DATABASE LINK sales;
```

To close a database link connection in your user session, you must have the ALTER SESSION system privilege.

Note: Before closing a database link, first close all cursors that use the link and then end your current transaction if it uses the link.

MAINTAINING REFERENTIAL INTEGRITY IN A DISTRIBUTED SYSTEM

If a part of a distributed statement fails, for example, due to an integrity constraint violation, the database returns error number ORA-02055. Subsequent statements or procedure calls return error number ORA-02067 until a ROLLBACK or ROLLBACK TO SAVEPOINT is issued.

Design your application to check for any returned error messages that indicate that a portion of the distributed update has failed. If you detect a failure, you should roll back the entire transaction before allowing the application to proceed.

The database does not permit declarative referential integrity constraints to be defined across nodes of a distributed system. In other words, a declarative referential integrity constraint on one table cannot specify a foreign key that references a primary or unique key of a remote table. Nevertheless, you can maintain parent/child table relationships across nodes using triggers. If you decide to define referential integrity across the nodes of a distributed database using triggers, be aware that network failures can limit the accessibility of not only the parent table, but also the child table. For example, assume that the child table is in the sales database and the parent table is in the hq database.

If the network connection between the two databases fails, some DML statements against the child table (those that insert rows into the child table or update a foreign key value in the child table) cannot proceed because the referential integrity triggers must have access to the parent table in the hq database.

TUNING DISTRIBUTED QUERIES

The local Oracle Database server breaks the distributed query into a corresponding number of remote queries, which it then sends to the remote nodes for execution. The remote nodes execute the queries and send the results back to the local node. The local node then performs any necessary post-processing and returns the results to the user or application.

Using Collocated Inline Views

The most effective way of optimising distributed queries is to access the remote databases as little as possible and to retrieve only the required data. For example, assume you reference five remote tables from two different remote databases in a distributed query and have a complex filter (for example, WHERE r1.salary + r2.salary > 50000). You can improve the performance of the query by rewriting the query to access the remote databases once and to apply the filter at the remote site. This rewrite causes less data to be transferred to the query execution site. Rewriting your query to access the remote database once is achieved by using collocated inline views.

The following terms need to be defined:

* Collocated
* Inline view: A SELECT statement that is substituted for a table in a parent SELECT statement. The embedded SELECT statement, shown within the parentheses is an example of an inline view:

```
SELECT e.empno,e.ename,d.deptno,d.dname
    FROM (SELECT empno, ename from
        emp@orcl.world) e, dept d;
```

* Collocated inline view: An inline view that selects data from multiple tables from a single database only. It reduces the amount of times that the remote database is accessed, improving the performance of a distributed query.

Oracle recommends that you form your distributed query using collocated inline views to increase the performance of your distributed query. Oracle Database cost-based optimisation can transparently rewrite many of your distributed queries to take advantage of the performance gains offered by collocated inline views.

Using Cost-based Optimisation

In addition to rewriting your queries with collocated inline views, the cost-based optimisation method optimises distributed queries according to the gathered statistics of the referenced tables and the computations performed by the optimiser.

For example, cost-based optimisation analyses the following query. The example assumes that table statistics are available. Note that it analyses the query inside a CREATE TABLE statement:

```
CREATE TABLE AS (
            SELECT l.a, l.b, r1.c, r1.d, r1.e,r2.b, r2.c
            FROM local l, remote1 r1, remote2 r2
                WHERE l.c = r.c
                AND r1.c = r2.c
                AND r.e > 300
            );
```

and rewrites it as:

```
CREATE TABLE AS (
              SELECT l.a, l.b, v.c, v.d, v.e
              FROM (
                    SELECT r1.c, r1.d, r1.e, r2.b, r2.c
                    FROM remote1 r1, remote2 r2
                    WHERE r1.c = r2.c
                    AND r1.e > 300
                  ) v, local l
              WHERE l.c = r1.c
            );
```

The alias v is assigned to the inline view, which can then be referenced as a table in the preceding SELECT statement. Creating a collocated inline view reduces the amount of queries performed at a remote site, thereby reducing costly network traffic.

Cost-Based Optimisation Work

The main task of optimisation is to rewrite a distributed query to use collocated inline views.

This optimisation is performed in three steps:

* All mergeable views are merged.
* Optimiser performs collocated query block test.
* Optimiser rewrites query using collocated inline views.

After the query is rewritten, it is executed and the data set is returned to the user.

While cost-based optimisation is performed transparently to the user, it is unable to improve the performance of several distributed query scenarios. Specifically, if your distributed query contains any of the following, cost-based optimisation is not effective:

* Aggregates
* Subqueries
* Complex SQL

If your distributed query contains one of these elements, see "Using Hints" to learn how you can modify your query and use hints to improve the performance of your distributed query.

Setting Up Cost-Based Optimisation

After you have set up your system to use cost-based optimisation to improve the performance of distributed queries, the operation is transparent to the user.

In other words, the optimisation occurs automatically when the query is issued.

Setting Up the Environment

To enable cost-based optimisation, set the OPTIMISER_MODE initialisation parameter to CHOOSE or COST.

You can set this parameter by:

* Modifying the OPTIMISER_MODE parameter in the initialisation parameter file
* Setting it at session level by issuing an ALTER SESSION statement

Issue one of the following statements to set the OPTIMISER_MODE initialisation parameter at the session level:

```
ALTER SESSION OPTIMISER_MODE = CHOOSE;
ALTER SESSION OPTIMISER_MODE = COST;
```

Analysing Tables

For cost-based optimisation to select the most efficient path for a distributed query, you must provide accurate statistics for the tables involved. You do this using the DBMS_STATS package or the ANALYSE statement.

Note: You must connect locally with respect to the tables when executing the DBMS_STATS procedure or ANALYSE statement. For example, you cannot execute the following:

ANALYSE TABLE remote@remote.com COMPUTE STATISTICS;

You must first connect to the remote site and then execute the preceding ANALYSE statement, or the equivalent DBMS_STATS procedure.

The following DBMS_STATS procedures enable the gathering of certain classes of optimiser statistics:

* GATHER_INDEX_STATS
* GATHER_TABLE_STATS
* GATHER_SCHEMA_STATS
* GATHER_DATABASE_STATS.

For example, assume that distributed transactions routinely access the scott.dept table. To ensure that the cost-based optimiser is still picking the best plan, execute the following:

```
BEGIN
      DBMS_STATS.GATHER_TABLE_STATS ('scott', 'dept');
END;
```

Using Hints

If a statement is not sufficiently optimised, then you can use hints to extend the capability of cost-based optimisation. Specifically, if you write your own query to utilise collocated inline views, instruct the cost-based optimiser not to rewrite your distributed query.

Additionally, if you have special knowledge about the database environment (such as statistics, load, network and CPU limitations, distributed queries, and so forth), you can specify a hint to guide cost-based optimisation. For example, if you have written your own optimised query using collocated inline views that are based on your knowledge of the database environment, specify the NO_MERGE hint to prevent the optimiser from rewriting your query.

This technique is especially helpful if your distributed query contains an aggregate, subquery, or complex SQL. Because this type of distributed query cannot be rewritten by the optimiser, specifying NO_MERGE causes the optimiser to skip the steps.

The DRIVING_SITE hint lets you define a remote site to act as the query execution site. In this way, the query executes on the remote site, which then returns the data to the local site. This hint is especially helpful when the remote site contains the majority of the data.

Using the NO_MERGE Hint

The NO_MERGE hint prevents the database from merging an inline view into a potentially non-collocated SQL statement. This hint is embedded in the SELECT statement and can appear either at the beginning of the SELECT statement with the inline view as an argument or in the query block that defines the inline view.

```
/* with argument */
SELECT/*+NO_MERGE(v)*/t1.x, v.avg_y
    FROM t1, (SELECT x, AVG(y) AS avg_y FROM t2 GROUP
  BY x) v,
    WHERE t1.x = v.x AND t1.y = 1;
/* in query block */
SELECT t1.x, v.avg_y
      FROM t1, (SELECT/*+NO_MERGE*/x, AVG(y) AS avg_y FROM
t2 GROUP BY x) v,
      WHERE t1.x = v.x AND t1.y = 1;
```

Typically, you use this hint when you have developed an optimised query based on your knowledge of your database environment.

Using the DRIVING_SITE Hint

The DRIVING_SITE hint lets you specify the site where the query execution is performed. It is best to let cost-based optimisation determine where the execution should be performed, but if you prefer to override the optimiser, you can specify the execution site manually.

Following is an example of a SELECT statement with a DRIVING_SITE hint:

```
SELECT/*+DRIVING_SITE(dept)*/* FROM emp, dept@remote.com
       WHERE emp.deptno = dept.deptno;
```

Analysing the Execution Plan

An important aspect to tuning distributed queries is analysing the execution plan. The feedback that you receive from your analysis is an important element to testing and verifying your database. Verification becomes especially important when you want to compare plans. For example, comparing the execution plan for a distributed query optimised by cost-based optimisation to a plan for a query manually optimised using hints, collocated inline views, and other techniques.

Preparing the Database to Store the Plan

Before you can view the execution plan for the distributed query, prepare the database to store the execution plan. You can perform this preparation by executing a script. Execute the following script to prepare your database to store an execution plan:

```
SQL> @UTLXPLAN.SQL
```

Note: The utlxplan.sql file can be found in the $ORACLE_HOME/rdbms/admin directory.

After you execute utlxplan.sql, a table, PLAN_TABLE, is created in the current schema to temporarily store the execution plan.

Generating the Execution Plan

After you have prepared the database to store the execution plan, you are ready to view the plan for a specified query. Instead of directly executing a SQL statement, append the statement to the EXPLAIN PLAN FOR clause. For example, you can execute the following:

```
    EXPLAIN PLAN FOR
SELECT d.dname
    FROM dept d
        WHERE d.deptno
          IN (SELECT deptno
              FROM emp@orc2.world
                GROUP BY deptno
                    HAVING COUNT (deptno) >3
                    )
/
```

HANDLING ERRORS IN REMOTE PROCEDURES

When the database executes a procedure locally or at a remote location, four types of exceptions can occur:

* PL/SQL user-defined exceptions, which must be declared using the keyword EXCEPTION
* PL/SQL predefined exceptions such as the NO_DATA_FOUND keyword
* SQL errors such as ORA-00900 and ORA-02015
* Application exceptions generated using the RAISE_APPLICATION_ERROR() procedure

When using local procedures, you can trap these messages by writing an exception handler such as the following:

```
BEGIN
  ...
EXCEPTION
    WHEN ZERO_DIVIDE THEN
    /*... handle the exception */
END;
```

Notice that the WHEN clause requires an exception name. If the exception does not have a name, for example, exceptions generated with RAISE_APPLICATION_ERROR, you can assign one using PRAGMA_

EXCEPTION_INIT. For example:

```
DECLARE
    null_salary EXCEPTION;
    PRAGMA EXCEPTION_INIT(null_salary, -20101);
BEGIN
    ...
    RAISE_APPLICATION_ERROR(-20101, 'salary is missing');
...
EXCEPTION
    WHEN null_salary THEN
    ...
END;
```

When calling a remote procedure, exceptions can be handled by an exception handler in the local procedure. The remote procedure must return an error number to the local, calling procedure, which then handles the exception as shown in the previous example. Note that PL/SQL user-defined exceptions always return ORA-06510 to the local procedure.

Therefore, it is not possible to distinguish between two different user-defined exceptions based on the error number. All other remote exceptions can be handled in the same manner as local exceptions.

9

Reliability of Computer Networking

In computer networking, a reliable protocol is one that provides reliability properties with respect to the delivery of data to the intended recipient(s), as opposed to an unreliable protocol, which does not provide notifications to the sender as to the delivery of transmitted data. A reliable multicast protocol may ensure reliability on a per-recipient basis, as well as provide properties that relate the delivery of data to different recipients, such as, *e.g.*, total order, atomicity, or virtual synchrony.

Reliable protocols typically incur more overhead than unreliable protocols, and as a result, are slower and less scalable. This often is not an issue for unicast protocols, but it may be a problem for multicast protocols. TCP, the main protocol used in the Internet today, is a reliable unicast protocol. UDP, often used in computer games or other situations where speed is an issue and the loss of a little data is not as important because of the transitory nature of the data, is an unreliable protocol.

Often, a reliable unicast protocol is also connection-oriented. For example, the TCP/IP protocol is connection-oriented, with the virtual circuit ID consisting of source and destination IP addresses and port numbers. Some unreliable protocols are connection-oriented as well. These include ATM and Frame Relay, on which a substantial part of all Internet traffic is passed.

RELIABILITY PROPERTIES

In the context of distributed protocols, reliability properties specify the guarantees that the protocol provides with respect to the delivery of messages to the intended recipient(s). An example of a reliability property for a unicast protocol is "at least once", *i.e.,* at least one copy of the message is guaranteed to be delivered to the recipient.

Reliability properties for multicast protocols can be expressed on a per-recipient basis (simple reliability properties), or they may relate the fact of delivery or the order of delivery among the different recipients (strong reliability properties). In the context of multicast protocols, strong reliability properties express the guarantees that the protocol provides with respect to the delivery of messages to different recipients. An example of a strong reliability property is last copy recall, meaning that as long as at least a single copy of a message remains available at any of the recipients, every other recipient that does not fail eventually also receives a copy. Strong reliability properties such as this one typically require that messages are retransmitted or forwarded among the recipients.

An example of a reliability property stronger than last copy recall is atomicity. The property states that if at least a single copy of a message has been delivered to a recipient, all other recipients will eventually receive a copy of the message. In other words, each message is always delivered to either all or none of the recipients. One of the most complex strong reliability properties is virtual synchrony.

Strong reliability properties are offered by group communication systems (GCS) such as ISIS, Appia framework, Spread, JGroups or QuickSilver Scalable Multicast. The QuickSilver Properties Framework is a flexible platform that allows strong reliability properties to be expressed in a purely declarative manner, using a simple rule-based language, and automatically translated into a hierarchical protocol.

RELIABILITY DATABASE AND SYSTEM ANALYSIS

Reaching a 20% or greater penetration of the electrical demand in the US, as outlined in the DOE 20% report, requires continuing public confidence in the quality, durability, and reliability of wind turbines throughout the fleet. The Reliability programme aims to ensure the fleet is operating at high performance levels, judged both by energy delivery and low operating costs. This task will measure, analyse, document and publish current and emerging performance, as well as target potential issues as early as possible. To accomplish this, the programme will initiate a widespread tracking system to monitor reliability of the fleet, archived in a national reliability database. The national database will be analysed to determine the systemic sources of unreliability. The programme can use these analyses to initiate technology improvement projects where critical issues are discovered to be negatively impacting fleet performance.

SYSTEM PERFORMANCE AND BLADE TESTING

Full scale testing of prototype wind turbine blades is vital to asses the structural and aerodynamic performance of advanced concepts. Through a series of projects, Sandia has developed three advanced blade designs which are in the process of being evaluated by structural and aerodynamic testing. Sandia will continue to conduct both laboratory and field testing of advanced blades in the future, and provide the necessary results to industry to ensure the viability of the unique features of the designs. Additionally, results from the blade testing will provide the critical information needed to validate and improve our design codes.

RELIABILITY COLLABORATION AND SYSTEM ANALYSIS

The objective of Reliability Collaboration and System Analysis programme is to characterise reliability performance issues and identify opportunities for improving reliability and availability performance of the national wind energy infrastructure. A system for gathering, protecting, managing and disseminating reliability data at the point of operations for all critical stakeholders, including manufacturers, developers, financiers, and operators themselves is being created. The information will also be used to guide DOE programme R&D investment through identification of critical issues (TIOs). It will determine relative impact of component failures and provide data for root cause of component failures.

The information will be used to guide industry action for improved equipment performance and operating practices in several ways, including the following:

- Provide industry benchmarking with aggregated statistics to assess their own equipment and practices,
- Identify best practices, improvements and opportunities, as well as potential pitfalls for industry,
- Give specific feedback assessments to partners: operators, owners, asset managers, and equipment suppliers, and finally
- Facilitate a culture change in wind plant operation to more effectively monitor and utilise reliability information.

The long-term objective will be an industry led and funded programme that serves industry needs through high value-added management of Reliability, Availability, and Maintenance (RAM) data.

Certification and Standards

Wind turbine standards aim to insure that turbines are installed with the appropriate strength and durability. When a site is chosen, a site assessment determines whether that location will be adequately covered by the design specifications. Sites can have critical conditions that create a hazard for deployment from such local conditions as atmospheric events or earthquakes. This task seeks to lay out a systematic framework for site risk assessment so that these conditions can be assessed. This task provides the link from atmospheric science, which characterises the environment, to the impact of these conditions on turbine deployment risk. The objective is to provide a clear pathway for developers to assess whether a particular site is completely covered by the standard design conditions, needs design modification to mitigate a particular risk, or should be insured to cover a rare but devastating event.

RELIABILITY IN CONNECTED SYSTEMS

From hardware, software, and maintenance perspectives, reliability is expensive, so it is very important to understand the reliability requirements of your application. While an application with no reliability requirement is rare, implementing an application with more reliability than is required can be a waste of time and resources. For this reason, it is important to understand the reliability issues of connected systems, so you can architect a solution that will provide the required level of reliability, while not wasting resources by providing reliability that is not required.

In service-oriented architecture (SOA) or connected systems, services communicate with each other through well-defined message formats, which means that the reliability of the connected systems application will be influenced strongly by the reliability of the messaging infrastructure it relies on to communicate between services. We will use the example of services in an automated-teller banking application to illustrate the various degrees of messaging reliability and how they are achieved. Message handling between services is generally more complex than client/server messaging, because client/server messaging can rely on the user to make some decisions about how to handle various error situations and time-outs, while the server initiating the message exchange in server-to-server messaging must make all the decisions that the end user would normally make in a client/server interaction.

INFRASTRUCTURE BURDEN

Many service-oriented applications achieve better throughput by using asynchronous messaging. With asynchronous messaging, a service sends a message to another service without waiting for a response to the message before continuing.

The service processes many more requests, because it doesn't waste time waiting for responses to requests that it makes to other services, but it puts the burden of ensuring that the message is delivered and processed on the messaging infrastructure. The choice of synchronous or asynchronous message handling is usually determined by the business requirements of the application. For example, if a customer is trying to withdraw money from an automated-teller machine (ATM), making an asynchronous request to check the customer's balance and proceeding to dispense the money without waiting for a response from the balance check is generally not a sound business decision. This scenario doesn't necessarily rule out an asynchronous request, however.

The ATM might dispatch a balance request as soon as the customer selects the withdrawal option, and then let the customer enter an amount while the balance check is proceeding asynchronously. Once the withdrawal amount is entered and the balance is received, the ATM application can make the decision on whether to dispense the cash. Let's look at how the ATM handles the balance-request message. The ATM service will send the balance-request message to the account service to get the customer's account balance. At this point, one of three things will happen: The balance will be returned successfully, an error will be returned, or the request will time out because the result was not returned in a timely manner. If the balance is returned, the ATM service continues with the transaction.

If an error is returned, the ATM uses its business logic to work with it-maybe using a cached copy of the balance, or dispensing or not dispensing the cash depending on the amount requested. The hardest one to work with is the time-out. A time-out may mean the message got lost in transit, the message arrived at the account service but the response was delayed for some reason, or the response was sent and then lost on the way back. In most cases, the best response is to try again and hope that it will work better next time. If the message was lost on the way the first time, it may get through this time. If the response was slow, the original response might arrive before the second request times out. Unless the account service is unreachable or completely gone, a retry should succeed eventually. Depending on what the problem was, the balance request might have been processed multiple times, or multiple results may be received; but as long as the ATM service is prepared to work with them, these aren't serious issues.

If the message was sent asynchronously, the ATM service might not have the information around to resend the message when a retry is required, so the messaging infrastructure will need to keep a copy of the messages it sends and resend them if required. For this type of simple request message, keeping a copy of the message in memory is probably adequate, because if the ATM loses power, the customer will have to start over anyway. If the ATM service needs a response even after a power loss, the message will have to be put into some persistent storage, and the messaging system will have to resend it when it restarts.

MESSAGE DELIVERY

For the synchronous version of this request, a simple SOAP Web service will provide the required degree of reliability. Error handling and time-out handling are the responsibility of the ATM service, so it will determine the level of reliability for the request. For the asynchronous version of the balance request, either the WS-RM channel in the Windows Communication Foundation (WCF) or express delivery in MSMQ will provide the required reliability, if the request doesn't have to survive system failures. If the message has to survive a system restart, MSMQ recoverable delivery is the appropriate choice. These messaging systems will handle the time-outs and retries that are required to deliver the message and the response, so the ATM service doesn't have to include this logic.

Now that we understand the reliability issues with a balance request, let us move on to the balance-change request that happens after the cash is dispensed. The reliability requirements for this message are a lot higher, because if it doesn't get delivered successfully, the bank will have given the customer cash without reducing the customer's account balance. While the customer is not likely to complain, the bank will not be happy if this situation happens regularly.

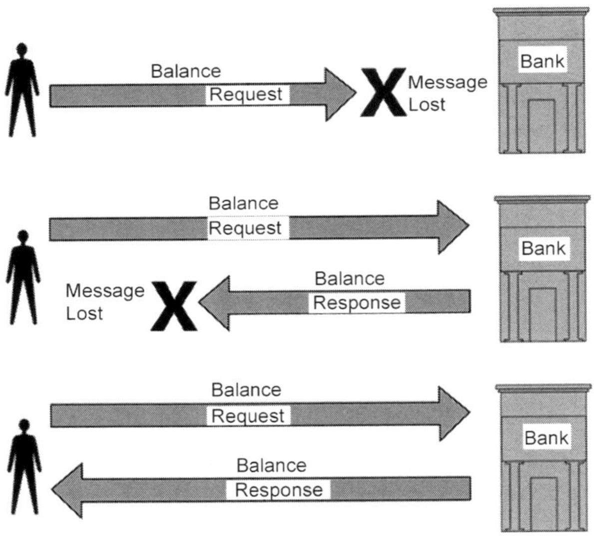

Fig. Balance Request.

The balance-change message must get delivered and processed in the face of any number of network and system failures. The memory-based retry mechanism obviously is not adequate for this task, because a system failure will lose the copy of the message being kept for retries. Keeping a persisted copy of the message for retries may also be an issue, because it is possible for multiple copies of the message to be delivered because of retries.

If the message decreases the customer account balance by $200, for example, delivering the message multiple times can lead to customer dissatisfaction. The retries required to ensure reliable message delivery work only if the messages are idempotent. An idempotent message can be delivered any number of times without violating the business constraints of the application. Some messages are naturally idempotent. For example, a message that changes a customer's address can be executed multiple times without ill effects. Other messages are not naturally idempotent, so the messaging system must make them idempotent to prevent the damage that can be done when a message is processed more than once.

This transaction is normally done by keeping a list of messages that have already been processed; if the same message is received more than once, it will not be processed more than once. Most messaging systems don't keep a copy of the incoming messages, but the sender assigns an identifier to each message and the receiver keeps track of the identifiers it has seen before. These identifiers must be kept until the message destination is sure that the source has thrown the message away, because if the source fails, the message might be sent again days later when the source restarts.

The list of processed messages must also be persistent, because the destination service may fail between retries. The destination must also keep track of the message that was sent in response to the incoming message, because the source will keep sending the original message until it receives the response, and the reason for the retry might be that the original response message was lost.

CHOOSE A MESSAGE INFRASTRUCTURE

Unless you are willing to persist and track the messages in your service logic, you will need a reliable messaging infrastructure to provide this level of reliability. Microsoft has three options for this infrastructure: MSMQ recoverable messaging, SQL Server Service Broker, and BizTalk. Which option you choose depends on your reliability requirements and application design. Service Broker and BizTalk provide more reliable message storage than MSMQ, because they store messages in a SQL Server database while MSMQ stores them in a file.

If your application can work with the occasional loss of messages when a file is lost or corrupted, MSMQ will be adequate for your needs. Some MSMQ applications guard against the potential loss of messages by storing a copy of the message in a database. If you are going to store messages, using Service Broker (which stores messages in the database, anyway) is significantly more efficient.

Service Broker and BizTalk provide roughly the same degree of reliability and defence against message, loss because they both store messages in the database. Service Broker's message handling is built into the database server logic, so Service Broker talks directly from the SQL Server process to the TCP/IP sockets, which is much more efficient than the BizTalk approach of an external process calling into the database to store messages in a table. While the Service Broker can deliver significantly more messages per second than

BizTalk, BizTalk offers a large number of features-message transformation, data-dependent message routing, multiple message transports, orchestration, and so on-that Service Broker doesn't offer.

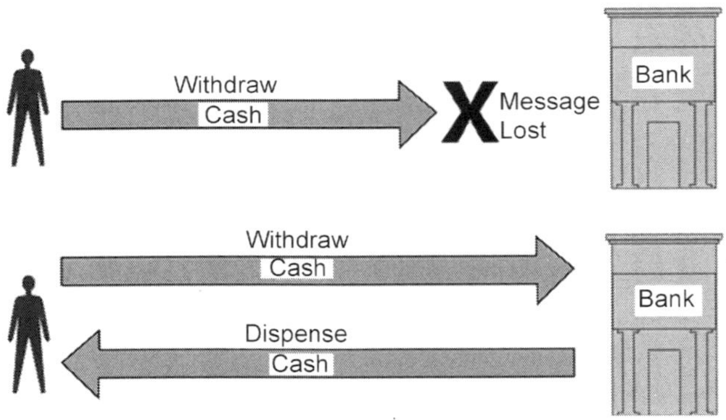

Fig. Withdraw-cash Request, Harmless Retry.

In general, if reliable transfer of messages between databases is all your application requires, Service Broker is a better choice, because it is more lightweight and efficient at transferring messages than BizTalk. If, on the other hand, your application requires the message manipulation, data integrations, or orchestration features that BizTalk provides, Service Broker is probably not the right solution. While MSMQ recoverable messaging doesn't provide the reliability levels that the SQL Server-based options provide, it does have the advantage of not requiring SQL Server at both messaging endpoints. If supporting a database at both endpoints is not an option and the application's reliability requirements can be met by MSMQ, MSMQ is probably the right choice as the messaging infrastructure. If both of the communicating services require data storage, however, the extra reliability of storing messages in the database is worthwhile.

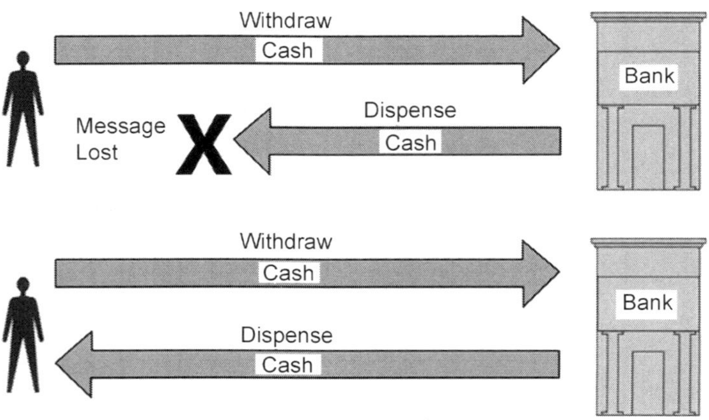

Fig. Withdraw-cash-request Retry, Where the Customer Loses Money.

In our ATM example, the ATM service will require local data storage for auditing, local storage of data for offline operation, and storage of reference data, so there will probably be a database in the ATM, anyway, and one of the SQL Server-based options is appropriate. The choice between Service Broker and BizTalk depends on the nonmessaging requirements of the application, the resources available at the ATM, and the message-volume requirements.

EXECUTION RELIABILITY

The reliability in message delivery from one service to another. Not surprisingly, we found that the amount of reliability required depends on what the application is doing and how critical the message data is to the application. Here, we will assume that messages are transferred with the required degree of reliability to a service and examine the reliability requirements for the service processing the messages.

One of the unique requirements of a service that processes asynchronous messages is that receiving a message from the queue is a "pull" operation. In other words, when a message arrives in a queue, it will sit there until an application executes a "receive" operation to retrieve and process the message. This requirement means that an asynchronous service must ensure that it executes when there are messages in the queue to be processed. The most common way to achieve this requirement is to make the service a Windows service managed by the Windows Service Control Manager (SCM). The SCM will ensure the service is started when Windows starts, and can be configured to restart the service if it fails for some reason.

While this configuration generally provides the required level of reliability and is generally the preferred solution when messages arrive at a constant rate, it can cause problems if the message load varies significantly. If the service is configured with enough resources to handle peak loads, it will be wasting resources when the message load is low; and if it is configured to handle the average load, it will get far behind during peak loads. BizTalk messaging runs as a Windows service, so a BizTalk application can rely on the Windows service to be there to handle incoming messages.

MSMQ addresses the message-load problem with triggers that start a messaging-processing service each time a message arrives in the queue. While this processing works well when messages arrive infrequently, when message load is high, the overhead of starting 1,000 copies of the services can be more than the service logic itself.

Service Broker provides a feature called activation to solve this problem. When a message arrives in an empty queue, Service Broker will start a stored procedure to handle the message. This stored procedure will wait in a loop for more messages to arrive and continue in this loop until the queue is empty. If Service Broker determines that the stored procedure is not keeping up with the messages coming in, it will start additional copies of the stored procedure until there are enough copies running to keep up. When the message arrival rate decreases, the queue will be empty and the extra copies will exit. Then, there will always be approximately the right number of resources available to service the incoming messages. Because Service Broker starts these procedures, it will be notified if one fails and replace the failing copy. If the service is an external application instead of a stored procedure, Service Broker provides events that an external application can subscribe to that will notify the service when more resources are required to process messages in a queue.

LOST MESSAGE

The other reliability issue that service execution must work with is a service failure while processing a message. If a service deletes a message from the queue as soon as it has received it and then fails before completely processing the message, that message is effectively lost. Similarly, if the service waits until it has completely processed the message before removing it from the queue, a failure between the processing step and the message removal will result in the message still being in the queue when the service restarts, and it will be processed again.

As mentioned earlier, processing the same message multiple times is not a problem if the message is a balance query, but processing a withdrawal twice can be irritating to the customer involved. The only real way to ensure that each message is processed "exactly once" is for the message processing and the queue deletion to be part of the same transaction. If there is a failure in processing, both the processing changes and the message deletion are rolled back, so everything is back to the way it was before the message was received.

A single commit operation commits both the message-receive and the message-processing actions. Similarly, if processing the message generates an outgoing message, the "send" of the outgoing message should be part of the transaction to avoid the situation where the service rolls back, but the response message is still sent. This type of message processing is called transactional messaging. Most reliable messaging infrastructures support transactional messaging.

Because the messages are stored in a different file from the database, MSMQ transactional messaging requires a two-phase commit to ensure both parts of the transaction are committed. Because Service Broker SEND and RECEIVE commands are TSQL commands, the messaging and data-update operations in a Service Broker service can be executed from the same SQL Server connection and be part of the same SQL Server transaction. Therefore, a two-phase commit is not required, which makes Service Broker's implementation of transactional messaging significantly more efficient than MSMQ's implementation. Again, transactional messaging is required to make a non-idempotent service behave like an idempotent service, to eliminate the issues caused by message retries. If the service is inherently idempotent, transactional messaging is not required. If transactional messaging is not used, the service requester must be prepared to receive a response multiple times, sometimes over a long time span.

DATA RELIABILITY

Now, we will look at the impact of data on service reliability. Most services access data while processing service messages, so data reliability is tightly bound to service reliability.

One of the unique aspects of asynchronous service execution is that, in many cases, the service messages are valuable business objects. In our ATM service, for example, if balance-change messages are lost because of a failure, the account balance is not changed and the bank loses money. For this reason, storing messages in the database-so they enjoy the same reliability, redundancy, and availability protections that the rest of the data stored there enjoy-makes a lot of sense. If the balance-change messages in our example are stored in the same database as the accounts, they will be lost only if the accounts also are lost. The backups, log backups, and Storage Area Network (SAN) features used to ensure that the bank-account information is not lost apply also to the balance-change messages, making the reliability of the service extremely high. If your message-reliability requirements are high, Service Broker or BizTalk have significant reliability advantages, because they store messages in the database.

One of the new features of SQL Server 2005 that can improve service reliability is database mirroring (DBM). DBM provides reliability by maintaining a secondary copy of a database that is maintained transactionally consistent with the primary database, by applying each transaction that commits on the primary to the secondary copy before returning control to the service. If the primary fails, the secondary copy of the database can become the primary in a few seconds.

Service Broker takes advantage of database mirroring to improve messaging reliability. If the account database is a DBM pair of databases, the Service Broker database in the ATM will open network connections to both the primary and secondary databases, and send messages to the primary. If the secondary database becomes the primary, Service Broker is notified immediately and messages are routed to the new primary with no user intervention or interruption.

Highly data-intensive services can take advantage of another feature in SQL Server 2005 to improve reliability. The integration of the Common Language Runtime (CLR) into the SQL Server engine means that the service logic can run into the database also. Therefore, for a Service Broker service, the logic, messages, execution environment, security context, and data for a service can be in the same database.

This single-location storage has many advantages in a system with high reliability requirements. Database servers generally have the hardware and software features to maintain the high reliability required by a database. This reliability can now apply to all aspects of the service implementation. In the unlikely event of a service failure, the whole environment of the service can be restored to a transactionally consistent state with the database recovery features. Not only is the data saved, but any operations in progress are rolled back and restarted in the same execution and security environment that they were in at the time of failure.

The loosely coupled, asynchronous nature of service-oriented applications imposes some unique reliability requirements. When architecting services, the level of reliability required for the service must be understood and taken into account. Microsoft offers a variety of infrastructures for implementing services that offer different levels of reliability. Choosing the right infrastructure involves matching the level of reliability required against the capabilities of the infrastructure. The new features of SQL Server 2005 provide a service-hosting infrastructure that offers unprecedented levels of reliability for services that require very high reliability levels.

RELIABILITY DATABASES: STATE OF THE ART AND PERSPECTIVES

The fundamental works on reliability theory have established the mathematical basis for the evaluation of the reliability of complex systems computed from the knowledge of component reliability and also for the construction of reliable systems from relatively unreliable components.

Today reliability and safety analysis becomes an important part of each technological system design or investigation process.

Problems to be solved can be divided into two main groups:

- Reliability and safety analysis of hazardous plants, comparing the values of their reliability and safety parameters, increasing safety level of the plant, etc.;
- Prognoses of the values of reliability and safety parameters for new plants which are to be constructed.

So, the necessity exists to obtain complete and exact data concerning equipment functioning, accidents and their consequences, maintenance operations and their costs that can be used for the solution of problems from the first group in the classification. The best case would be if such information were collected from the same equipment (specific failure data) or from analogous equipment in similar conditions. In the case of the second group of problems we must use the information on equipment to be planned for implementation combined with expert judgements on new equipment reliability parameters or using standard values or standard reliability models. So, there is a need for reliability data collection in relation to all types of components from the field records of installations and operations, in order to allow us to analyse, compare, or predict the reliability levels of complex systems.

We can define at least three categories of users of reliability databases:

- Risk and reliability analysts for analysing and predicting a reliability of complex systems;
- Maintenance engineers for measuring and optimising the maintenance performance;
- Component designers for analysing and optimising the component performance.

All of these specialists need different types of data. The risk analyst needs to compute system availability or probability of mission success or failure. For this he needs to know the availability of components and failure rates. Availability can be estimated from failure on demand if downtime has been properly included in the database. The maintenance engineer needs to measure maintenance performance. The operational data conflates the effects of maintenance and the intrinsic reliability of the component. Also he wants to know what the failure behaviour of the component would be in the case it were not maintained. The component designer is primarily interested in failure mechanisms that reveal the weak points of design. Hence, he is interested in distinguishing failure modes according to failure mechanisms. Where this is not possible, engineering knowledge is used to infer failure mechanisms from other information. The scope of this survey is description of the data sources that can be used for the analysis of reliability of hazardous industrial plants and installations.

HISTORICAL REVIEW OF DATA

Collection of necessary empirical data for the prediction of future event probabilities has a long history. Architects used design rules of thumb to capture experience of the ages and thereby produce buildings of incredible longevity and reliability. At least before the 17th century the safe passage events and mortality events were collected and analysed to uncover prospective underlying classes; then associated class attributes formed a basis for the insurance industry.

One of the first designs for which reliability and risk databases may have been developed were that of the automobile and aircraft when they were converted from a plaything of the rich to means of transport for a broad spectrum of population. Such transport must be reliable and safe, and this fact becomes a basis for gathering of maintenance statistics and attempts at redesigning or replacing of frequently failed items.

First Generation of Failure Data Source

The earliest broad-based published source of reliability data may well have been the.Martin Titan Handbook. This widely distributed source contained generic failure rates on a wide range of electrical, electronic, electromechanical, and mechanical.parts and assemblies.. The Titan Handbook was the first known source to standardise the presentation of failure rates in terms of failures per 106 hours eliminating the necessity for conversions.

Reliability Data, Second Generation

The Titan Handbook sets the stage for more ambitious programmes to collect and organise reliability data.

The brightest examples of these efforts are:

- MIL-Handbook-217
- Failure Rate Data Bank (FARADA)
- RADC Non-Electronic Reliability Notebook.

All of these second-generation sources were built upon the experience of the Titan Handbook (using the constant hazard exponential model and base failure rates per 106 hours) and have survived in some form to the present day. When the computer-aided systems appeared, special databases being managed by software tools became the areas for reliability data collections. Computer utilisation permits the user to recover data more rapidly and to analyse them statistically.

The first computer aided database was GIDEP (Government Industry Data Exchange Programme) also known as FARADA created under the sponsorship of US Army Material Command, Air Force Logistic Command, and Air Force Systems Command.

Third Generation

The main deficiency of the previous generation of reliability data source was represented by the constant failure rates and non-adequacy of the hazard model to the whole spectrum of environmental conditions and possible reasons of failure. Researchers began to seek improvements by designing new databases that addressed these problems. Range estimations were introduced for estimated mean values to address the problem of heterogeneous sub-populations. These estimates attempted to gauge the actual uncertainty of the underlying mixture distributions through various percentile grouping approaches, thereby preserving the dispersion in the data and reducing the possibility for misuse. Failure rate estimates were separated into time-related and demand-related categories.

The failure modes were divided into catastrophic, degraded, and incipient; efforts moved into the commercial nuclear power industry and to the offshore oil and chemical industry. The improvement of data analysis techniques and also of hardware and software tools has initiated the growth of database performances. It should be noted that the extent to which a database has been developed varies according to the domain of its application.

A NON-BLOCKING COMMITMENT PROTOCOL

A distributed transaction requires a commitment protocol to ensure that all sites agree whether the transaction commits or aborts. A non-blocking commitment protocol is one that permits at least some sites to terminate (Le.. commit or abort) in spite of the occurrence of any single failure before or during execution of the protocol.

The standard centralised two-phase commitment protocol is not non-blocking because if a prepared subordinate loses contact with the coordinator (either because the coordinator crashes or because of a network failure). Then the subordinate must remain prepared until the failure is repaired and communication with the coordinator is re-established. Until then, the subordinate continues to hold write locks for the transaction and is said to be blocked.

Blocking is undeSirable because if the data at the subordinate is more valuable than that at the coordinator. Then the unavailability of data at the blocked subordinate may be more harmful than the unavailability of the coordinator. An example of this situation is when a data-rich mainframe serves as a subordinate to transactions initiated by user-controlled workstations. Also, if data is replicated, then data access protocols can overcome a crashed site, but not a blocked site.

In the absence of failures, non-blocking commitment protocols are inherently slower than blocking protocols, and so non-blocking commitment is not suitable for all applications.

Its main uses are:

- For applications that are willing to sacrifice some performance in return for higher availability.
- For large transactions. If the cost of commitment is a small part of the whole cost of a transaction. Then the advantages of non-blocking commitment make it desirable.
- For transactions executed at sites spanning a wide area. In such a configuration. Subordinates remain prepared longer and network failures are more likely.
- For systems in which transaction management code runs in the same address space as user-written code. In such a system the coordinator can be expected to fail more often because user-written code is presumably more error-prone.

This chapter describes a non-blocking commitment protocol that permits at least some functioning sites to terminate in spite of any single site crash or network partition.

This is optimal resiliency, since, Skeen has shown that no protocol can be nonblocking despite any two failures and since, it is likewise impossible to ensure that all sites can terminate during a single partition. The protocol uses the quorum consensus technique to avoid blocking during partition and is a centralised protocol that becomes gradually decentralised as failures occur. It can be viewed as an improved version of a similar protocol described.

The improvements are:

- An optimisation that, typically, allows the processing of read-only sites and read-only transactions to be as fast as with the Presumed Abort variation of two-phase commit).
- Addition of the ability for all sites to forget (Le.. expunge data structures pertaining to) the transaction after it is terminated. This is an important practical feature and correctly adding this ability to a non-blocking protocol is not as obvious as it may seem. A protocol that forgets too soon is incorrect, yet no existing specification of any non-blocking commitment protocol indicates how to forget.
- Design such that all actions to be taken both before and after a failure are integrated into a single protocol. Normally. The non-blocking problem is divided into four sub-protocols:
  1. A "commit protocol" executed before the failure.
  2. A post-failure "termination protocol" executed by sites that survive the failure.
  3. A post-failure "recovery protocol" executed by crashed sites once they recover.
  4. In addition, centralised termination protocols typically make use of an additional "election protocol" for selecting a replacement coordinator.

Having one rather than three or four protocols eases the tasks of reasoning about and implementing the protocol.

In addition, this chapter presents the following advantages over previous descriptions of quorum-based non-blocking protocols:

- Elucidation of several performance optimisations beyond the read-only optimisation.
- A complete specification that includes all knowledge needed to implement the protocol - including exactly when to write log records and what the contents of log records and messages should be.
- Detailed arguments about the safety and liveness of the protocol.
- Analysis of normal case (Le.. failure-free) performance and comparison with measured results of an implementation.
- Discussion of a depressing fact about quorum-based non-blocking commit protocols: they are effective only for transactions involving at least three sites. This fact is fundamental but has never before been explicitly mentioned in several discussions of quorum-based non-blocking commit protocols.

PROTOCOL DESCRIPTION

Assumptions

It is assumed that when the commit protocol begins the operations comprising the transaction are finished; *i.e.,* the transaction is not spreading to new sites while the commit protocol executes. The only assumptions that must be made about the environment are that each site has a single stable storage log that can be written atomically, that communication is point-to-point and that possible failures are described by a failure model:

- Any process or site may fail at any time but must be "fail stop" meaning that a failure results in the site or process halting immediately then losing its volatile memory.
- The fail stop condition implies that malicious failures do not occur. Specifically, processes do not "tell lies" no network message will be undetectably altered and the network will not spontaneously create good messages. Messages may however be lost duplicated or reordered. No bound on delivery time is assumed.
- Any two sites may lose the ability to communicate, either in one or both directions and the network may partition. A partition is the separation of a completely connected network into exactly two completely connected subnetworks that cannot communicate with one another. The typical cause of partition is the crash of a gateway.
- Failure is detected by timing out on an expected message. It is not possible to determine the type of failure.
- Every failure is eventually repaired.

This model matches closely the events that do and do not happen in the real world. Although the protocol is independent of the methods used for concurrency control and recovery. This chapter is written as if the recovery method is logging, the concurrency control method is locking and each site has a transaction controller that executes the commitment protocol and controls the dropping of locks. These conventions are adopted only in order to be precise in discussing the actions required at various times. Also, the communicating entities are called "sites" that communicate via a "network," although the protocol applies more generally to processes communicating via any sort of communication system governed by the failure model.

Operation Without Failures

In the absence of failures, the non-blocking commitment protocol has three phases. In the first "prepare phase" the coordinator tries to have all sites become prepared to either commit or abort. The purpose of the second "replication phase" is to have the coordinator replicate at subordinate sites the information that it will use to make the commit/abort decision, namely whether all sites are prepared. (Recording the fact that all sites are prepared is referred to as joining the commit group. Recording the perception that some site is not prepared is referred to as joining the abort group.) In the third "notify phase" the coordinator makes the decision and informs subordinates of the outcome. After the third phase - once all sites have committed or aborted - there is an additional seventh message. The atomic commitment point occurs during the replication phase once enough sites have recorded the information given to them by the coordinator. As in two-phase commit, all sites retain the ability to "abort unilaterally" before they prepare. The first and third phases of this protocol correspond closely to the two phases of two-phase commit.

Beyond having three centralised phases, the other salient aspects of the protocol are that a subordinate does not forever await messages from the coordinator but instead times out and itself becomes another coordinator and that a crashed site assumes the role of a coordinator when it recovers.

The precise steps of the protocol for an update transaction are:

- The coordinator prepares by dropping its read locks and forcing a prepare log record that contains the list of its write locks the quorum sizes and the list of subordinates.
- The coordinator sends prepare asynchronously to all subordinates, then awaits responses. The prepare message must contain enough information to allow the subordinate to later behave as a coordinator: the list of sites involved in the transaction and the two quorums sizes.
- Each subordinate drops its read locks and attempts to prepare. To prepare, the subordinate forces a prepare log record that contains its write locks, the quorum sizes and the list of all sites. It then sends prepare-ack (yes) to the coordinator. If the site cannot prepare it sends prepare-aele (no), undoes its updates, drops its write locks and spools an abort record. To "spool" a log record means to write it into a log buffer: the next log force will write the entire buffer into the log.
- The coordinator waits until either all prepare-ack messages are received or a timeout occurs. If all sites are prepared, then the coordinator forces an in-group log record. The record should contain the state of all sites, the state of the coordinator being in-group/commit. It then sends join-group (commit) which also contains state of all sites as known to the coordinator. If some site is unprepared or a timeout occurred, then the coordinator forces the in-group log record with the coordinator state being in-group/abort. It then sends join-group (abort) to all subordinates. This message also lists every site and its state.
- A subordinate that receives the join-group message joins the specified group provided it is not already in a group. It does so by forcing an in-group log record that contains the list of all sites and

their states. It then sends in-group back to the coordinator. If the subordinate times out waiting for join-group. Then it becomes a coordinator in the prepared state.

- The coordinator collects in-group messages. Checking if a quorum is formed. While no quorum exists, the coordinator must continue to resent join-group to those subordinate sites not yet in a group. Once a quorum exists, the coordinator either commits or aborts. Committing is easy: the coordinator forces an outcome log record that specifies commit. To abort, updates are undone, write locks are dropped, and then an outcome log record specifying abort is spoiled. After committing or aborting, the coordinator sends outcome to all subordinates. The outcome message and log record need not include any extra information beyond that which indicates whether to commit or abort.
- A subordinate that receives outcome commits or aborts just as the coordinator did. It then replies with outcome-ack. As at the coordinator the log record need not include extra information. If the subordinate times out waiting for the outcome, it becomes a coordinator in the appropriate in-group state.
- The coordinator res ends outcome until it receives outcome-ack from all subordinates. It then sends forget to all sites, and forgets the transaction. Forgetting is accomplished by spooling a done record into the log buffer. The purpose of a done record is to indicate that this transaction's portion of the log can be reclaimed.
- A subordinate that receives forgets in the same way the coordinator does. If it times out, it becomes a coordinator and sends outcome to all sites. Which will reply with outcome-ack. Clearly, the coordinator should retransmit unacknowledged messages a few times to prevent needless subordinate timeouts. The messages sent between coordinator and subordinate when a transaction commits without failure. The three phases are obvious. The extra message is necessary if sites are to be able to forget according to three steps of reasoning.

First, a site with no record of a transaction can join the abort group. Second, it is possible for one site to be committed while another is still trying to gather an abort quorum. So if a subordinate were to commit and then forget, it could join the abort group after having forgotten. In this fashion a single site could join both the commit group and, later, the abort group and allow the same transaction to commit at some sites and abort at others. To ensure correctness, no site forgets until all sites (including those that may have crashed or been isolated by partition) have acknowledged the outcome. While forgetting thus can be delayed by a failure, this is not blocking, since, locks have been dropped.

DATA CONSISTENCY

Data consistency summarises the validity, accuracy, usability and integrity of related data between applications and across an IT enterprise. This ensures that each user observes a consistent view of the data, including visible changes made by the user's own transactions and transactions of other users or processes. Data Consistency problems may arise at any time but are frequently introduced during or following recovery situations when backup copies of the data are used in place of the original data.

Various kinds of data consistency have been identified. These include Application Consistency, Transaction Consistency and Point-in-Time (PiT) Consistency.

POINT-IN-TIME CONSISTENCY

Data is point-in-time consistent if all of the interrelated data components (either a group of data sets or a set of logical volumes) are as they were at any single instant in time. Point-in-time consistency is an important property of backup files and a critical objective of software that creates backups. It is also relevant to the design of disk memory systems, specifically relating to what happens when they are unexpectedly shut down.

As a relevant backup example, consider a web site with a database, which needs to be operational around the clock, but also must be backed up with regularity to protect against disaster. Database is stored on servers in the form of one or several very large files which require minutes or hours to back up. These large files - as with any database - contain numerous data structures which reference each other by location. For example, some structures are indexes which permit the database subsystem to quickly find search results. If the data structures cease to reference each other properly, then the database can be said to be corrupted.

Counter Example

The importance of point-in-time consistency can be illustrated with what would happen if a backup were made without it. Database is a huge file, which has an important index located 20% of the way through, and saves article data at the 75% mark. Consider a scenario where an editor comes and creates a new article at the same time a backup is being performed, which is being made as a simple "file copy" which copies from the beginning to the end of the large file(s) and doesn't consider data consistency - and at the time of the article edit, it is 50% complete. The new article is added to the article space (at the 75% mark) and a corresponding index entry is added (at the 20% mark).

Because the backup is already halfway done and the index already copied, the backup will be written with the article data present, but with the index reference missing. As a result of the inconsistency, this file is considered corrupted. In real life, a real database may be edited thousands of times per hour, and references are virtually always spread throughout the file and can number into the millions, billions, or more. A sequential "copy" backup would literally contain so many small corruptions that the backup would be completely unusable without a lengthy repair process which could provide no guarantee as to the completeness of what has been recovered.

A backup process which properly accounts for data consistency ensures that the backup is a snapshot of how the entire database looked at a single moment. It would ensure that the backup was written without the added article at the 75% mark, so that the article data would be consistent with the index data previously written.

Disk Caching Systems

Point-in-time consistency is also relevant to computer disk subsystems. Specifically, operating systems and file systems are designed with the expectation that the computer system they are running on could lose power, crash, fail, or otherwise cease operating at any time. When properly designed, they ensure that data will not be unrecoverably corrupted if the power is lost. Operating systems and file systems do this by ensuring that data is written to a hard disk in a certain order, and rely on that in order to detect and recover from unexpected shutdowns.

On the other hand, rigorously writing data to disk in the order that maximizes data integrity also impacts performance. A process of write caching is used to consolidate and re-sequence write operations such that they can be done faster by minimizing the time spent moving disk heads. Data consistency concerns arise when write caching changes the sequence in which writes are carried out, because it there exists the possibility of an unexpected shutdown that violates the operating system's expectation that all writes will be committed sequentially.

For example, in order to save a typical document or picture file, an operating system might write the following records to a disk in the following order:

- Journal entry saying file XYZ is about to be saved into sector 123.
- The actual contents of the file XYZ are written into sector 123.
- Sector 123 is now flagged as occupied in the record of free/used space.
- Journal entry noting the file completely saved, and its name is XYZ and is located in sector 123.

The operating system relies on the assumption that if it sees item #1 is present (saying the file is about to be saved), but that item #4 is missing (confirming success), that the save operation was unsuccessful and so it should undo any incomplete steps already taken to save it (*e.g.*, marking sector 123 free since, it never was properly filled, and removing any record of XYZ from the file directory). It relies on these items being committed to disk in sequential order. Suppose a caching algorithm determines it would be fastest to write these items to disk in the order 4-3-1-2, and starts doing so, but the power gets shut down after 4 get written, before 3, 1 and 2, and so those writes never occur. When the computer is turned back on, the file system would then show it contains a file named XYZ which is located in sector 123, but this sector really does not contain the file. (Instead, the sector will contain garbage, or zeroes, or a random portion of some old file - and that is what will show if the file is opened).

Further, the file system's free space map will not contain any entry showing that sector 123 is occupied, so later, it will likely assign that sector to the next file to be saved, believing it is available. The file system will then have two files both unexpectedly claiming the same sector (known as a cross-linked file). As a result, a write to one of the files will overwrite part of the other file, invisibly damaging it.

A disk caching subsystem that ensures point-in-time consistency guarantees that in the event of an unexpected shutdown, the four elements would be written one of only five possible ways: completely (1-2-3-4), partially (1, 1-2, 1-2-3), or not at all.

High-end hardware disk controllers of the type found in servers include a small battery back-up unit on their cache memory so that they may offer the performance gains of write caching while mitigating the risk of unintended shutdowns. The battery back-up unit keeps the memory powered even during a shutdown so that when the computer is powered back up, it can quickly complete any writes it has previously committed. With such a controller, the operating system may request four writes (1-2-3-4) in that order, but the controller may decide the quickest way to write them is 4-3-1-2. The controller essentially lies to the operating system and reports that the writes have been completed in order (a lie that improves performance at the expense of data corruption if power is lost), and the battery backup hedges against the risk of data corruption by giving the controller a way to silently fix any and all damage that could occur as a result.

If the power gets shut off after element 4 has been written, the battery backed memory contains the record of commitment for the other three items and ensures that they are written ("flushed") to the disk at the next available opportunity.

TRANSACTION CONSISTENCY

A transaction is a logical unit of work that may include any number of file or database updates. Transaction consistency is also frequently referred to as atomicity. A good example of the importance of transaction consistency is a database that handles the transfer of money.

Suppose a money transfer requires two operations: writing a debit in one place, and a credit in another. If the system crashes or shuts down when one operation has completed but the other has not, and there is nothing in place to correct this, the system can be said to lack transaction consistency. With a money transfer, it is desirable that either the entire transaction completes, or none of it completes. Both of these scenarios keep the balance in check. Transaction consistency ensures just that - that a system is programmed to be able to detect incomplete transactions when powered on, and undo (or "roll back") the portion of any incomplete transactions that are found.

Application Consistency

Application Consistency is similar to Transaction consistency, but instead of data consistency within the scope of a single transaction, data must be consistent within the confines of many different transaction streams from one or more applications.

CONSISTENT NETWORK DEVICE NAMING

BENEFIT TO FEDORA

System Administrators can then use BIOS-provided names, which are consistent and not arbitrarily named, for their network ports. This eliminates the confusion that non-deterministic naming brings, and eliminates the use of hard-coded MAC address based port renaming which a) is racy and error-prone, and b) introduces state into an otherwise stateless system. This change affects most desktop, notebook, and server-class systems.

Limitations

Not all add-in cards have a method to expose their Linux interface name(s) to external port mapping, biosdevname may provide incorrect names for such. Discussions are ongoing on the netdev mailing list to standardize a method of exposing such mapping.

How To Test

- System-Under-Test can be just about any system. Systems that expose SMBIOS 2.6 Type 9 and Type 41 fields are preferred, but the code will work on systems that expose the legacy PCI IRQ Routing Table as well.
- biosdevname must be installed on the target system.
- erase/etc/udev/rules.d/70-persistent-net.rules file. This is where naming is persisted across reboots.
- reboot the system
- Following reboot:
  - /sbin/ifconfig -a must show LAN-on-Motherboard ports named em[1234]
  - em[1234] must correspond to the chassis labels. Verify using ethtool -p em[1234] and watch the lights blink.

- Installing using Anaconda:
  - anaconda should present network devices to use, having the new naming convention.

User Experience

Ethernet NICs embedded on the motherboard will be named em[1234] rather than ethX. PCI add-in card NICs will be named p<slot>p<port>_<vf>.

Linux guests running under virtualisation platforms such as KVM, Xen, VMware Workstation or ESX, or Microsoft Hyper-V will not have their devices renamed.

System Administrators may disable this feature by passing "biosdevname=0" on the kernel command line.

Release Notes

Servers often have multiple Ethernet ports, either embedded on the motherboard, or on add-in PCI cards. Linux has traditionally named these ports ethX, but there has been no correlation of the ethX names to the chassis labels - the ethX names are non-deterministic. Starting in Fedora 15, Ethernet ports will have a new naming scheme corresponding to physical locations, rather than ethX. Ethernet ports embedded on server motherboards will be named em<port_number>, while ports on PCI cards will be named p<slot_number>p<port_number>, corresponding to the chassis labels. Additionally, if the network device is an SR-IOV Virtual Function or has Network Partitioning (NPAR) capability, the name will have a suffix of _<virtual_function> or _<partition>.

By changing the naming convention, system administrators will no longer have to guess at the ethX to physical port mapping, or invoke workarounds on each system to rename them into some "sane" order.

This feature affects all physical systems that expose network port naming information in SMBIOS 2.6 or later (specifically field types 9 and 41). Dell PowerEdge 10G and newer servers (PowerEdge 1950 III family, PowerEdge R710 family, and newer), and HP ProLiant G6 servers and newer are known to expose this information, as do some newer desktop models. Furthermore, most older systems expose some information in the PCI IRQ Routing Table, which will be consulted if information is not provided by SMBIOS. Fedora running as a guest virtual machine will continue to use the ethX names.

Existing installations upgraded to Fedora 15 will not see a change in names unless/etc/udev/rules.d/70-persistent-net.rules is deleted and the HWADDR lines are removed from all/etc./sysconfig/network-scripts/ifcfg-* files, and those files are renamed to use the new device names. You may continue to write rules in/etc/udev/rules.d/70-persistent-net.rules to change the device names to anything you wish. Such will take precedence over this physical location naming scheme. Such rules may look like:

```
SUBSYSTEM=="net", ACTION=="add", DRIVERS=="?*", ATTR{address}=="00:11:22:33:44:55", ATTR{type}=="1", KERNEL=="eth*", NAME="public"
```

This feature may be disabled by passing "biosdevname=0" on the kernel command line, in which case, behaviour will revert to using ethX names.

Upgrading from an earlier version of Fedora (including 15-Alpha or -Beta) to Fedora 15 may result in a change of network device names from an earlier biosdevname naming scheme to the final naming scheme described here. Configuration files must be manually adjusted accordingly.

DETECTION OF INCONSISTENCY IN UML MODELS

Maintaining consistency in a large, evolving design model is difficult. Changes to the model may introduce inconsistencies, which then need to be detected and resolved.Adesign model is inconsistent if it contains conflicting information about the system, and/or violates predefined constraints. Such constraints include both good practices for this kind of design and specific requirements from the stakeholders for this system. The term inconsistency refers to a single instance of such conflict or violation. To manually identify and resolve design inconsistencies can be tedious and error prone. Computer assistance in handling design consistency issues is inevitably required.

Recently, a number of research teams have made progress in providing computerbased design consistency checking, notably the xlinkit tool, Argo/UML, and the process-oriented design guidance approach. Inconsistency has also been recognised as a major challenge in requirements engineering, and van Lamsweerde has developed a typology of inconsistencies that occur in goal-based requirements models. However, as yet, no such typology has been developed for inconsistency in design models.

For UML, constraints expressed in OCL are intended to maintain the well-formedness of the UMLsemantics. We are interested in a broader class of inconsistencies, including problems related to information redundancy, nonconformance to standards and requirements, and the propagation of change through a model as it evolves. Our goal is to develop a software design environment that automates the detection and resolution of design inconsistencies in design models. Observations of software developers suggest that designers often tolerate inconsistencies in their models because the alternatives may be to leave information out, or to make premature design decisions.

Hence, a support environment should not try to prevent inconsistency, and needs to be flexible in the manner in which it indicates the presence of inconsistencies to the designer. Our approach is to detect and track inconsistencies automatically as the design model is edited, and to suggest likely resolutions where possible. Our approach uses a production system running in the background of an editor. The production rules recognise inconsistencies, and track them by adding entries to the working memory of the production system. The use of a production system gives us a powerful pattern matching approach to inconsistency detection, and allows rules to modify the behaviour of other rules, depending on the context. We define a classification scheme of design inconsistencies that occur in the design representation, and develop our production rules based on these classes of inconsistencies.

CLASSES OF DESIGN INCONSISTENCY

We can analyse software design consistency from two perspectives. One is the design description, which is concerned with maintaining a consistent representation of the design. Another is the actual design, which is concerned with building the actual system where inconsistencies may arise from implementing design concepts. We present three classes of inconsistencies within the design description: redundancy, conformance to constraints and standards, and change. These classes cover syntactic and semantic inconsistencies of the description language, and language-independent constraints and standards. Examples are drawn for each class in UML.

Redundancy One of the most frequently occurring inconsistency sources is redundancy of information. More specifically, a redundancy occurs when a design artifact (perhaps partial) is represented multiple times, possibly in varying views. Redundancies can occur either in design or data representation.

Design related redundancy arises when two design units have common elements, or overlap, in the representation. For example, a structural redundancy refers to an overlap between several structural and/or behavioural diagrams. It is known as structure clash in the context of requirements specifications. Such redundancy may be desirable since, it can provide additional information to a requirement specification from different perspectives, and describe the behaviour of a design unit under various scenarios. For instance, in modelling feature interactions, two kinds of feature dependence relations can be introduced, specialisation and interference. In both cases, there is redundant information.

DETECTION AND RESOLUTION OF DATA INCONSISTENCIES

The development of Information Systems, network communications and the World Wide Web, has permitted access to autonomous, distributed and heterogeneous data sources. An increasing number of databases, especially those published on the Web, are becoming available to external users. User requests are converted to queries over several data sources with different information quality. Integration of schemas on existing databases into a global unified schema is an approach developed over 20 years ago. However information quality can not be guaranteed after integration, because data quality is dependent on the design of the information and its provenance. Even greater levels of inconsistency exist when information is retrieved from different information sources.

On the other hand, different expectations exist on the quality of the information, depending on the user. A casual user on the Web does not expect complete and precise information, but what is the available information in the shorter possible time. A professional user expects accuracy and completeness of the information retrieved in order to make a decision irrespective of the time it could take, to retrieve the data, although speed is still likely to be a lesser priority.

User priorities, data inconsistencies and data quality differences among the participating sources have not been fully addressed in the processes and optimisations of information integration, such as query processing, query planning and hierarchical structuring of results to the user.

The aim of this paper is to establish the context and background on data quality for information retrieval from distributed heterogeneous systems with regard to the following issues:

- How the information quality has been modelled and measured.
- Which quality dimensions are more useful for query processing.
- Which quality criteria have been more determinant as user priorities for classification of the final result set.
- Discussion on how these approaches have been developed, and highlight new topics for further research.

The background on the establishment of information quality criteria, models and assessment. Some issues are presented in order to help query answering and ranking of query results using priorities given by the user.

DATA INTEGRATION IN HETEROGENEOUS DATABASE SYSTEMS

Data integration is the process of extracting and merging data from multiple heterogeneous sources to be loaded into an integrated information resource. Solving structural, syntactical and semantic heterogeneities between source and target data has been a complex problem for data integration for a number of years. One solution to this problem has been developed through the use of a single global database schema that represents the integrated information with mappings from global schema to local schemas, where each query to the global schema is translated to queries to the local databases using these mappings.

The use of domain ontology, metadata, transformation rules, user, and system constraints have resolved the majority of the problems of domain mismatch associated with schematic integration and global schematic approaches. However, even when all the mappings, semantic and structure heterogeneity are solved in the global schema, consistency may not have been achieved, because the information provided by the sources may be mutually inconsistent. This problem has remained because it is impossible to capture all the information and avoid null values. At the same time, each autonomous component database deals with its own properties or domain constraints on information, such as accuracy, reliability, availability, timeliness and cost of information access.

Several approaches to solve inconsistency between databases have been implemented:

- By reconciliation of data, also known as data fusion: different values become just one using a fusion function (*i.e.,* average, highest, majority), depending on the data semantic.
- On the basis of individual data properties: associated with each information source (*i.e.,* cost of retrieving information, how recent is the information, level of authority associated with this source, or accuracy and completeness of information). These properties can be specified at different levels: the global schema design level, the query itself or in the users profile.

The definitions of data quality models and some information quality measurement methods are presented.

Data Quality (DQ) vs. Information Quality (IQ)

"High data quality has been defined as data that is fit for use by data consumers and is treated independent of the context in which data is produced and used" Data quality has been characterised by quality criteria or dimensions such as accuracy, completeness, consistency and timeliness. However there is no general agreement on data quality dimensions.

Data Quality Classifications

A definition of quality dimensions and a framework for analysis of data quality as a research area was first proposed by Richard Wang *et.al.*

An ontologically based approach was developed by Yair Wand *et. al.,* this model analysed data quality based on discrepancies between the representation mapping from real world (RW) to information system (IS) and vice versa, through design and operation activities involved in the construction of an information system as an internal view. A real world system is said to be properly represented if there exists an exhaustive mapping, and no two states in RW are mapped into the same state in IS. Four intrinsic data quality dimensions were identified: complete, unambiguous, meaningful and correct. Additionally mapping problems and data deficiency repairs were suggested.

MEASURING DATA QUALITY IN HETEROGENEOUS DATABASES

Database integration is divided in two main problems, intensional and extensional inconsistencies. Intensional are related to resolving the schematic differences between the component databases, this issue is also known as semantic heterogeneity. Extensional inconsistencies are related to reconciling the data differences among the participating databases.. Information integration is the process of merging multiple query results into a single response to the user.

There are several important areas of related work to consider.

- Data integration techniques have been developed based on data quality aspects within an object oriented data model, and data quality information stored in metadata. Quality aspects such as timeliness, accuracy and completeness were considered in the process of database integration. The main aspect was the assumption that quality of the data stored at different sites can be different and the quality varies over time. Query language extensions were necessary to support the specification of data quality goals for global queries and thus data integration. In the case of data conflicts between semantically equivalent objects, the object with best data quality must be chosen. If no conflicts exist between objects but their quality level is different, the integrated objects need to be grouped to allow the ranking of the results.
- The project MULTIPLEX addressed the problem of extensional inconsistencies and a Data Quality Model for Relational Databases. MULTIPLEX was based on accuracy and completeness as quality criteria, this model assigned a quality specification for each instance of a relation, and these quality specifications were calculated by extending the relational algebra. The quality of answers was calculated by the measure of arbitrary queries from the overall quality specification of the database. In the case of multiple sets of records as possible answers to one query, each set of records has an individual quality specification. A voting scheme, using probabilistic arguments, identifies the best set of records to provide a complete and sound answer and a ranking of tuples in the answer space. The conflict resolution strategy, and the quality estimates are addressed by the multi database designer.
- An enhancement of the Multiplex system FUSIONPLEX stores information features or quality criteria scores in metadata, the considered quality dimensions are timestamp, accuracy, availability, clearance and cost of retrieval. Inconsistencies are resolved by data fusion, allowing the user to define data quality estimation on a vector of features weights, performance thresholds and a fusion function at attribute level, as required. This approach reconciles the conflicting values at attribute level using an intermediate result named polyinstance, which contains the inconsistencies. First the polyinstance is divided in polytuples, and using the feature weights and the threshold, members of each polytuple are discarded. Second

each polytuple is separated into mono-attribute polytuples using the primary key, assuming that the same value of the primary key between databases refers to the same object but with different data values, and attribute values are discarded based on corresponding feature values. Finally the mono-attribute tuples are joined back together resulting in single tuples.

- Information Quality Reasoning: Selection of data sources, and optimisation of query planning by considering user priorities has been also addressed in by the definition of a quality model and a quality assessment method under the following assumptions:
- Query processing: Concerned with efficiently answering a user query to a single or multi database. In this context efficiency means speed.
- Query planning: Is concerned with finding the best possible answer given some cost or time constraint. Query planning involves regarding many query execution plans across different, autonomous sources that together form the complete result.
- Information Quality reasoning is defined as the integration of information quality aspects, to the process of planning and optimising queries against databases and information systems. Such aspects are related through the establishment of information quality criteria, assessment methods and measure.

Commonly the information sources on the web are classified by counting the appearances of certain words and using statistics to determine the most "relevant sources". In this approach information sources were selected by using Data Envelopment Analysis method (DEA) and the following quality dimensions, understandability, extent, availability, time and price. Discarding sources with poor quality before executing the query.

However different sources have different quality scores and they must be fused to determine the best quality result, the quality fusion can be done in two ways:

- Applying a fusion function per each quality criteria and find the best combination to query such as fused time as the maximum of the individual scores or fused process as the sum of the individual prices.
- Computing the information quality score using different quality criteria such as availability, price, accuracy, completeness, amount response time for each plan and thus a ranking of the plans using Simple Additive Weighting method (SAW).

The completeness of the query result derived from different sources is approached in considering the number of results (coverage) and the number of attribute values in the result (density). Completeness is calculated as the product between the density and the coverage of the corresponding set of information sources. In the Seminar "Data Quality on the Web", it was established that it is essential to first concentrate on developing expressive data quality models, once such models are in place, develop tools that help users and IT managers to capture and analyse the state of data quality in an information system.

INCONSISTENCY DETECTION FRAMEWORK

Conventionally, consistency control protocols, such as strong consistency protocols or optimistic consistency protocols that increase the availability while tolerate relaxed inconsistency among nodes, are predefined and deployed before the system starts to run an application. We refer to this scheme as inconsistency avoidance.

While inconsistency avoidance can be effective in a small-scale networked system, such as a small cluster, it has some drawbacks in an Internet-scale environment, such as Grid. In this environment, a strong consistency protocol can be very costly to maintain because of the membership maintenance and strict protocol enforcement cost.

On the other hand, optimistic consistency protocol relieves the costly maintenance and strict enforcement burden associated with strong consistency protocols; however, it also does not suit the large-scale distributed system because it is predefined.

In an environment where many applications are deployed, providing a predefined consistency protocol can be either overkill when an application does not need that strong consistency, or insufficient when an application needs stronger ones.

IDF (INCONSISTENCY DETECTION FRAMEWORK)

Thus, we propose a framework to detect inconsistency in a timely manner when it occurs instead of avoiding it in the first place. We refer this as inconsistency detection.

IDF's primary advantages are:

- First, it removes the costly membership management requirement that is used to enforce a consistency in the first place. Instead, it detects the inconsistency when it happens. That makes the system scalable. Besides, by ensuring that the potential inconsistent behaviour be detected in a timely manner, a system can combine the results (if the results are combinable), break the tie or alert the users so that they can resolve the conflict as soon as possible using appropriate resolution protocols.
- Second, after the inconsistency is detected, the system can respond based on the application semantics. That is, it resolves the inconsistency when it is needed, while letting the detected inconsistency continue to exist when it is tolerable or even preferred.

System Overview

As an alternative to inconsistency avoidance, the inconsistency detection framework detects inconsistency among nodes in a timely manner. In this framework, multiple applications share data and services through the support of the Internet-scale middleware and the inconsistencies among them are detected by the detector.

Upon detection, the detector consults with the inconsistency level monitor before reaction is initiated. Based on the applications' semantics, if the inconsistency is tolerable, the detector does not react; otherwise, the detector informs the inconsistency resolution model to resolve this inconsistency.

10

Distributed Database Programming

Distributed database programming describes the distributed relational database management portion of the i5/OS® licensed programme. Distributed relational database management provides applications with access to data that is external to the applications and typically located across a network of computers. This information is intended primarily for application programmers responsible for the development, administration, and support of a distributed relational database on one or more System i™ products. Application programmers who are not familiar with the i5/OS database can also get a view of the total range of database support provided by the i5/ operating system (i5/OS). Application programmers can use this information in the system context in which distributed relational database applications run. Before using this information, you should be familiar with general programming concepts and terminology, and have a general understanding of the System i environment and the i5/OS operating system.

INTRODUCTION TO DISTRIBUTED DATABASE PROGRAMMING

i5/OS® distributed relational database support consists of an implementation of IBM® Distributed Relational Database Architecture™ (DRDA®) and integration of other SQL clients through Application Requester Driver (ARD) programmes. i5/OS and the DB2 Universal Database™ for iSeries™ Query Manager and SQL Development Kit combine to provide this support. This topic describes distributed relational database and how it is used on the i5/OS operating system. In addition, an example distributed relational database called Spiffy Corporation is described. This fictional company uses the System i™ product in a distributed relational database application programme.

DISTRIBUTED RELATIONAL DATABASE AND THE AS/400 SYSTEM

Distributed relational database support on the AS/400* system consists of an implementation of IBM* Distributed Relational Database Architecture*

(DRDA*) and integration of other SQL clients by use of Application Requester Driver (ARD) programmes. The Operating System/400 (OS/400) and the DB2 UDB for iSeries Query Manager and SQL Development Kit combine to provide this support. This chapter describes distributed relational database and how it is used on the AS/400 system. It defines some general concepts of distributed relational database, outlines the IBM DRDA implementation, and provides an overview of the current DRDA implementation on the AS/400 system. Finally, an example corporation named Spiffy is described. This fictional company uses AS/400 systems in a distributed relational database application programme. This sample of the Spiffy Corporation forms the background for all examples used in this manual.

All data on the AS/400 system is stored in a single relational database. DB2 UDB for AS/400 provides all the database management functions for this AS/400 relational database. Distributed relational database support on the system is an integral part of the OS/400 programme, just as is support for communications, work management, security functions and other functions.

The AS/400 system can be part of a distributed relational database network with other systems that support a DRDA implementation. The AS/400 system can be an AR or an AS in either like or unlike environments. Distributed relational database implementation on the AS/400 system supports remote unit of work (RUW) and distributed unit of work (DUW). 1 RUW allows you to submit multiple requests to a single database within a single unit of work, and DUW allows requests to multiple databases to be included within a single unit of work. For example, using DUW support you can decrement the inventory count of a part on one system and increment the inventory count of a part on another system within a unit of work, and then commit changes to these remote databases at the conclusion of a single unit of work using a two-phase commit process. DB2 UDB for AS/400 does not support distributed requests, so you can only access one database with each SQL statement. The level of support provided in an application programme depends on the level of support available on the target systems and the order in which connections and updates are made.

In addition to DRDA access, ARD programmes can be used to access databases that do not support DRDA. Connections to relational databases accessed through ARD programmes are treated like connections to unlike systems. Such connections can coexist with connections to DRDA application servers, connections to the local relational database, and connections which access other ARD programmes.

On AS/400, the distribution functions of snapshots and replication, introduced in Other Distributed Relational Database terms and concepts, are not automatically performed by the system. You can install and configure the DataPropagator Relational Capture and Apply product on AS/400 to perform these functions. Also, you can use these functions in user-written application programmes. On AS/400, the distributed request function that is discussed in Other Distributed Relational Database terms and concepts is not directly supported. However, the DataJoiner product can perform distributed queries, joining tables from a variety of data sources. DataJoiner works synergistically with DataGuide, a comprehensive information catalogue in the IBM Information Warehouse family of products. DataGuide provides a graphical user interface to complete information listings about a company's data resources.

The OS/400 programme includes run-time support for SQL. You do not need the DB2 UDB for AS/400 Query Manager and SQL Development Kit licensed programme installed on a DB2 UDB for AS/400 application requester or application server to process distributed relational database requests or to create an SQL collection on an AS/400. However, you do need the DB2 UDB for AS/400 Query Manager and SQL Development Kit programme to precompile programmes with SQL statements, run interactive SQL, or run DB2 UDB for AS/400 Query Manager.

SECURITY FOR AN AS/400 DISTRIBUTED RELATIONAL DATABASE

A distributed relational database administrator is faced with two security issues to resolve:

- System to system protection
- Identification of users at remote sites.

When two or more systems are set up to access each other's databases, it may be important to make sure that the other side of the communications line is the intended location and not an intruder. For DRDA access to a remote relational database, the AS/400 system use of advanced programme-to-programme communications (APPC) and Advanced Peer-to-Peer Networking (APPN) communications configuration capabilities provides options for you to do this network level security.

The second concern for the distributed relational database administrator is that data security is maintained by the system that stores the data. In a distributed relational database, the user has to be properly authorised to have access to the database (according to the security level of the system) whether the database is local or remote. Distributed relational database network users must be properly identified with a user ID on the application server (AS) for any jobs they run on the AS. DRDA support using both APPC/APPN and TCP/IP communications protocols provides for the sending of user IDs and passwords along with connection requests.

This chapter discusses security topics that are related to communications and DRDA access to remote relational databases. The significant differences between conversation-level security in an APPC network connection and the corresponding level of security for a TCP/IP connection initiated by a DRDA application. In remaining security discussions, the term user also includes remote users starting communications jobs.

DISTRIBUTED RELATIONAL DATABASE PROCESSING

A relational database is a set of data stored in one or more tables in a computer. A table is a two-dimensional arrangement of data consisting of horizontal rows and vertical columns as shown in Table below. Each row contains a sequence of values, one for each column of the table. A column has a name and contains a particular data type (for example, character, decimal, or integer).

Table. A Typical Relational Table

Item	*Name*	*Supplier*	*Quantity*
78476	Baseball	ACME	650
78477	Football	Imperial	228
78478	Basketball	ACME	105
78479	Soccer ball	ACME	307

Tables can be defined and accessed in several ways on the AS/400 system. One way to describe and access tables on the system is to use a language like Structured Query Language (SQL). SQL is the standard IBM database language and provides the necessary consistency to enable distributed data processing across different system operating environments. Another way to describe and access tables on the AS/400 system is to describe physical and logical files using data description specifications (DDS) and access tables using file interfaces (for example, read and write high-level language statements).

SQL uses different terminology from that used on the AS/400 system. For most SQL objects there is a corresponding system object on the AS/400 system. The relationship between SQL relational database terms and AS/400 system terms.

Table. Relationship of SQL Terms to System Terms

SQL Term	*System Term*
Collection. Consists of a library, a journal, a journal receiver, an SQL catalog, and an optional data dictionary. A collection groups related objects and allows you to find the objects by name.	**Library**. Groups related objects and allows you to find the objects by name.
Table. A set of columns and rows.	**Physical file**. A set of records.
Row. The horizontal part of a table containing a serial set of columns.	**Record**. A set of fields.
Column. The vertical part of a table of one data type.	**Field**. One or more bytes of related information of one data type.

View. A subset of columns and rows of one or more tables.	**Logical file**. A subset of fields and/or records of up to 32 physical files.
Index. A collection of data in the columns of a table, logically arranged in ascending or descending order.	A type of logical file
Package. An object that contains control structures for SQL statements to be used by an application server.	**SQL Package**. Has the same meaning as the SQL term.
Catalog. A set of tables and views that contain information about tables, packages, views, indexes, and constraints. The catalog views in QSYS2 contain information about all tables, packages, views, indexes, and constraints on the AS/400 system. Additionally, an SQL collection will contain a set of these views that only contains information about tables, packages, views, indexes, and constraints in the collection.	No similar object. However, the Display File Description (DSPFD) and Display File Field Description (DSPFFD) commands provide some of the same information that querying an SQL catalog provides.

A distributed relational database exists when the application programmes that use the data and the data itself are located on different systems. The simplest form of a distributed relational database, the application programme runs on one system, and the data is located on another system.

When using a distributed relational database, the system on which the application programme is run is called the application requester (AR), and the system on which the remote data resides is called the application server (AS).

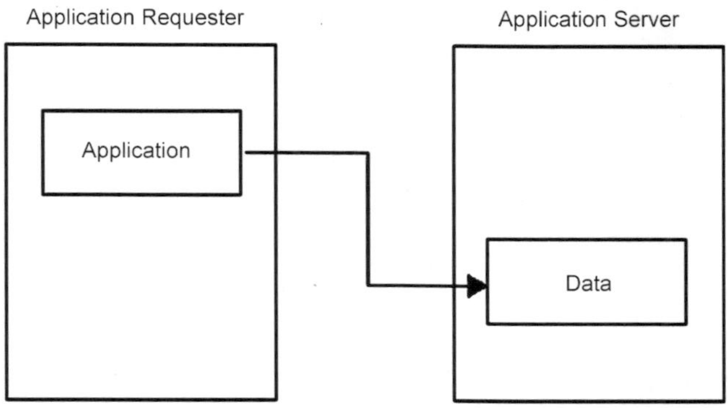

Fig. A Distributed Relational Database.

A unit of work is one or more database requests and the associated processing that make up a completed piece of work. A simple example is taking a part from stock in an inventory control application programme. An inventory programme can tentatively remove an item from a shop inventory account table and then add that item to a parts reorder table at the same location. The term transaction is another expression used to describe the unit of work concept. The unit of work is not complete until the part is both removed from the shop inventory account table and added to a reorder table.

When the requests are complete, the application programme can commit the unit of work. This means that any database changes associated with the unit of work are made permanent. With unit of work support, the application programme can also roll back changes to a unit of work. If a unit of work is rolled back, the changes made since, the last commit or rollback operation are not applied. Thus, the application programme treats the set of requests to a database as a unit.

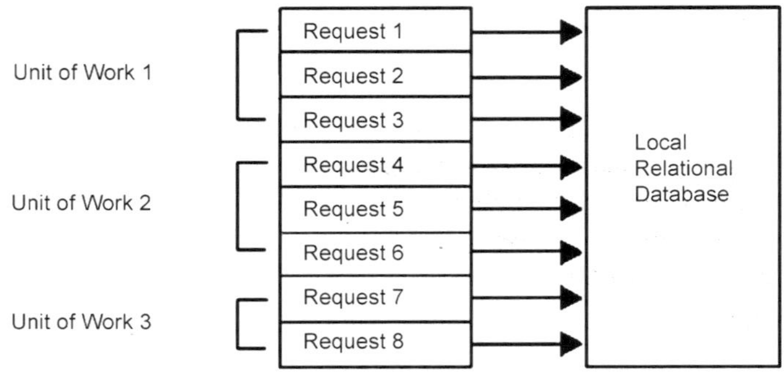

Fig. Unit of Work in a Local Relational Database.

Problem Analysis for a Distributed Relational Database

Problem analysis needs to be managed in a distributed database environment. Problem analysis involves both identifying and resolving problems for applications that are processed across a network of servers.

Consider the following:

- Distributed database processing problems manifest themselves in various ways. For example, an error return code may be passed to a distributed database application by the server that detects the problem. In addition, responses may be slow, wrong, or nonexistent.
- Tools are available to diagnose distributed database processing problems. For example, each distributed relational database product provides trace functions that can assist in diagnosing distributed data processing problems.
- When server failures are detected by an iSeries server, the server logs information about programme status immediately after the failure is detected.

DISTRIBUTED UNIT OF WORK

The application-directed distributed unit of work facility also provides for the remote preparation and execution of SQL statements in the same fashion as remote unit of work. Like remote unit of work, an activation group at system A can connect to an application server at system B and run any number of static or dynamic SQL statements that reference objects at B before ending the unit of work. All objects referenced in a single SQL statement must be managed by the same application server. However, unlike remote unit of work, any number of application servers can participate in the same unit of work. A commit or rollback operation ends the unit of work.

Distributed unit of work (DUW) enables a user or application programme to read or update data at multiple locations within a unit of work. Within one unit of work, an application running in one system can direct SQL requests to multiple remote database management systems using the SQL supported by those systems. For example, the shop inventory programme can perform updates to the inventory table on one system and the accounts receivable table on another system within one unit of work.

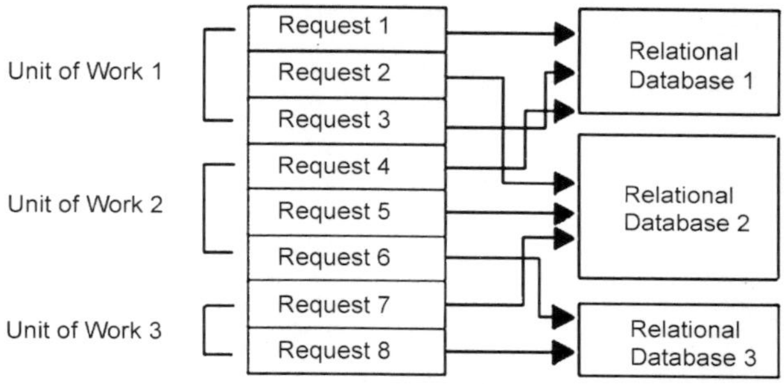

Fig. Distributed Unit of Work in a Distributed Relational Database.

The target of the requests is controlled by the user or application with SQL statements such as CONNECT TO and SET CONNECTION. Each SQL statement must refer to data at a single location. When the application is ready to commit the work, it initiates the commit; commitment coordination is performed by a synchronisation-point manager.

Distributed unit of work allows:

- Update access to multiple database management systems in one unit of work, or
- Update access to one or more database management systems with read access to other database management systems in one unit of work.

Whether an application can update a given database management system in a unit of work is dependent on the level of DRDA (if DRDA is used to access the remote relational database) and the order in which the connections and updates are made.

REMOTE UNIT OF WORK

A unit of work is a single logical transaction. It consists of a sequence of SQL statements in which either all of the operations are successfully performed, or the sequence as a whole is considered unsuccessful. A remote unit of work lets a user or application programme read or update data at one location per unit of work. It supports access to one database within a unit of work. While an application programme can access several remote databases, it can only access one database within a unit of work. Remote unit of work (RUW) is a form of distributed relational database processing in which an application programme can access data on a remote database within a unit of work.

A remote unit of work can include more than one relational database request, but all requests must be made to the same remote database. All requests to a relational database must be completed (either committed or rolled back) before requests can be sent to another relational database.

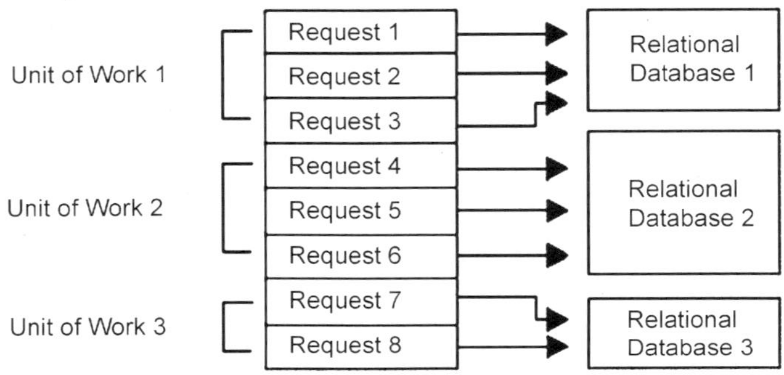

Fig. Remote Unit of Work in a Distributed Relational Database.

Remote unit of work is application-directed distribution because the application programme must connect to the correct relational database system before issuing the requests. However, the application programme only needs to know the name of the remote database to make the correct connection. Remote unit of work support enables an application programme to read or update data at more than one location. However, all the data that the programme accesses within a unit of work must be managed by the same relational database management system. For example, the shop inventory application programme must commit its inventory and accounts receivable unit of work before it can read or update tables that are in another location.

In remote unit of work processing, each computer has an associated relational database management system and an associated application requester programme that help process distributed relational data requests. This allows you or your application programme to request remote relational data in much the same way as you request local relational data.

REMOTE UNIT OF WORK FOR DISTRIBUTED RELATIONAL DATABASES

The remote unit of work facility provides for the remote preparation and execution of SQL statements. An application process at computer system "A" can connect to an application server at computer system "B" and, within one or more units of work, execute any number of static or dynamic SQL statements that reference objects at "B". After ending a unit of work at B, the application process can connect to an application server at computer system C, and so on.

Most SQL statements can be remotely prepared and executed, with the following restrictions:

- All objects referenced in a single SQL statement must be managed by the same application server.
- All of the SQL statements in a unit of work must be executed by the same application server.

At any given time, an application process is in one of four possible connection states:

Connectable and connected. An application process is connected to an application server, and CONNECT statements can be executed.

If implicit connect is available:

- The application process enters this state when a CONNECT TO statement or a CONNECT without operands statement is successfully executed from the connectable and unconnected state.
- The application process may enter this state from the implicitly connectable state if any SQL statement other than CONNECT RESET, DISCONNECT, SET CONNECTION, or RELEASE is issued.

Whether or not implicit connect is available, this state is entered when:

- A CONNECT TO statement is successfully executed from the connectable and unconnected state.
- A COMMIT or ROLLBACK statement is successfully issued, or a forced rollback occurs from the unconnectable and connected state.

Unconnectable and Connected. An application process is connected to an application server, but a CONNECT TO statement cannot be successfully executed to change application servers. The application process enters this state from the connectable and connected state when it executes any SQL statement other than the following: CONNECT TO, CONNECT with no operand, CONNECT RESET, DISCONNECT, SET CONNECTION, RELEASE, COMMIT, or ROLLBACK. Connectable and unconnected. An application process is not connected to an application server. CONNECT TO is the only SQL statement that can be executed; otherwise, an error (SQLSTATE 08003) is raised. Whether or not implicit connect is available, the application process enters this state if an error occurs when a CONNECT TO statement is issued, or an error occurs within a unit of work, causing the loss of a connection and a rollback. An error that occurs because the application process is not in the connectable state, or because the server name is not listed in the local directory, does not cause a transition to this state.

If implicit connect is not available:

- The application process is initially in this state
- The CONNECT RESET and DISCONNECT statements cause a transition to this state.

Implicitly connectable (if implicit connect is available). If implicit connect is available, this is the initial state of an application process. The CONNECT RESET statement causes a transition to this state. Issuing a COMMIT or ROLLBACK statement in the unconnectable and connected state, followed by a DISCONNECT statement in the connectable and connected state, also results in this state.

Availability of implicit connect is determined by installation options, environment variables, and authentication settings. It is not an error to execute consecutive CONNECT statements, because CONNECT itself does not remove the application process from the connectable state. It is, however, an error to execute consecutive CONNECT RESET statements. It is also an error to execute any SQL statement other than CONNECT TO, CONNECT RESET, CONNECT with no operand, SET CONNECTION, RELEASE, COMMIT, or ROLLBACK, and then to execute a CONNECT TO statement. To avoid this error, a CONNECT RESET, DISCONNECT (preceded by a COMMIT or ROLLBACK statement), COMMIT, or ROLLBACK statement should be executed before the CONNECT TO statement.

OTHER DISTRIBUTED RELATIONAL DATABASE TERMS AND CONCEPTS

An overview of additional distributed relational database concepts. On IBM systems, some of this support is provided by DataHub, DataJoiner, and DataPropagator Relational products. In addition, you can use some of these concepts as part of AS/400 application programmes.

DB2 UDB for iSeries supports both the remote unit of work and distributed unit of work with APPC communications. Remote unit of work is also supported with TCP/IP communications. A degree of processing sophistication beyond the distributed unit of work is a distributed request. This type of distributed relational database access enables a user or application programme to issue a single SQL statement that can read or update data at multiple locations.

The distributed relational database do not have to differ from one another. Some tables can be exact or partial copies of one another. Extracts, snapshots, and replication are terms that describe types of copies using distributed processing. Extracts are user-requested copies of tables. The copies are extracted from one database and loaded into another specified by the user. The unloading and loading process may be repeated periodically to obtain updated data. Extracts are most useful for one-time or infrequent occurrences, such as read-only copies of data that rarely changes.

Snapshots are read-only copies of tables that are automatically made by a system. The system refreshes these copies from the source table on a periodic basis specified by the user--perhaps daily, weekly, or monthly. Snapshots are most useful for locations that seek an automatic process for receiving updated information on a periodic basis. Data replication means the system automatically updates copies of a table. It is similar to snapshots because copies of a table are stored at multiple locations. Data replication is most effective for situations that require high reliability and quick data retrieval with few updates.

Tables can also be split across computer systems in the network. Such a table is called a distributed table. Distributed tables are split either horizontally by rows or vertically by columns to provide easier local reference and storage. The columns of a vertically distributed table reside at various locations, as do the rows of a horizontally distributed table. At any location, the user still sees the table as if it were kept in a single location. Distributing tables is most effective when the request to access and update certain portions of the table come from the same location as those portions of the table.

DISTRIBUTED RELATIONAL DATABASE ARCHITECTURE SUPPORT

Distributed Relational Database Architecture™ (DRDA®) support for distributed relational database processing is used by IBM® relational database products. DRDA support defines protocols for communication between an application programme and a remote relational database. DRDA support provides distributed relational database management in both IBM and non-IBM environments.

In IBM environments, relational data is managed with the following programmes:

- DB2 for OS/390
- DB2 for VSE and VM
- DB2 Connect Personal Edition
- DB2 Connect Enterprise Edition
- DB2 Universal Database Workgroup Edition
- DB2 Universal Database Enterprise Edition
- DB2 Universal Database Extended Enterprise Edition
- DB2 UDB for iSeries support in the OS/400 licensed programme on AS/400.

DRDA support provides the structure for access to database information for relational database managers operating in like and unlike environments. For example, access to relational data between two or more AS/400 systems is distribution in a like environment, and access to relational data between an AS/400 system and systems using the DB2 database manager is distribution in an unlike environment.

SQL is the standard IBM database language. It provides the necessary consistency to enable distributed data processing across like and unlike operating environments. Within DRDA support, SQL allows users to define, retrieve, and manipulate data across environments that support a DRDA implementation.

DISTRIBUTED RELATIONAL DATABASE FUNCTION AND SQL

A distributed relational database consists of a set of SQL objects that are spread across interconnected computer systems. These relational databases can be of the same type (for example, the DB2® for i5/OS® database) or of different types (DB2 for z/OS®, DB2 for VSE and VM, or non-IBM database management systems that support Distributed Relational Database Architecture™ (DRDA®)). Each relational database has a relational database manager to manage the tables in its environment. The database managers communicate and cooperate with each other in a way that allows a given database manager access to run SQL statements on a relational database on another system.

The application requester supports the application side of a connection. The application server is the local or remote database to which an application requester is connected. DB2 for i5/OS provides support for DRDA to allow an application requester to communicate with application servers. In addition, DB2 for i5/OS can call exit programmes to allow access to data on other database management systems that do not support DRDA. These exit programmes are called application requester driver (ARD) programmes.

DISTRIBUTED RELATIONAL DATABASE ON I5/OS

DB2 Universal Database™ for i5/OS® provides all the database management functions for i5/OS. Distributed relational database support on the system is an integral part of the operating system, just as is support for communications, work management, security functions and other functions.

The i5/OS operating system can be part of a distributed relational database network with other systems that support a Distributed Relational Database Architecture™ (DRDA®) implementation. i5/OS can be an application requester (AR) or an application server (AS) in either like or unlike environments. Distributed relational database implementation on the i5/OS operating system supports remote unit of work (RUW) and distributed unit of work (DUW). RUW allows you to submit multiple requests to a single database within a single unit of work, and DUW allows requests to multiple databases to be included within a single unit of work.

Using DUW support, you can decrement the inventory count of a part on one system and increment the inventory count of a part on another system within a unit of work, and then commit changes to these remote databases at the conclusion of a single unit of work using a two-phase commit process. DB2 Universal Database for iSeries™ does not support distributed requests, so you can only access one database with each SQL statement. The level of support provided in an application programme depends on the level of support available on the application server (AS) and the order in which connections and updates are made.

In addition to DRDA access, application requester driver (ARD) programmes can be used to access databases that do not support DRDA. Connections to relational databases accessed through ARD programmes are treated like connections to unlike servers. Such connections can coexist with connections to DRDA application servers, connections to the local relational database, and connections which access other ARD programmes.

On the i5/OS operating system, the distribution functions of snapshots and replication are not automatically performed by the system. You can install and configure the DataPropagator™ for iSeries, V8.1 product on i5/OS to perform these functions. Also, you can use these functions in user-written application programmes. On the i5/OS operating system, the distributed request function is not directly supported. However, the DataJoiner® product can perform distributed queries, joining tables from a variety of data sources. DataJoiner works synergistically with DataGuide, a comprehensive information catalogue in the IBM® Information Warehouse family of products. DataGuide provides a graphical user interface to complete information listings about a company's data resources.

The i5/OS licensed programme includes runtime support for SQL. You do not need the DB2® UDB for iSeries Query Manager and SQL Development Kit licensed programme installed on a DB2 UDB for iSeries application requester or application server to process distributed relational database requests or to create an SQL collection on i5/OS. However, you need the DB2 Universal Database for iSeries Query Manager and SQL Development Kit programme to precompile programmes with SQL statements, to run interactive SQL, or to run DB2 Universal Database for iSeries Query Manager.

CHARACTER CONVERSION WITH CDRA

Not only can there be differences in encoding schemes (such as EBCDIC versus ASCII), but there can also be differences related to language. For instance, systems configured for different languages can assign different characters to the same code, or different codes to the same character. For example, a system configured for U.S. English can assign the same code to the character } that a system configured for the Danish language assigns to å. But those two systems can assign different codes to the same character such as $. If data is to be shared across different systems, character data needs to be seen by users and applications the same way.

In other words, a PS/2 user in New York and an AS/400 user in Copenhagen both need to see a $ as a $, even though $ may be encoded differently in each system. Furthermore, the user in Copenhagen needs to see a }, if that is the character that was stored at New York, even though the code may be the same as a Danish å. In order for this to happen, the $ must be converted to the proper character encoding for a PS/2 system (that is, U.S. English character set, ASCII), and converted back to Danish encoding when it goes from New York to Copenhagen (that is, Danish character set, EBCDIC). This sort of character conversion is provided for by AS/400 as well as the other IBM distributed relational database managers. This conversion is done in a coherent way in accordance with the Character Data Representation Architecture (CDRA).

CDRA specifies the way to identify the attributes of character data so that the data can be understood across systems, even if the systems use different character sets and encoding schemes. For conversion to happen across systems, each system must understand the attributes of the character data it is receiving from the other system. CDRA specifies that these attributes be identified through a coded character set identifier (CCSID). All character data in DB2, SQL/DS, and the OS/400 database management systems have a CCSID, which indicates a specific combination of encoding scheme, character set, and code page. All character data in an Extended Services environment has a code page only (but the other database managers treat that code page identification as a CCSID). A code page is a specific set of assignments between characters and internal codes. For example, CCSID 37 means encoding scheme 4352 (EBCDIC), character set 697 (Latin, single-byte characters), and code page 37 (USA/Canada country extended code page). CCSID 5026 means encoding scheme 4865 (extended EBCDIC), character set 1172 with code page 290 (single-byte character set for Katakana/Kanji), and character set 370 with code page 300 (double-byte character set for Katakana/Kanji).

DB2, SQL/DS, the OS/400 system, and DDCS/2 include mechanisms to convert character data between a wide range of CCSID-to-CCSID pairs and CCSID-to-code page pairs. Character conversion for many CCSIDs and code pages is already built into these products. For a complete list and description of all CCSIDs registered in CDRA.

DRDA AND CDRA SUPPORT

One of the interesting possibilities in a distributed relational database is that the database may not only span different types of computers, but those computers may be in different countries or regions. The same systems, such as AS/400 systems, can encode data differently depending on the language used on the system. Different types of systems encode data differently. For instance, a System/390* system, an AS/400 system, and a PS/2* system encode numeric data in their own unique formats. In addition, a System/390 system and an AS/400 system use the EBCDIC encoding scheme to encode character data, while a PS/2 system uses an ASCII encoding scheme.

For numeric data, these differences do not matter. Unlike systems that provide DRDA support automatically convert any differences between the way a number is represented in one computer system to the way it is represented in another. For example, if an AS/400 application programme reads numeric data from a DB2 database, DB2 sends the numeric data in

System/390 format and the OS/400 database management system converts it to AS/400 numeric format. However, the handling of character data is more complex, but this too can be handled within a distributed relational database.

APPLICATION REQUESTER DRIVER PROGRAMMES

An application requester driver (ARD) programme is a type of exit programme that enables SQL applications to access data managed by a database management system other than DB2 UDB for iSeries.

AS/400 calls the ARD programme during the following operations:

- The package creation step of SQL precompiling, performed using the CRTSQLPKG or CRTSQLxxx commands, when the relational database (RDB) parameter matches the RDB name corresponding to the ARD programme.
- Processing of SQL statements when the current connection is to an RDB name corresponding to the ARD programme.

These calls allow the ARD programme to pass the SQL statements and information about the statements to a remote relational database and return results back to the system. The system then returns the results to the application or the user. Access to relational databases accessed by ARD programmes appear like access to DRDA application servers in the unlike environment. The ARD programme is registered in the system by use of the Add Relational Database Directory Entry (ADDRDBDIRE) command. One of the parameters that is specified is the library in which the programme is located. For a system configured with independent auxiliary storage pools, the ARD programme must reside in a library in the system database (a library that is part of the system ASP or a configured basic ASP).

COMPLEMENT DATABASE ACCESS AND APPLICATION REQUESTER DRIVER PROGRAMMES

To complement database access provided by products that implement DRDA®, DB2 UDB for iSeries provides an interface for writing exit programmes on a DB2 UDB for iSeries application requester to process SQL requests. Such an exit programme is called an application requester driver.

The server calls the ARD programme during the following operations:

- During package creation performed using the CRTSQLPKG or CRTSQLxxx commands, when the relational database (RDB) parameter matches the RDB name corresponding to the ARD programme.
- Processing of SQL statements when the current connection is to an RDB name corresponding to the ARD programme.

These calls allow the ARD programme to pass the SQL statements and information about the statements to a remote relational database and return results back to the system. The system then returns the results to the application or the user. Access to relational databases accessed by ARD programmes appears like access to DRDA application servers in the unlike environment. However, not all DRDA function is supported in the ARD environment. Examples of function not supported are Large objects (LOBs) and long passwords (passphrases).

DISTRIBUTED RELATIONAL DATABASE ON THE ISERIES SERVER

DB2 UDB for iSeries provides all the database management functions for the iSeries™ system relational database and any configured user databases. Distributed relational database support on the system is an integral part of the OS/400 programme, just as is support for communications, work management, security functions and other functions. The iSeries system can be part of a distributed relational database network with other servers that support a DRDA® implementation. The iSeries system can be an application requester (AR) or an application server (AS) in either like or unlike environments. Distributed relational database implementation on the iSeries system supports remote unit of work (RUW) and distributed unit of work (DUW). RUW allows you to submit multiple requests to a single database within a single unit of work, and DUW allows requests to multiple databases to be included within a single unit of work.

For example, using DUW support you can decrement the inventory count of a part on one server and increment the inventory count of a part on another `server within a unit of work, and then commit changes to these remote databases at the conclusion of a single unit of work using a two-phase commit process. DB2 UDB for iSeries does not support distributed requests, so you can only access one database with each SQL statement. The level of support provided in an application programme depends on the level of support available on the application server (AS) and the order in which connections and updates are made. In addition to DRDA access, ARD programmes can be used to access databases that do not support DRDA. Connections to relational databases accessed through ARD programmes are treated like connections to unlike servers. Such connections can coexist with connections to DRDA application servers, connections to the local relational database, and connections which access other ARD programmes.

On the iSeries server, the distribution functions of snapshots and replication, introduced in Other distributed relational database terms and concepts, are not automatically performed by the server. You can install and configure the DataPropagator Relational Capture and Apply product on iSeries servers to perform these functions. Also, you can use these functions in user-written application programmes.

On the iSeries server, the distributed request function is not directly supported. However, the DataJoiner® product can perform distributed queries, joining tables from a variety of data sources. DataJoiner works synergistically with DataGuide, a comprehensive information catalogue in the IBM® Information Warehouse family of products. DataGuide provides a graphical user interface to complete information listings about a company's data resources.

The OS/400 programme includes run-time support for SQL. You do not need the DB2 UDB for iSeries Query Manager and SQL Development Kit licensed programme installed on a DB2 UDB for iSeries application requester (AR) or application server (AS) to process distributed relational database requests or to create an SQL collection on an iSeries server. However, you do need the DB2 UDB for iSeries Query Manager and SQL Development Kit programme to precompile programmes with SQL statements, run interactive SQL, or run DB2 UDB for iSeries Query Manager.

DISTRIBUTED RELATIONAL DATABASE ON THE AS/400 SYSTEM

All data on the AS/400 system is stored in a single relational database. DB2 UDB for iSeries provides all the database management functions for this AS/400 relational database. Distributed relational database support on the system is an integral part of the OS/400 programme, just as is support for communications, work management, security functions and other functions. The AS/400 system can be part of a distributed relational database network with other systems that support a DRDA implementation. The AS/400 system can be an AR or an AS in either like or unlike environments. Distributed relational database implementation on the AS/400 system supports remote unit of work (RUW) and distributed unit of work (DUW).

1 RUW allows you to submit multiple requests to a single database within a single unit of work, and DUW allows requests to multiple databases to be included within a single unit of work. For example, using DUW support you can decrement the inventory count of a part on one system and increment the inventory count of a part on another system within a unit of work, and then commit changes to these remote databases at the conclusion of a single unit of work using a two-phase commit process. DB2 UDB for iSeries does not support distributed requests, so you can only access one database with each SQL statement. The level of support provided in an application programme depends on the level of support available on the target systems and the order in which connections and updates are made.

In addition to DRDA access, ARD programmes can be used to access databases that do not support DRDA. Connections to relational databases accessed through ARD programmes are treated like connections to unlike systems. Such connections can coexist with connections to DRDA application servers, connections to the local relational database, and connections which access other ARD programmes. On AS/400, the distribution functions of snapshots and replication, introduced in Other Distributed Relational

Database terms and concepts, are not automatically performed by the system. You can install and configure the DataPropagator Relational Capture and Apply product on AS/400 to perform these functions. Also, you can use these functions in user-written application programmes.

On AS/400, the distributed request function. However, the DataJoiner product can perform distributed queries, joining tables from a variety of data sources. DataJoiner works synergistically with DataGuide, a comprehensive information catalogue in the IBM Information Warehouse family of products. DataGuide provides a graphical user interface to complete information listings about a company's data resources.

The OS/400 programme includes run-time support for SQL. You do not need the DB2 UDB for iSeries Query Manager and SQL Development Kit licensed programme installed on a DB2 UDB for iSeries application requester or application server to process distributed relational database requests or to create an SQL collection on an AS/400. However, you do need the DB2 UDB for iSeries Query Manager and SQL Development Kit programme to precompile programmes with SQL statements, run interactive SQL, or run DB2 UDB for iSeries Query Manager.

MANAGING AN AS/400 DISTRIBUTED RELATIONAL DATABASE

Managing a distributed relational database on the AS/400 system requires broad knowledge of the resources and tools within the OS/400 licensed programme. This book provides an overview of the various functions available with the operating system that can help you administer a distributed relational database on AS/400 systems. This guide explains distributed relational database functions and tasks in a network of AS/400 systems (a like environment). Differences between AS/400 distributed relational database functions in a like and unlike environment are presented only in a general discussion in this guide. Considerations for different distributed relational database platforms working with AS/400 distributed relational database.

CONSIDERATIONS FOR IMPLEMENTING A DISTRIBUTED RELATIONAL DATABASE

A properly implemented distributed relational database makes it easy to access a database on a remote system, process a database file without knowing where it resides, and move parts of a database to another system without requiring changes to the application programmes.

PLANNING AND DESIGN FOR DISTRIBUTED RELATIONAL DATABASES

The first requirement for the successful operation of a distributed relational database is thorough planning. The needs and goals of your enterprise must be considered when making the decision to use a distributed relational database. How you code an application programme, where it resides in relation to the data, and the network design that connects application programmes to data are all important design considerations. Database design in a distributed relational database is more critical than when dealing with just one AS/400 relational database. With more than one AS/400 system to consider, you must develop a consistent management strategy across the network. Operations that require particular attention when forming your strategy are: general operations, networking protocol, system security, accounting, problem analysis, and backup and recovery processes.

CONFIGURING COMMUNICATIONS FOR DRDA IMPLEMENTATION

The communications support for the DRDA implementation on the AS/400 is based on the AS/400 Distributed Data Management (DDM) Architecture. This support includes both native TCP/IP connectivity as well as the IBM Systems Network Architecture (SNA) through advanced programme-to-programme communications (APPC), with or without Advanced Peer-to-Peer Networking* (APPN*), and High-Performance Routing (HPR). In addition, OS/400 provides for APPC, and therefore DDM and distributed relational database access, over TCP/IP using AnyNet* support. AnyNet is not required for DRDA remote unit of work support over TCP/IP, but might be useful for distributed unit of work function over TCP/IP.

DEVELOPING A SECURITY STRATEGY FOR DISTRIBUTED RELATIONAL DATABASES

The AS/400 system has security functions built into the operating system to limit access to the data resources of an application server. Security options range from simple physical security to full password security coupled with authorisation to commands and data objects. Users must be properly authorised to have access to the database whether it is local or remote. They must also have proper authorisation to collections, tables, and other relational database objects necessary to run their application programmes. This typically means that distributed database users must have valid user profiles for the databases they use throughout the network. Security planning must consider user and application programme needs across the network. Security for an AS/400 Distributed Relational Database provides information on the security considerations for an AS/400 distributed relational database.

SETTING UP APPLICATION REQUESTERS

The run-time support for an AS/400 distributed relational database is provided by the OS/400 programme. Therefore, when the operating system is installed, distributed relational database support is installed. However, some setup work is required to make the application requesters and application servers ready to send and receive work. One or more subsystems can be used to control interactive, batch, spoiled, and communications jobs. All the systems in the network must also have their relational database directory set up with connection information. Finally, you may wish to put data into the tables of the application servers throughout the network. The relational database directory contains database names and values that are translated into communications network parameters.

You add an entry for each database in the network, including the local database. Each directory entry consists of a unique relational database name and corresponding communications path information. For access provided by ARD programmes, the ARD programme name must be added to the relational database directory entry.

There are a number of ways to enter data into a database. You can use an SQL application programme, some other high-level language application programme, or one of these methods:

- Interactive SQL
- OS/400 query management
- Data file utility (DFU)
- Copy File (CPYF) command.

Monitoring Distributed Relational Database Administrative and Operational Tasks

As a database administrator in a distributed relational database network, you may need to locate and monitor work being done on any one of several systems.

Work management functions on the AS/400 system provide effective ways to track this work by allowing you to do the following:

- Work with jobs in the network
- Work with the communications networks, controllers, devices, modes, and sessions
- Manage the DDM TCP/IP server
- Enable DDM conversations
- Grant and remove authority for users
- Stop work on a remote system.

Ensuring Data Protection and Availability for a Distributed Relational Database

The AS/400 system provides a wide array of functions to ensure that data on systems in a distributed relational database network is available for use. These include save/restore functions of the system, journal management and access path journaling, commitment control, auxiliary storage pools, checksum protection, mirrored protection and the uninterruptible power supply. While the system operator for each AS/400 system is typically responsible for backup and recovery of that system's data, you should address provisions for network redundancy and data redundancy to provide optimum data availability.

Monitoring Performance for a Distributed Relational Database

No matter what kind of application programmes you are running on a system, performance can always be a concern. For a distributed relational database, network, system, and application performance are all crucial. System performance can be affected by the size and organisation of main and auxiliary storage. There can also be performance gains if you know the strengths and weaknesses of SQL programmes.

Handling Problems within a Distributed Relational Database

When a problem occurs within a distributed relational database, it is necessary to first identify where the problem originates. The problem may be on the application server or application requester. When the database problem is located properly in the network, you may further isolate the problem as a user problem, a problem with an application programme, an AS/400 system problem, or communications problem in order to correct the error.

Programming Applications for the Distributed Relational Database Environment

Programmers can write high-level language programmes that use SQL statements for AS/400 distributed application programmes. The main differences from programmes written for local processing only are the ability to connect to remote databases and to create SQL packages. The CONNECT SQL statement can be used to explicitly connect an application requester to an application server, or the name of the relational database can be specified when the programme is created to allow an implicit connection to occur. Also, the SET CONNECTION, RELEASE, and DISCONNECT statements can be used to manage connections for applications that use distributed unit of work.

An SQL package is an AS/400 object used only for distributed relational databases. It can be created as a result of the precompile process of SQL or can be created from a compiled programme object. An SQL package resides on the application server. It contains SQL statements, host variable attributes, and access plans which the application server uses to process an application requester's request. Because application programmes can connect to many different systems, programmers may need to pay more attention to data conversion between systems. The AS/400 system provides for conversion of various types of data, including coded character set identifier (CCSID) support for the management of character information.

SPIFFY CORPORATION DISTRIBUTED RELATIONAL DATABASE

The Spiffy Corporation is used in several IBM manuals to describe distributed relational database support. In this manual, this fictional company has been changed somewhat to illustrate AS/400 support for DRDA in an AS/

400 network. Examples used throughout this manual illustrate particular functions, connections, and processes. These may not correspond exactly to the examples used in other distributed relational database publications but an attempt has been made to make them look familiar.

Though the Spiffy Corporation is a fictional enterprise, the business practices described here are modelled after those in use in several companies of similar construction. However, this example does not attempt to describe all that can be done using a distributed relational database, even by this example company.

DATA REDUNDANCY IN YOUR DISTRIBUTED RELATIONAL DATABASE NETWORK

Data redundancy in a distributed relational database also provides different ways for users on the distributed relational database network to access a database on the network. The considerations a distributed relational database administrator examines to create a data redundancy strategy are more complex than ensuring communications paths are available to the data.

Tables can be replicated across systems in the network, or a snapshot of data can be used to provide data availability. DB2® DataPropagator™ can provide this capability.

The following figure shows that a copy of the MP000 system distributed relational database can be stored on the KC000 system, and a copy of the KC000 system distributed relational database can be stored on the MP000 system. The client from one region can link to the other server to query or to update a replicated copy of their relational database.

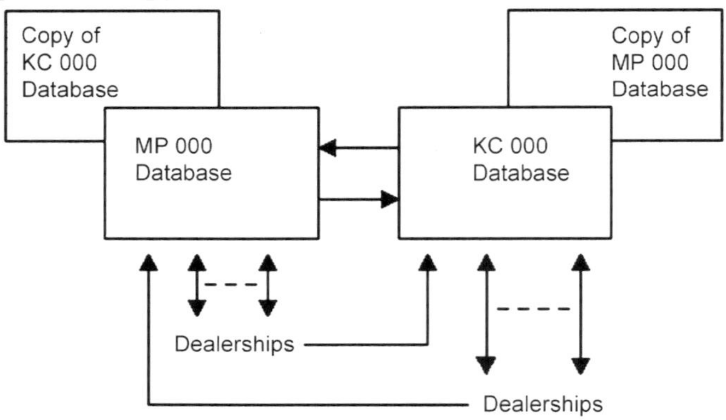

Fig. Data Redundancy.

The administrator must decide what is the most efficient, effective strategy to allow distributed relational database processing. Alternative strategies might include these scenarios. One alternative might be that when MP000 is unavailable, its clients connect to the KC000 system to query a read-only snapshot of the MP000 distributed relational database so service work can be scheduled. DB2 DataPropagator can provide a read-only copy of the tables to a remote system on a regular basis. For the Spiffy Corporation, this might be at the end or the beginning of each business day. In this example, the MP000 database snapshot provides a 24-hour-old, last-point-in-time picture for dealerships to use for scheduling only.

When the MP000 system is back on line, its clients query the MP000 distributed relational database to completely process inventory requests or other work queried on the read-only copy. Another alternative might be that Spiffy Corporation wants dealership users to be able to update a replicated table at another server when their regional server is unavailable.

For example, a client that normally connects to the MP000 database can connect to a replicated MP000 database on the KC000 system to process work. When the MP000 system is available again, the MP000 relational database can be updated by applying journal entries from activity that originated in its replicated tables at the KC000 location. When these journal entries have been applied to the original MP000 tables, distributed relational database users can access the MP000 as a server again.

Journal management processes on each regional system update all relational databases. The amount of journal management copy activity in this situation should be examined because of potential adverse performance effects on these systems.

SETTING UP A RELATIONAL DATABASE DIRECTORY

The Spiffy Corporation network example illustrates how the relational database directory is set up and used on systems in a distributed relational database network. The example assumes the use of Advanced Programme-to-Programme Communication (APPC) for communications, as opposed to TCP/IP, which would be simpler to set up. However, some elements of the example are protocol-independent. The RDB directory entries needed for APPC use are also needed in a TCP/IP network, but the parameters differ. Host names or IP addresses and port identifications would replace logical unit (LU) names, device descriptions, modes, TPNs, and so forth.

A simple relationship to consider is the one between two regional offices as shown in the following figure:

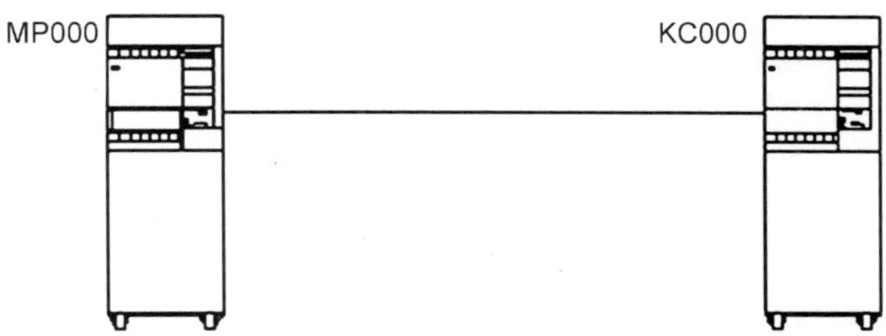

Fig. Relational Database Directory Set up for Two Systems.

The relational database directory for each regional office must contain an entry for the local relational database and an entry for the remote relational database because each system is both a client and a server. The commands to create the relational database directory for the MP000 system are:

```
ADDRDBDIRE RDB(MP000) RMTLOCNAME(*LOCAL) TEXT('Minneapolis
region database')

ADDRDBDIRE RDB(KC000) RMTLOCNAME(KC000) TEXT('Kansas City
region database')
```

In the preceding example, the MP000 system identifies itself as the local relational database by specifying *LOCAL for the RMTLOCNAME parameter. There is only one relational database on a System i® platform. You can simplify identification of your network relational databases by making the relational database names in the RDB directory the same as the system name. The entry for the local location can have the same name as the local system name, and the entry for the remote location name can have the same name as the remote system name.

Note: The system name is specified on the SYSNAME parameter of the Change Network Attributes (CHGNETA) command. The local system is identified on the LCLLOCNAME parameter of the CHGNETA command during communications configuration. Remote locations using SNA (APPC) are identified with the RMTCPNAME parameter on the Create Controller Description (APPC) (CRTCTLAPPC) command during communications configuration. Using the same names for system names, network locations, and database names can help avoid confusion, particularly in complex networks.

The corresponding entries for the KC000 system relational database directory are:

```
ADDRDBDIRE RDB(KC000) RMTLOCNAME(*LOCAL) TEXT('Kansas City
region database')

ADDRDBDIRE RDB(MP000) RMTLOCNAME(MP000) TEXT('Minneapolis
region database')
```

A more complex example to consider is that of a regional office to its dealerships. For example, to access relational databases in the network shown in the following figure, the relational database directory for the MP000 system must be expanded to include an entry for each of its dealerships.

A sample of the commands used to complete the MP000 relational database directory to include all its dealer databases is as follows:

```
PGM
ADDRDBDIRE RDB(MP000) RMTLOCNAME(*LOCAL) +
TEXT('Minneapolis region database')
ADDRDBDIRE RDB(KC000) RMTLOCNAME(KC000)
```

```
TEXT('Kansas City region database')
ADDRDBDIRE RDB(MP101) RMTLOCNAME(MP101)
TEXT('Dealer database MP101')
ADDRDBDIRE RDB(MP002) RMTLOCNAME(MP110)
TEXT('Dealer database MP110')
.
.
.
ADDRDBDIRE RDB(MP215) RMTLOCNAME(MP201)
TEXT('Dealer database MP201')
ENDPGM
```

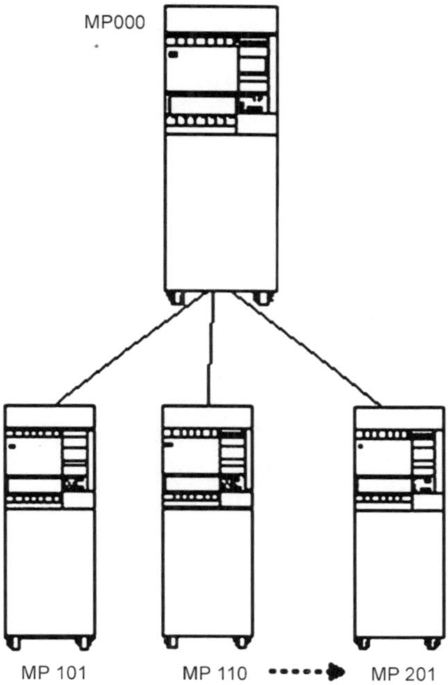

Fig. Relational Database Directory Set up for Multiple Systems.

In the preceding example, each of the region dealerships is included in the Minneapolis relational database directory as a remote relational database.

Because each dealership can serve as a client to MP000 and to other dealership servers, each dealership must have a relational database directory that has an entry for itself as the local relational database, and have the regional office and all other dealers as remote relational databases. The database administrator has several options to create a relational database directory at each dealership system.

The most time-consuming and error-prone method is to create a relational database directory at each system by using the Add Relational Database Directory Entry (ADDRDBDIRE) command to create each directory entry on all systems that are part of the MP000 distributed relational database network. A better alternative is to create a control language (CL) programme like the one shown in the preceding example for the MP000 system. The distributed relational database administrator can copy this CL programme for each of the dealership systems.

To customise this programme for each dealership, the database administrator changes the remote location name of the MP000 system to MP000, and changes the remote location name of the local dealership to *LOCAL. The distributed relational database administrator can distribute the customised CL programme to each dealership to be run on that system to build its unique relational database directory.

A third method is to write a programme that reads the relational database directory information sent to an output file as a result of using the Display Relational Database Directory Entry (DSPRDBDIRE) command. This programme can be distributed to the dealerships, along with the output file containing the relational database directory entries for the MP000 system. Each system can read the MP000 output file to create a local relational database directory. The Change Relational Database Directory Entry (CHGRDBDIRE) command can then be used to customise the MP000 system directory for the local system.

SPIFFY ORGANISATION AND SYSTEM PROFILE

Spiffy Corporation is a national product distributor that sells and services automobiles, among other products, to retail customers through a network of regional offices and local dealerships. Given the high competitiveness of today's automobile industry, the success of an operation like the Spiffy Corporation depends on high-quality servicing and timely delivery of spare parts to the customer. To meet this competition, Spiffy has established a vast service network incorporated within its dealership organisation.

The dealership organisation is headed by a central vehicle distributor that is located in Chicago, Illinois. There are several regional distribution centres across North America. Two of these are located in Minneapolis, Minnesota and Kansas City, Missouri. These centres minimize the distribution costs of vehicles and spare parts by setting up regional inventories. The Minneapolis regional centre serves approximately 15 dealerships while the Kansas City centre serves as many as 30 dealerships.

Spiffy is in the process of building up a nationwide integrated telecommunications network. For the automobile division they are setting up a network of AS/400 systems for the regional distributions centres and the dealerships. These are connected to an IBM 3090* at the central vehicle distributor. This network is considered a vital business asset for maintaining the competitive edge. The central distributor runs OS/390 on its IBM 3090 system with DB2 and relevant decision support software. This system is used because of the large amounts of data that must be handled at any one time in a variety of application programmes. The central vehicle distributor system is not dedicated to automobile division data processing. It must handle work and processes for the corporation that do not yet operate in a distributed database environment. The regional centres are running AS/400 Model 650 e-systems. They use APPC/APPN with SNADS and 5250 Display Station Pass-through using an SDLC protocol.

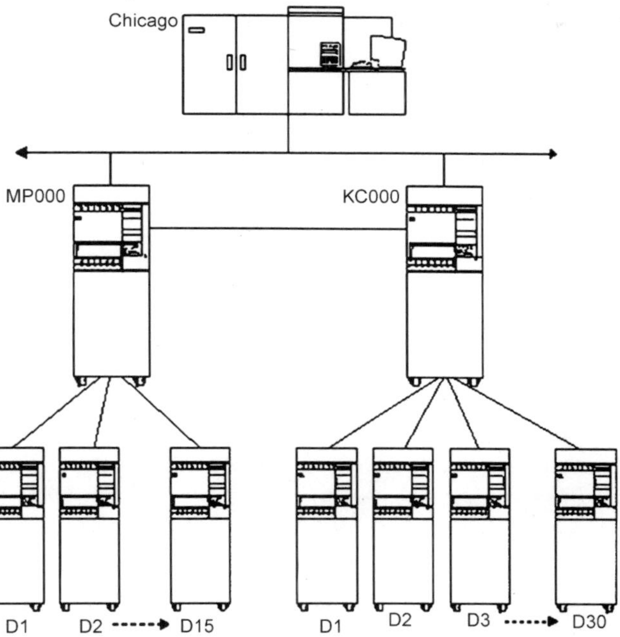

Fig. The Spiffy Corporation System Organisation.

All of the dealerships use AS/400 systems but they may range in size from a Model 600 e-system in the smaller enterprises up to a Model 640 e-system in the largest. These systems are connected to the regional office using SDLC protocol. The largest dealerships have a part time programmer and a system operator to tend to the data processing functioning of the enterprise. Most of the installations do not employ anyone with programming expertise and some of the smaller locations do not employ anyone with more than a very general knowledge of computers.

Business Processes of the Spiffy Corporation Automobile Service

The Spiffy Corporation automobile division has business practices that are automated in this distributed relational database environment. To keep the examples from becoming more complicated than necessary, consider just those functions in the company that pertain to vehicle servicing. Dealerships can have a list of from 2000 to 20,000 customers. This translates to 5 service orders per day for a small dealership and up to 50 per day for a large dealership. These service orders include scheduled maintenance, warranty repairs, regular repairs, and parts ordering.

The dealers stock only frequently needed spare parts and maintain their own inventory databases. Both regional centres provide parts when requested. Dealer inventories are also stocked on a periodic basis by a forecast-model-controlled batch process.

Distributed Relational Database Administration for the Spiffy Corporation

Each dealership manages its data processing resources and procedures as a stand-alone enterprise. Spiffy Corporation requires that each dealership have one or more AS/400 systems and that those systems must be available to the network at certain times. However, the size of the system and the number of business processes that are automated on it are determined by each dealership's needs and the resources available to it.

The Spiffy Corporation requires all dealerships to be active in the inventory distributed relational database. Since, the corporation operates its own dealerships, it has a full complement of dealership software that may or may not access the distributed relational database environment. The Spiffy dealerships use the full set of software tools. Most of the private franchises use them also since, they are tailored specifically to the Spiffy Corporation way of doing business.

The regional distribution centres manage the inventory for their region. They also function as the database administrator for all distributed database resources used in the region. The responsibilities involved vary depending on the level of data processing competency at each dealership. The regional centre is always the first contact for help for any dealership in the region. The Minneapolis regional distribution centre has a staff of AS/400 programmers with a wide range of experience and knowledge about the systems and the network.

The dealership load is about one half that of other regional centres to allow this centre to focus on network-wide AS/400 support functions. These functions include application programme development, programme maintenance, and problem handling.

The following are the database responsibilities for each level of activity in the network:

Dealerships:

- Perform basic operation and administration of system
- Enroll local users.

Regional distribution centres:

- Set up data processing for new dealerships
- Disperse database resources for discontinued dealerships

- Enroll network users in region
- Maintain inventory for region
- Develop service plans for dealerships
- Operate help desk for dealerships.

In addition to the regional distribution centre activities above, the Minneapolis AS/400 competency centre does the following activities:

- Develop applications for AS/400 network
- Operate help desk for regional centres
- Tune database performance
- Alert focal point
- Resolve database problems.

Examples used throughout this manual are associated with one or more of these activities. Many examples show the process of obtaining a part from inventory in order to schedule customer service or repairs.

Others show distributed relational database administration tasks used to set up, secure, monitor, and resolve problems for systems in the Spiffy Corporation distributed relational database network.

PLANNING AND DESIGN FOR DISTRIBUTED RELATIONAL DATABASE

To prepare for a distributed relational database, you must understand both the needs of the business and relational database technology. Because the planning and design of a distributed relational database are closely linked to each other, this chapter combines these topics when discussing the following related tasks:

- Identifying your needs and expectations
- Designing the application, data, and network
- Putting together a management strategy

IDENTIFYING EXPECTATIONS FOR A DISTRIBUTED RELATIONAL DATABASE

When analysing your needs and expectations of a distributed relational database, consider the following:

1. Data needs. What data is pertinent to your plans, who will need it, for what reason, and how often?
2. Distributed relational database capabilities. Do the requirements lend themselves to a distributed relational database solution?
3. Goals and directions. If a distributed relational database appears to be a viable solution, what short-term and long-term goals can be met?

Data Needs for Distributed Relational Databases

The first step in your analysis is to determine which factors affect your data and how they affect it. Ask yourself the following questions.

- What locations are involved?
- What kind of transactions do you envision?
- What data is needed for each transaction?
- What dependencies do items of data have on each other, especially referential limitations? For example, will information in one table need to be checked against the information in another table? (If so, both tables must be kept at the same location.)
- Does the data currently exist? If so, where is it located? Who "owns" it (that is, who is responsible for maintaining the accuracy of the data)?
- What priority do you place on the availability of the needed data? Integrity of the data across locations? Protection of the data from unauthorised access?
- What access patterns do you envision for the data? For instance, will the data be read, updated, or both? How frequently? Will a typical access return a lot of data or a little data?
- What level of performance do you expect from each transaction? What response time is acceptable?

Distributed Relational Database Capabilities

The second step in your analysis is to decide whether or not your data needs lend themselves to a distributed relational database solution.

Applications where most database processing is done locally and access to remote data is needed only occasionally are typically good candidates for a distributed relational database.

Applications with the following requirements are usually poor candidates for a distributed relational database:

- The data is kept at a central site and most of the work that a remote user needs to do is at the central site.
- Consistently high performance, especially consistently fast response time, is needed. It takes longer to move data across a network.
- Consistently high availability, especially twenty-four hour, seven-day-a-week availability, is needed. Networks involve more systems and more in-between components, such as communications lines and communications controllers, which increases the chance of breakdowns.
- A distributed relational database function that you need is not currently available or announced.

Designing Distributed Relational Database Applications

Distributed relational database applications have different requirements from applications developed solely for use on a local database. To properly plan for these differences, design your applications with the following in mind:

- Take advantage of the distributed unit of work (DUW) function where appropriate.

Note: The current AS/400 implementation of DRDA limits you to one-phase commit capability where TCP/IP is used. However, you can still interoperate with one-phase commit servers in an application compiled with the *DUW connection management option under certain restrictions. For example, if the first connection made from the application is to an AS/400 over TCP/IP, updates can be made to that system, but any subsequent connections will be read-only.

- Code programmes using common interfaces.
- Consider dividing a complex application into smaller parts and placing each piece of the application in the location best suited to process it. One good way to distribute processing in an application is to make use of the SQL CALL statement to run a stored procedure at a remote location where the data to be processed resides. The stored procedure is not limited to SQL operations when it runs on a DB2/400 application server; it can use integrated database input/ output or perform other types of processing.
- Investigate how the initial database applications will be prepared, tested, and used.
- Take advantage, when possible, of SQL set-processing capabilities. This will minimize communication with the application servers. For example, update multiple rows with one SQL statement whenever you can.
- Be aware that database updates within a unit of work must be done at a single site if the RUW connection method is used when the programmes are prepared, or if the other nodes in the distributed application do not support DUW.
- Keep in mind that the DUW connection method restricts you from directing a single statement to more than one relational database.
- Performance is affected by the choice of connection management methods. Use of the RUW connection management method might be preferable if you do not have the need to switch back and forth among different remote relational databases. This is because more overhead is associated with the two-phase commit protocols used with DUW connection management.

However, if you have to switch frequently among multiple remote database management systems, use DUW connection management. When running with DUW connection management, communication conversations to one database management system do not have to be ended when you switch the connection to another database management system. In the like environment, this is not as big a factor as in the unlike environment, since, conversations in the like environment can be kept active by use of the default

DDMCNV(*KEEP) job definition attribute. Even in the like environment, however, a performance advantage can be gained by using DUW to avoid the cost of closing cursors and sending the communication flow to establish a new connection.

- The connection management method determines the semantics of the CONNECT statement. With the RUW connection management method, the CONNECT statement ends any existing connections prior to establishing a new connection to the relational database. With the DUW connection management method, the CONNECT statement does not end existing connections.

Network Considerations for a Distributed Relational Database

The design of a network directly affects the performance of a distributed relational database. To properly design a distributed relational database that works well with a particular network, do the following:

- Because the line speed can be very important to application performance, provide sufficient capacity at the appropriate places in the network to achieve efficient performance to the main distributed relational database applications.
- Evaluate the available communication hardware and software and, if necessary, your ability to upgrade.
- For APPC connections, consider the session limits and conversation limits specified when the network is defined.
- Identify the hardware, software, and communication equipment needed (for both test and production environments), and the best configuration of the equipment for a distributed relational database network.
- Consider the skills that are necessary to support TCP/IP as opposed to those that are necessary to support APPC. Also consider the additional functionality offered by APPC (that is, two-phase commit).
- Take into consideration the initial service level agreements with end user groups (such as what response time to expect for a given distributed relational database application), and strategies for monitoring and tuning the actual service provided.
- Develop a naming strategy for database objects in the distributed relational database and for each location in the distributed relational database system. A location is a specific relational database management system in an interconnected network of relational database management systems that participate in distributed relational database. Consider the following when developing this strategy:
  - The fully qualified name of an object in a distributed database

system has three (rather than two) parts, and the highest-level qualifier identifies the location of the object.

— Each location in a distributed relational database system should be given a unique identification; each object in the system should also have a unique identification. Duplicate identifications can cause serious problems. For example, duplicate locations and object names may cause an application to connect to an unintended remote database, and once connected, access an unintended object. Pay particular attention to naming when networks are coupled.

11

Database Integration

This document provides instructions for integrating Openfire authentication, users, and groups with your custom database tables. This is useful when your users already have accounts in an external system and you do not wish to duplicate those accounts in Openfire. If your user information is available via an LDAP directory rather than custom database tables. Simple integration with a custom database lets users authenticate using their existing username and password. Optionally, you can configure Openfire to load user profile and group information from your custom database. Any group in Openfire can be designated as a shared group, which means that you can pre-populate user's rosters using groups.

BACKGROUND OF DATABASE

The integration requires that you enter customised database queries to access your database.

CONFIGURATION

In order to configure your server to integrate with your custom database tables:

- Stop Openfire.
- Edit conf/openfire.xml in your Openfire installation folder as described below using your favourite editor.
- Restart Openfire.

Database Connection Settings

You must specify the connection string for your database as well as the JDBC driver.

- jdbcProvider.driver -- the class name of the JDBC driver used to connect to your custom database. The driver must also be in the Openfire classpath (for example, by placing it into the "lib/" directory of your Openfire installation.
- jdbcProvider.connectionString -- the full connection string for the database. Please consult your database driver documentation for

syntax. Warning: it's common for connection string to contain "&" characters. That character has special meaning in XML, so you should escape it using "&".

A sample config file section (note: the "..." sections in the examples indicate areas where the rest of the config file would exist):

```
<jive>
  ...
  <jdbcProvider>
  <driver>com.mysql.jdbc.Driver</driver>
      <connectionString>jdbc:mysql://localhost/
dbname?user=username&amp;password=secret</connectionString>
  </jdbcProvider>
  ...
</jive>
```

Authentication Integration

The simplest possible integration with a custom external database is authentication integration. Use the following settings to enable authentication integration.

- provider.auth.className -- set the value to org.jivesoftware.openfire.auth.JDBCAuthProvider.
- jdbcAuthProvider.passwordSQL -- the SQL String to select a user's password. The SQL statement should contain a single "?" character, which will be dynamically replaced with a username when being executed.
- jdbcAuthProvider.passwordType -- the type of the password. Valid values are
  - "plain" (the password is stored as plain text)
  - "md5" (the password is stored as a hex-encoded MD5 hash)
  - "sha1" (the password is stored as a hex-encoded SHA-1 hash)
  - "sha256" (the password is stored as a hex-encoded SHA-256 hash)
  - "sha512" (the password is stored as a hex-encoded SHA-512 hash)

If this value is not set, the password type is assumed to be plain.

Below is a sample config file section:

```
<jive>
...
<provider>
<auth>
<className>org.jivesoftware.openfire.auth.JDBCAuthProvider</
className>
```

```
</auth>
</provider>
<jdbcAuthProvider>
<passwordSQL>SELECT password FROM user_account WHERE
username=?</passwordSQL>
<passwordType>plain</passwordType>
</jdbcAuthProvider>
...
</jive>
```

You'll most likely want to change which usernames are authorised to login to the admin console. By default, only the user with username "admin" is allowed to login. However, you may have different users in your LDAP directory that you'd like to be administrators. The list of authorised usernames is controlled via the admin.authorisedUsernames property. For example, to let the usersnames "joe" and "jane" login to the admin console:

```
<jive>
...
<admin>
...
<authorizedUsernames>joe, jane</authorizedUsernames>
</admin>
...
</jive>
```

User Integration

Optionally, Openfire can load user data from your custom database. If you enable user integration you must also enable authentication integration. Use the following settings to enable user integration.

- provider.user.className— set the value to org.jivesoftware.openfire.user.JDBCUserProvider.
- jdbcUserProvider.loadUserSQL— the SQL statement to load the name and e-mail address of a user (in that order) given a username. The SQL statement should contain a single "?" character, which will be dynamically replaced with a username when being executed.
- jdbcUserProvider.userCountSQL— the SQL statement to load the total number of users in the database.
- jdbcUserProvider.allUsersSQL— the SQL statement to load all usernames in the database.
- jdbcUserProvider.searchSQL— the SQL statement fragment used to search your database for users. the statement should end with "WHERE"— the username, name, and e-mail fields will then be dynamically appended to the statement depending on the search. If this value is not set, searching will not be enabled.

- usernameField— the name of the username database field, which will be used for searches.
- nameField— the name of the name database field, which will be used for searches.
- e-mailField— the name of the e-mail database field, which will be used for searches.

Below is a sample config file section. Note that the single provider section must include all providers that should be configured:

```
<jive>
...
<provider>
<auth>
<className>org.jivesoftware.openfire.auth.JDBCAuthProvider</
className>
</auth>
<user>
<className>org.jivesoftware.openfire.user.JDBCUserProvider</
className>
</user>
</provider>
<jdbcAuthProvider>
<passwordSQL>SELECT password FROM user_account WHERE
username=?</passwordSQL>
<passwordType>plain</passwordType>
</jdbcAuthProvider>
<jdbcUserProvider>
<loadUserSQL>SELECT name,email FROM myUser WHERE
username=?</loadUserSQL>
<userCountSQL>SELECT COUNT(*) FROM myUser</userCountSQL>
<allUsersSQL>SELECT username FROM myUser</allUsersSQL>
<searchSQL>SELECT username FROM myUser WHERE</searchSQL>
<usernameField>username</usernameField>
<nameField>name</nameField>
<emailField>email</emailField>
</jdbcUserProvider>
...
</jive>
```

Group Integration

Openfire can load group data from your custom database. If you enable group integration you must also enable authentication integration; you'll also likely want to enable user integration. Use the following settings to enable group integration.

- provider.group.className — set the value to org.jivesoftware. openfire.group.JDBCGroupProvider.
- jdbcGroupProvider.groupCountSQL — the SQL statement to load the total number of groups in the database.
- jdbcGroupProvider.allGroupsSQL — the SQL statement to load all groups in the database.
- jdbcGroupProvider.userGroupsSQL — the SQL statement to load all groups for a particular user. The SQL statement should contain a single "?" character, which will be dynamically replaced with a username when being executed.
- jdbcGroupProvider.descriptionSQL — the SQL statement to load the description of a group. The SQL statement should contain a single "?" character, which will be dynamically replaced with a group name when being executed.
- jdbcGroupProvider.loadMembersSQL — the SQL statement to load all members in a group. The SQL statement should contain a single "?" character, which will be dynamically replaced with a group name when being executed.
- jdbcGroupProvider.loadAdminsSQL — the SQL statement to load all administrators in a group. The SQL statement should contain a single "?" character, which will be dynamically replaced with a group name when being executed.

Below is a sample config file section. Note that the single provider section must include all providers that should be configured:

```
<jive>
...
<provider>
<auth>
<className>org.jivesoftware.openfire.auth.JDBCAuthProvider</
className>
</auth>
<user>
<className>org.jivesoftware.openfire.user.JDBCUserProvider</
className>
</user>
<group>
<className>org.jivesoftware.openfire.group.JDBCGroupProvider</
className>
</group>
</provider>
<jdbcAuthProvider>
<passwordSQL>SELECT password FROM user_account WHERE
username=?</passwordSQL>
```

```
<passwordType>plain</passwordType>
</jdbcAuthProvider>
<jdbcUserProvider>
<loadUserSQL>SELECT name,email FROM myUser WHERE
username=?</loadUserSQL>
<userCountSQL>SELECT COUNT(*) FROM myUser</userCountSQL>
<allUsersSQL>SELECT username FROM myUser</allUsersSQL>
<searchSQL>SELECT username FROM myUser WHERE</searchSQL>
<usernameField>username</usernameField>
<nameField>name</nameField>
<emailField>email</emailField>
</jdbcUserProvider>
<jdbcGroupProvider>
<groupCountSQL>SELECT count(*) FROM myGroups</
groupCountSQL>
<allGroupsSQL>SELECT groupName FROM myGroups</allGroupsSQL>
<userGroupsSQL>SELECT groupName FROM myGroupUsers WHERE
username=?</userGroupsSQL>
<descriptionSQL>SELECT groupDescription FROM myGroups WHERE
groupName=?</descriptionSQL>
<loadMembersSQL>SELECT username FROM myGroupUsers WHERE
groupName=? AND isAdmin='N'</loadMembersSQL>
<loadAdminsSQL>SELECT username FROM myGroupUsers WHERE
groupName=? AND isAdmin='Y'</loadAdminsSQL>
</jdbcGroupProvider>
...
</jive>
```

DATA INTEGRATION

Data integration involves combining data residing in different sources and providing users with a unified view of these data. This process becomes significant in a variety of situations, which include both commercial (when two similar companies need to merge their databases) and scientific (combining research results from different bioinformatics repositories, for example) domains. Data integration appears with increasing frequency as the volume and the need to share existing data explodes. It has become the focus of extensive theoretical work, and numerous open problems remain unsolved. In management circles, people frequently refer to data integration as "Enterprise Information Integration" (EII).

HISTORY

Issues with combining heterogeneous data sources under a single query interface have existed for some time. The rapid adoption of databases after the 1960s naturally led to the need to share or to merge existing repositories. This merging can take place at several levels in the database architecture. One popular solution is implemented based on data warehousing. The warehouse system extracts, transforms, and loads data from heterogeneous sources into a single common queriable schema so data becomes compatible with each other. This approach offers a tightly coupled architecture because the data is already physically reconciled in a single repository at query-time, so it usually takes little time to resolve queries. However, problems arise with the "freshness" of data, which means information in warehouse is not always up-to-date. Therefore, when an original data source gets updated, the warehouse still retains outdated data and the ETL process needs re-execution for synchronisation. Difficulties also arise in constructing data warehouses when one has only a query interface to summary data sources and no access to the full data. This problem frequently emerges when integrating several commercial query services like travel or classified advertisement web applications.

As of 2009 the trend in data integration has favored loosening the coupling between data and providing a unified query-interface to access real time data over a mediated schema, which allows information to be retrieved directly from original databases. This approach may need to specify mappings between the mediated schema and the schema of original sources, and transform a query into specialised queries to match the schema of the original databases. Therefore, this middleware architecture is also termed as "view-based query-answering" because each data source is represented as a view over the (nonexistent) mediated schema. Formally, computer scientists term such an approach "Local As View" (LAV) - where "Local" refers to the local sources/ databases. An alternate model of integration has the mediated schema functioning as a view over the sources. This approach, called "Global As View" (GAV) - where "Global" refers to the global (mediated) schema - has attractions owing to the simplicity of answering queries by means of the mediated schema. However, it is necessary to reconstitute the view for the mediated schema whenever a new source gets integrated and/or an already integrated source modifies its schema.

As of 2010 some of the work in data integration research concerns the semantic integration problem. This problem addresses not the structuring of the architecture of the integration, but how to resolve semantic conflicts between heterogeneous data sources. For example if two companies merge their databases, certain concepts and definitions in their respective schemas like "earnings" inevitably have different meanings. In one database it may mean profits in dollars (a floating-point number), while in the other it might represent the number of sales (an integer). A common strategy for the resolution of such problems involves the use of ontologies which explicitly define schema terms and thus help to resolve semantic conflicts. This approach represents ontology-based data integration. On the other hand, the problem of combining research results from different bioinformatics repositories requires bench-marking of the similarities, computed from different data sources, on a single criterion such as, positive predictive value. This enables the data sources to be directly comparable and can be integrated even when the natures of experiments are distinct.

As of 2011 it was determined that current data modelling methods were imparting data isolation into every data architecture in the form of islands of disparate data and information silos each of which represents a disparate system. This data isolation is an unintended artifact of the data modelling methodology that results in the development of disparate data models. Disparate data models, when instantiated as databases, form disparate databases. Enhanced data model methodologies have been developed to eliminate the data isolation artifact and to promote the development of integrated data models. One enhanced data modelling method recasts data models by augmenting them with structural metadata in the form of standardised data entities. As a result of recasting multiple data models, the set of recast data models will now share one or more commonality relationships that relate the structural metadata now common to these data models. Commonality relationships are a peer-to-peer type of entity relationships that relate the standardised data entities of multiple data models. Multiple data models that contain the same standard data entity may participate in the same commonality relationship. When integrated data models are instantiated as databases and are properly populated from a common set of master data, then these databases are integrated.

In 2012, high-throughput biological data, such as, phenotypic profiles, gene expression microarrays, protein sequences, Kyoto Encyclopaedia of Genes and Genomes (KEGG) pathway, and protein-protein interaction data are integrated through a weighted power scoring framework, called weighted power biological score (WPBS), for predicting the function of some of the unclassified yeast Saccharomyces cerevisiae genes. The relative power and weight coefficients of different data sources are estimated systematically by utilising functional annotations of classified genes, available from Saccharomyces Genome Database. Genes are then clustered by applying k-medoids algorithm on WPBS, and functional categories of 334 unclassified genes are predicted using a P-value cutoff 1 × 10^{?5}.

WEB APPLICATION

Consider a web application where a user can query a variety of information about cities (such as crime statistics, weather, hotels, demographics, etc.). Traditionally, the information must be stored in a single database with a single schema. But any single enterprise would find information of this breadth somewhat difficult and expensive to collect. Even if the resources exist to gather the data, it would likely duplicate data in existing crime databases, weather web sites, and census data. A data-integration solution may address this problem by considering these external resources as materialised views over a virtual mediated schema, resulting in "virtual data integration". This means application-developers construct a virtual schema - the mediated schema - to best model the kinds of answers their users want. Next, they design "wrappers" or adapters for each data source, such as the crime database and weather web site. These adapters simply transform the local query results (those returned by the respective web sites or databases) into an easily processed form for the data integration solution. When an application-user queries the mediated schema, the data-integration solution transforms this query into appropriate queries over the respective data sources. Finally, the virtual database combines the results of these queries into the answer to the user's query.

This solution offers the convenience of adding new sources by simply constructing an adapter or an application software blade for them. It contrasts with ETL systems or with a single database solution, which require manual integration of entire new dataset into the system. The virtual ETL solutions leverage virtual mediated schema to implement data harmonisation; whereby the data is copied from the designated "master" source to the defined targets, field by field. Advanced Data virtualisation is also built on the concept of object-oriented modelling in order to construct virtual mediated schema or virtual metadata repository, using hub and spoke architecture.

DEVELOPERS FREQUENTLY INTEGRATE INTO A SHARED MASTER

Although developers can experiment frequently in their own area, it's important to bring the different approaches back together again frequently. An application needs a shared master database that all work flows from. When a developer begins a task they copy the master into their own workspace, manipulate, and then integrate their changes back into the master. As a rule of thumb each developer should integrate once a day.

Let's take an example where Mike starts a development task at 10am (assuming he actually comes in that early). As part of this task he needs to change the database schema. If the change is easy, like adding a column, he just decides how to make the change himself, Mike also makes sure the column he wants to add does not already exist in the database, with the help of the data dictionary. If it's more complicated then he grabs the DBA and talks over the likely changes with him.

Once he's ready to begin he takes a copy of the database master and can modify both the database schema and code freely. As he's in a sandbox any changes he makes don't impact anyone else's. At some point, say around 3pm, he's pretty comfortable that he knows what the database change needs to be, even though he's not completely done with his programming task. At that point he grabs the DBA, and tells him about the change. At this point the DBA can raise any issues that Mike hasn't considered. Most of the time all is well and the DBA goes off and makes the change. The DBA makes the changes right away. Mike can continue to work on his task and commit his code any time he likes once the DBA has applied these changes to the master. You may well recognise this principle as similar to the practice of Continuous Integration, which is applied to source code management. Indeed this is really about treating the database as another piece of source code. As such the master database is kept under configuration management in much the same way as the source code. Whenever we have a successful build, the database is checked into the configuration management system together with the code, so that we have a complete and synchronised version history of both.

With source code, much of the pain of integration is handled by source code control systems. For databases there's a bit more effort involved. Any changes to the database need to done properly, as automated database refactorings. In addition the DBA needs to look at any database changes and ensure that it fits within the overall scheme of the database schema. For this to work smoothly, big changes shouldn't come as surprises at integration time - hence, the need for the DBA to collaborate closely with the developers. We emphasise integrating frequently because we've found that it's much easier to do frequent small integrations rather than infrequent large integrations. It seems that the pain of integration increases exponentially with the sise of the integration. As such doing many small changes is much easier in practice, even though it often seems counter-intuitive to many. This same effect's been noticed by people in the Software Configuration Management community for source code.

A DATABASE CONSISTS OF SCHEMA AND TEST DATA

When we talk about a database here, we mean not just the schema of the database, but also a fair amount of data. This data consists of common standing data for the application, such as the inevitable list of all the states in the US, and also sample test data such as a few sample customers.

The data is there for a number of reasons. The main reason is to enable testing. We are great believers in using a large body of automated tests to help stabilise the development of an application. Such a body of tests is a common approach in agile methods. For these tests to work efficiently, it makes sense to work on a database that is seeded with some sample test data, which all tests can assume is in place before they run. As well as helping test the code, this sample test data also allows to test our migrations as we alter the schema of the database. By having sample data, we are forced to ensure that any schema changes also handle sample data. In most projects we've seen this sample data be fictional. However in a few projects we've seen people use real data for the samples. In these cases this data's been extracted from prior legacy systems with automated data migration scripts. Obviously you can't migrate all the data right away, as in early iterations only a small part of the database is actually built. But the idea is to iteratively develop the migration scripts just as the application and the database are developed iteratively. Not just does this help flush out migration problems early, it makes it much easier for domain experts to work with the growing system as they are familiar with the data they are looking at and can often help to identify problem cases that may cause problems for the database and application design. As a result we are now of the view that you should try to introduce real data from the very first iteration of your project.

INTEGRATION AT THE DATABASE LEVEL

There are many ways you can commit commercial suicide, but there is possibly no slower and more agonising death than that produced by attempting that great architectural objective, the single authoritative database to which all applications talk. The theory is good, if we have a single database then we have all our business information in one place, accessible to all, easy to report against, reduced maintenance costs, consistency across all applications, and a host of other good objectives. However all these noble ideals hide a more fundamental problem, that the single database does not solve any of them, and makes most of them into far bigger problems.

ALL INFORMATION IN ONE PLACE - THE SINGLE AUTHORITY

On the face of it this sounds like a great objective - after all developers try to live by the maxim of Don't Repeat Yourself - and data in many place is a clear violation of that principle. Data that appears across many applications and across many storage mechanisms leads to all sorts of massive problems; inconsistency, duplication, replication, duplicated business logic and code, essentially all boiling down to - you end up with spaghetti data. Spaghetti data is much like spaghetti code - it sprawls, gets tangled up, and becomes hard to pull apart without covering yourself in pasta sauce. This is obviously a "bad thing".

So what is Wrong?

Well the first and most obvious thing that is wrong is that all applications have different requirements, and different "world views". Although there may in theory be some concept of a "Customer" for the organisation as a whole, even this most basic of data items varies widely between individual departments and even individual applications within a single department. You could approach this problem, as many database centric people would do, and say "that is the problem right there, we need to standardise all these applications to use the One True Customer". But that is missing the really important word in the definition of the problem... "requirements"... this is not accidental that the Customer is different to different parts of the business, it really *is* different. Your database guys could say "well your Customer in your application may be different as you have different requirements, but you will just have to fit it into our One True Customer", but this is then like trying to put snakes into a plastic bag - they really don't want to be in the bag, they don't fit too well in the bag, and sooner or later while putting one in some others are going to escape or bite your hand. And when your other department starts putting his snakes in the bag too you will be fighting for who gets to not be bitten.

And worse still - now you are trying to map from your requirements based Customer to the One True Customer, and spend an inordinate amount of time maintaining this translation layer in your application. When that One True Customer changes, as he undoubtedly will as new applications require he is expanded to deal with more data they require, every previous application needs to be revisited, large parts of it need to be re-written, and the whole application needs to be regression tested again. And you have to do this for every single application talking to your single authority database. You could just skip this stuff, and rely on your applications ignoring this new data, and rely on the database not caring if they correctly updated new data - but this really will come back to bite you - when that bag of snakes starts getting really large and really full - you really don't want to be the one trying to get new snakes into it.

True Authority Database

Well, in legacy terms it is easy to understand why database admins and database developers want it - it is their lifeblood, their whole raison d'etre. More importantly, it is the culture in which they were brought up - the data is the important thing, the data is the centre of the universe, the data must be consistent, uniform and pure. But leaving database developers aside, more importantly why would a corporation want the One True Authority Database (OTADB)? After all, the title of this post says this is "Commercial Suicide", so why hasn't this got through to management?

Well - the promise of OTADB is that it will reduce errors in duplication, reduce waste, reduce duplicated effort and reduce maintenance costs - all highly desirable business objectives. And indeed, from those that advocate this approach (those database admins and developers again), the OTADB sounds mighty attractive. On the face of it, it achieves all of these objectives.

Where it falls down is that this holy grail of software development is always just out of reach, they never quite manage to achieve it. Each application that is developed starts to make the OTADB worse, people start to hack things into it to get it to meet business requirements, not because developers want to hack things together, but precisely because the restriction of the OTADB *forces* them to do it that way if they are to deliver any kind of functionality at all. They blame these hacks for ruining their vision of the One True Authority Database, the database admins tell them that they have to fight the application teams to stop them messing up their nice database, but that the OTADB no longer meets the noble objectives as those pesky development teams have messed it up for everyone.

Wait a Minute

If anyone was to step back from those noble objectives and ask a far more fundamental question, the solution might actually be a lot more obvious than it may seem. While they are all noble objectives, largely actually made worse specifically by the OTADB approach, they are not the real business objective. Underlying all the other requirements, the ultimate business requirement that drives people (in particular database admins) to want a single database is so that they can see what their company looks like, in other words - so they can produce Management Information - reports to you and me.

This is the single and most fundamental requirement for a business - to have a clear, consistent, accurate and up to date picture of what their company looks. This is what management needs, it is what allows them to make decisions, allows them to identify problems and allows them to spot opportunities. So, we are going to all this effort, and believe me it is extensive and significant effort, all to support some reporting tools at the end of the day. Reporting tools have problems with data in different formats, with data that is inconsistent, with data that is disparate and distributed. So at some point in the past, the "accepted truth" became "we need one true authority database to be able to produce good reports"

Actually Reporting

This is almost so easy to deal with, it is silly. Perhaps it is because it is so obviously simple that is has been overlooked by many and rejected by others. Especially as it violates another one of those noble objectives... to provide quality reporting information, we duplicate more of our data. Yep - we duplicate it - after all reporting data is read only, so it doesn't matter if it is just a copy of other data. Reporting requirements are also very different to transactional requirements too, so we get the added benefit of being able to optimise that duplicated data for the reporting functions. Data in relational databases is actually very poor for query and reporting purposes, and there is a constant compromise to make it fast for all those applications to write to, that makes it poor to report on - and vice-versa. How this data gets into the reporting database isn't my direct concern in this blog post, suffice to say the "easy" way is to publish messages with data changes, and have a reporting application pick those up and persist them. My point here - is that splitting the reporting functions from the day-to-day business functions pays massive dividends. That still leaves us with one problem - what happens when disparate applications really do need to know about data in other applications? What happens when my call centre operatives are asked to update the address for one of the Customers. Now as each application has it's own view of the world, and it's own data stores, my accounting application does not have access to that change. Well, the solution to the "how does data get in the reporting databases" question is exactly the same one here - you published messages from your application when you have changes that the rest of the corporation may be interested in. Fire off a message saying "CustomerAddressUpdated" and any other application that is concerned can now listen for that message and deal with it as it sees fit.

INTEROPERABILITY ACROSS DATA ACCESS APIS THROUGH SQL UP-LEVELLING

SQL up-levelling provides the capability to write a SQL statement that can be executed across multiple databases, regardless of the databases' SQL implementation. For example, a SQL statement written against Oracle will also be interoperable with DB2. Each of the major database vendors implements certain functionality in a unique proprietary format.

The functionality differences from the ANSI SQL standard fall into the following broad categories:

- Date and time literal representation
- Syntax for outer joins
- Syntax for scalar functions
- Methods for invoking stored procedures
- Dynamic SQL statement format corrections
- Empty string and null conversions
- Long character string insertion support.

These proprietary SQL implementations impact the interoperability provided by open data access standards. Adoption of these open standards has enabled companies to reduce expenditures by delivering a high degree of interoperability among databases. The inability to provide SQL interoperability has hindered some organisations from realising the full benefits of adopting these open standards. DataDirect Technologies has long been an industry leader in providing companies the highest level of interoperability between databases. One of the key areas of interoperability is SQL up-levelling. DataDirect provides SQL up-levelling across all open data access APIs. This gives developers a common way to implement these types of functionality-using the same code-regardless of the backend DBMS.

SQL UP-LEVELLING ACROSS APIS

SQL up-levelling is not a new concept. DataDirect products have implemented SQL up-levelling from the beginning. In the ODBC data access standard, SQL up-levelling was implemented through escape clauses. The escape clauses provided a syntax for certain functions to be performed independently of database vendors' implementation of the SQL standard. When Java emerged as a cross-platform development environment, Sun also implemented these escape clauses in the JDBC API to provide a level of interoperability between databases. The ADO.NET data access standard, however, does not require that ADO.NET data providers implement proprietary SQL functions across databases in a standard way. This limitation weakens application portability across data sources with ADO.NET. DataDirect Technologies has overcome this shortcoming in the ADO.NET specification by implementing SQL up-levelling in all DataDirect Connect for ADO.NET managed data providers. In addition, DataDirect data providers are written in 100% managed code. This means that developers can take advantage of true database interoperability, while taking advantage of the performance and security features provided within the.NET Framework through 100% managed code.

ESCAPE CLAUSES AND SQL EXTENSIONS

SQL extensions are just that, extensions to the SQL standard that are unique to open data access standards. SQL extensions provide a consistent method of SQL up-levelling to access SQL features available in many databases, but that have not been incorporated into the SQL standard. These SQL extensions, hereafter referred to as escape syntax, provide a high degree of interoperability for developers lwho want to use common SQL statements across databases. Each database vendor typically implements these features in a proprietary SQL extension. The escape syntax provides a way of using these features in a common, standard format that is independent of the underlying database. Using the escape clause, the DataDirect ODBC and JDBC drivers and ADO.NET data providers can easily scan SQL statements for syntax that may require special processing to be understood by the database. The escape clause consists of a pair of curly braces "{ }" surrounding the SQL syntax and a one- or two-character identifier to denote the type of escape clause. The driver or data provider then translates these escape clauses into syntax that is accepted by the database. This provides the greatest level of interoperability for developers who want to maximize the use of SQL statements in applications, regardless of the database implementation.

Date and Time Literals

All major databases support, to some extent, the data types DATE, TIME, and TIMESTAMP or DATETIME. The date and time formats implemented by the database vendors vary greatly, so there is little consistency for developers to leverage. A good example is the DATE format; the format required by Oracle is mm dd, yyyy, while for DB2 it is yyyy-mm-dd. The various implementations can be problematic for developers using these formats in applications that access multiple databases. Escape clauses implement the SQL standard definition for the DATE data type, which is yyyy-mm-dd. To use a DATE data type across multiple databases, application developers use the format {d 'yyyy-mm-dd'}. For example, a developer writing a SQL statement that selects employees hired on October 11 or October 15, 2003, would use the following SQL syntax:

```
SELECT EmpName, HireDate
FROM Emp
WHERE HireDate = {d '2003-10-11'}
OR HireDate = {d '2003-10-15'}
```

DataDirect's Oracle JDBC driver would translate this syntax to the following:

```
SELECT EmpName, HireDate
FROM Emp
WHERE HireDate = 'Oct 11, 2003'
OR HireDate = 'Oct 15, 2003'
```

DataDirect's SQL Server JDBC driver translates the syntax to:

```
SELECT EmpName, HireDate
FROM Emp
WHERE HireDate = '10-11-2003'
OR HireDate = '10-15-2003'
```

The escape clauses for TIME and TIMESTAMP use the SQL standard format for the syntax of the literals, and are denoted by using the 't' and 'ts' character designations respectively. Thus TIME escape clause is implemented as {t 'hh:mm:ss'}, and the TIMESTAMP escape clause is implemented as {ts 'yyyy-mm-dd hh:mm:ss'}. DataDirect products implement these escape syntaxes for DATE and TIME literals in the same way across all data access APIs. This means that developers can use a single SQL statement across different vendors' databases, as well as across JDBC, ODBC, and ADO.NET.

Outer Joins

Database vendors also differ in their implementation of the outer join functionality. Outer joins provide a convenient way to match records from two tables by forming pairs of related rows from the two different tables. The difference between outer joins and inner joins is that, if no pairs of data match, the inner join does not return a row, whereas the outer join returns a null value for a column in the row with unmatched data. Outer joins are implemented in escape clauses via the following syntax:

```
{oj table1 LEFT|RIGHT|FULL OUTER JOIN table2 ON search
condition}
```

For a developer to write a query that shows all sales reps in the Raleigh sales office, the outer join escape syntax is:

```
SELECT emp.EmpName, office.City
```

```
FROM {oj emp LEFT OUTER JOIN office ON emp.EmpId
=office.EmpId}
WHERE emp.City = 'Raleigh'
```

DataDirect's Oracle ADO.NET data provider translates this statement to:

```
SELECT emp.EmpName, office.City
FROM cust, ord
WHERE emp.EmpId =office.EmpID (+) AND emp.City = 'Raleigh'
```

DataDirect's SQL Server ADO.NET data provider translates the syntax to:

```
SELECT emp.EmpName, office.City
FROM emp, office
WHERE emp.EmpId *= office.EmpId AND office.city = 'Raleigh'
```

As developers plan to leverage SQL statements across applications that access multiple databases from different vendors, the need for SQL up-levelling in often complex outer join statements becomes extremely important. Most ADO.NET data providers today do not support this SQL up-levelling, a capability that is not built into the ADO.NET specification.

In contrast, DataDirect has extended its successful implementation of SQL up-levelling capabilities to include its DataDirect Connect for ADO.NET data providers so developers can maximize SQL statement portability.

Scalar Functions

Database vendors implement scalar functions in various proprietary formats. The escape syntax provides the ability to perform scalar functions in a consistent manner across databases. Scalar functions operate against a single value, in contrast to aggregate functions which operate on a given set of values. The four main types of scalar functions are numeric, string, time and date, and system. The DataDirect product lines implement these scalar functions in a consistent manner across all APIs, allowing developers to leverage the maximum amount of SQL syntax reuse, regardless of database.

Numeric Functions

Numeric functions provide the ability to determine many mathematic values, such as sine, cosine, square root, absolute value and logarithms. Each of the many supported functions is called using the escape syntax, regardless of the database implementation. Data access components, however, can only provide access to functions that are available on the database backend. The following example shows how to call the square root function:

```
Select {fn SQRT(c_squared)} from table1 where
shape='triangle'
and type='isosceles'
```

String Functions

String functions enable a developer to manipulate strings within the SQL result set, for example, setting all characters in a string to upper case, or returning a certain portion of a string from beginning or end. Some of the string functions available to developers are UCASE, LCASE, RTRIM, LTRIM, LENGTH, and SUBSTRING. The following statement returns UCASE values for a row that is mixed case in the database.

```
SELECT {fn UCASE(LastName)} FROM emp WHERE office =
'Raleigh'
```

Time and Date Functions

The time and data functions are very useful when developers need to manipulate date and time values, obtain days of week, or get the current time to use in a SQL statement. The following example uses the DAYNAME function to retrieve the date and day of the week the order was placed for the customer Progress.

```
SELECT date,{fn DAYNAME(date)} FROM orders WHERE
customer='Progress'
```

System Functions

System functions include the ability to retrieve a database name for the current connection, and the ability to check for a NULL value and substitute with another value if the expression is a NULL. The following example uses the USER function in a Select statement to retrieve all the vacation days available for the current user.

```
SELECT VacationDays FROM emp WHERE EmpName={fn USER()}
```

Invoking Stored Procedures

Developers who want to maximize performance in applications typically use stored procedures whenever possible. Database vendors implement stored procedure syntax in proprietary formats, using different markers for the parameters accepted as arguments in the stored procedure. DataDirect provides an escape syntax that is consistent across all data access APIs.

The escape syntax used for stored procedure invocation is {call procedure_name (?,?)} where the "?" is the parameter marker if the stored procedure uses parameters. The "?" parameter marker is used across all commercially available databases and APIs, ensuring that stored procedure invocation code does not need to be changed to access different databases. A stored procedure call to return the property tax percentage for a particular county, which accepts the parameter of a county name, uses the following syntax:

```
{CALL county_prop_tax (?)}
```

where the bound parameter would be the county name submitted by the user. This method of invoking stored procedure ensures that developers who want to use stored procedures to maximize performance can do so in a consistent format across databases and data access APIs.

DYNAMIC SQL STATEMENT FORMATTING CORRECTIONS

Certain databases require a specific format for SQL statements that extend to more than one line. A good example of dynamic format correction is with "newline" characters in SQL statements. Databases such as DB2 do not recognise newline characters, so statements that use them generate database syntax errors. The DataDirect products for DB2 dynamically replace these newline characters with white space so that DB2 can process the SQL statement without syntax errors. The functionality is implemented by the driver and requires no action from the developer. This level of interoperability between databases with regard to the syntax of SQL statements is implemented across all APIs and is dependent on the underlying database syntactical requirements.

EMPTY STRING AND NULL CONVERSIONS

Developers writing SQL statements to the ANSI standard use two single quoted identifiers in a SQL statement to denote an empty string. However, databases such as Oracle use two single quoted identifiers to denote a null value. Developers who use database access components provided by database vendors are forced to keep track of these differences in their code, either by coding separate SQL statements or by programmatically altering the identifiers based on the underlying database's implementation. DataDirect provides this conversion dynamically to the developer. If a developer uses the following syntax in an application connected to Oracle:

```
INSERT INTO emp (FirstName, LastName, VacationDays)
VALUES ('Tom', 'Smith', '')
```

The DataDirect Connect for ODBC driver for Oracle alters the syntax to:

```
INSERT INTO emp (FirstName, LastName, VacationDays)
VALUES ('Tom', 'Smith', "")
```

Null values are unable to use operators and are forced to use ISNULL and ISNOTNULL conditions. This ensures that the correct values are inserted into the database and that all operator logic with regards to strings still applies.

12

One-Sample and Two-Sample Hypothesis Tests

One sample t-test is a statistical procedure that is used to know the mean difference between the sample and the known value of the population mean. In one sample t-test, we know the population mean. We draw a random sample from the population and then compare the sample mean with the population mean and make a statistical decision as to whether or not the sample mean is different from the population. In one sample size, sample size should be less than 30. For example, we can use this when we take a sample from the city and we know the mean of the country (population mean). If we want to know whether the city mean differs from the country mean and we want to compare the two means, we will use the statistical test known as the one sample t-test.

ASSUMPTIONS IN ONE SAMPLE T-TEST

- In one sample t-test, dependent variables should be normally distributed.
- In one sample t-test, samples drawn from the population should be random.
- In one sample t-test, cases of the samples should be independent.
- In one sample t-test, sample size should be less than 30.
- In one sample t-test, we should know the population mean.

PROCEDURE FOR ONE SAMPLE T-TEST

- Set up the hypothesis for one sample t-test:
  - Null hypothesis: In one sample t-test, null hypothesis assumes that there are no significance differences between the population mean and the sample mean.
  - Alternative hypothesis: In one sample t-test, the alternative hypothesis assumes that there is a significant difference between the population mean and the sample mean.

Calculate the standard deviation for one sample t-test by using this formula.

$$S = \sqrt{\frac{\sum (X - \overline{X})^2}{n-1}}$$

Where,

S = Standard deviation for one sample t-test

$\overline{X}$ = Sample mean

n = number of observations in sample

- Calculate the value of the one sample t-test, by using this formula:

$$t = \frac{\overline{X} - \mu}{S}\sqrt{n}$$

Where,

t = One sample t-test

μ = Population mean

- Calculate the degree of freedom by using this formula:

V = n – 1

Where,

V= degree of freedom

Hypothesis testing: In hypothesis testing for the one sample t-test, statistical decisions are made to decide whether or not the population mean and the same mean are different. In hypothesis testing, we will compare the calculated value with the table value. If the calculated value of the one sample t-test is greater than the table value, then we will reject the null hypothesis. Otherwise, we will reject the alternative hypothesis.

ONE SAMPLE T-TEST AND SPSS:

In most of the statistical software, one sample t-test options are available. In SPSS, to perform the one sample t-test, we use the following procedures:

- Click on the "SPSS 16" icon from the start menu.
- Click on the "open data" icon and select the "data one sample t-test."
- Click on the "analysis" option and select the "compare mean" option, from the analysis.
- Select "one sample t-test" from the compare mean option. As we click on the one sample t-test, the following window will appear:

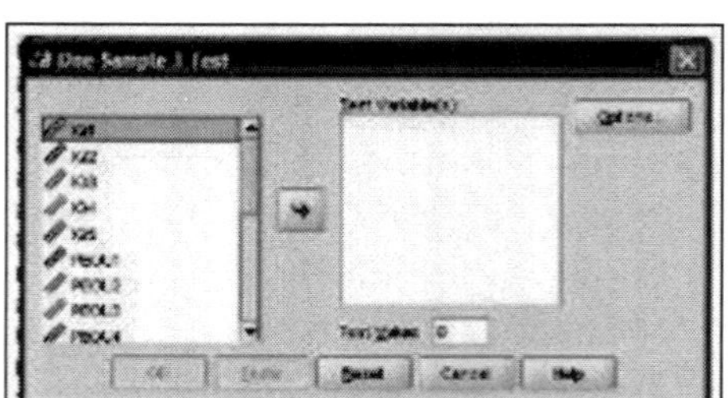

This window is called the one sample t-test window. In this window, select the dependent variable and insert them into the test variable box. Type the population mean value in the test value box.

Click on "option" and select the "percentage of confidence interval." As we click on the "ok" button, the result table for the one sample t-test will appear in front of us. The following table will appear in the result window.

TWO-SAMPLE HYPOTHESIS TESTS

TWO-SAMPLE HYPOTHESIS TEST

We will explain this by a example. This example compares the A-level count for a sample of Oxford University students getting BA and BSc degrees. The researcher believes the mean A-level count for BA students will be higher than that of BSc students.

The two-sample problem is examined visually using histograms and normal quantile plots and formally with a hypothesis test. Example #1 in the two-sample confidence interval module examines the assumptions underlying the test.

Problem Description

Measurements were made on a random sample of 40 students. The raw data is given in Appendix A of *Rees* and is reproduced as a set of variables in StatObjects.

The following variables were recorded:

ID: Student identification

Sex: The gender of the student (M = male; F = female)

Height: The height of the student (cm)

Siblings: Number of siblings

Distance: The distance form home to Oxford (km)

Degree: Type of degree (BA and BSc)

A-Level: A-level count

The shift in the centers of the two distribution is explored visually using the A-level histogram conditioning on the Degree Type. Select Normal Density from the Histogram popup menu to obtain the following plot for students seeking a BA degree:

Click on the right-hand side of the conditioning slider to display the A-level histogram for students in a BSc degree. Notice that both the sample mean (a measure of centre) and the sample standard deviation (a measure of spread or scale) both decrease (*i.e.,* it does appear that BSc students do receive lower A levels than BA students).

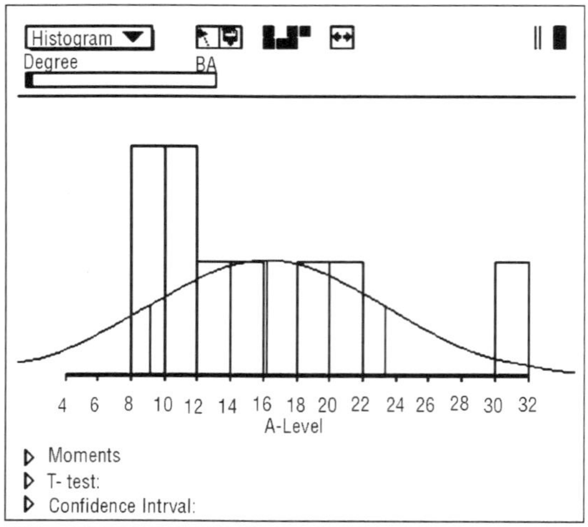

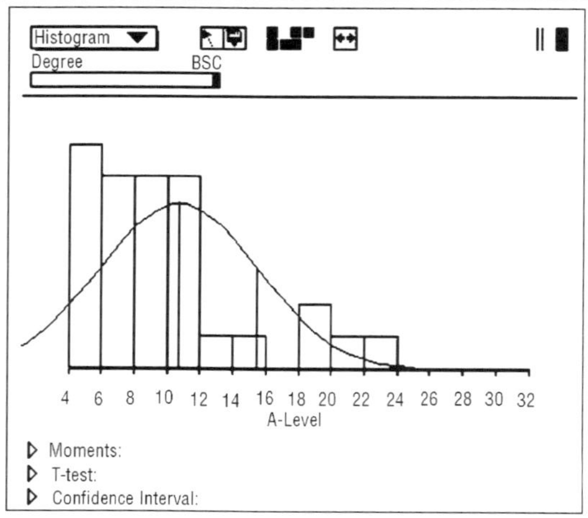

Select normalPlot from the Histogram popup menu to display the normal quantile plot. Select Robust Fit and Quantile LInes from the QuantPlot popup menu to show the following quantile plot:

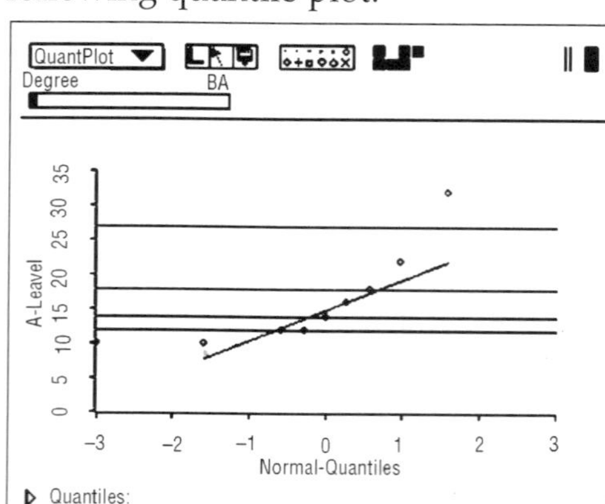

The intercept of the line (*i.e.*, the A-level value of the blue line for a normal-quantile value of 0) is an estimate of the centre and the slope is an estimate of the spread. Click on the right-hand side of theconditioning slider to display the A-leve normal quantile plot for students getting a BSc degree. Both the intercept and the slope decrease when BSc is selected. The BSc normal quantile plot is shown below.

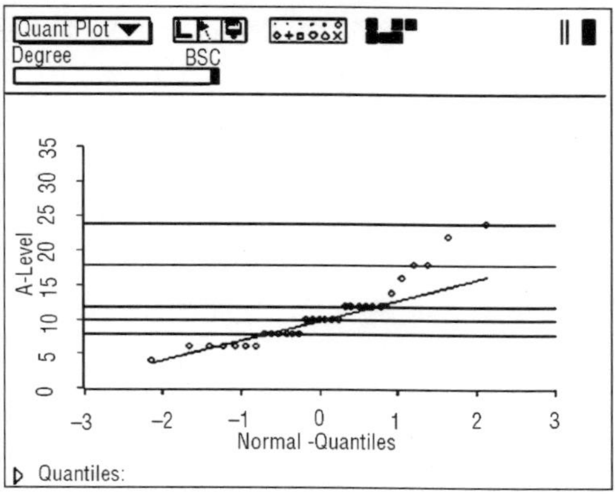

Thus, both the sample mean and standard deviation become smaller. We will now formally test that the population mean difference ($\mu_{BA} = \mu_{BSc}$) is 0. The formal test can be carried out using the A-level count by Degree dot plot. Click on the Means and Effect Test triangular reveal buttons and select Fit Means from the DotPlot popup menu to obtain the following plot:

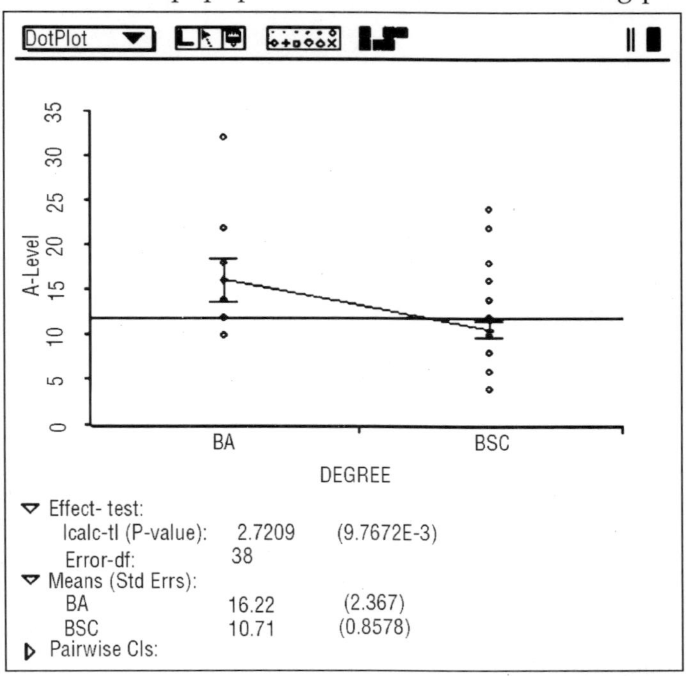

The interpretation of the error bars is given in Example #1 of the two-sample CI module. The sample BA A-level is clearly higher, but could the difference in means be attributable to chance, *i.e.*, is the observed difference too large to be considered plausible under the null hypothesis.

The calculated t-value is 2.72 based on 38 (= 9 + 31 –2) degrees of freedom. The probability of getting an observed t-value this large or larger assuming the null is true (*i.e.*, the P-value) is 0.0097 or about 1 in a 100. This is the two-sided alternative P-value and it supports the alternative hypothesis at a significancce level of 0.01. Since the BA sample mean exceeds the BSc mean, the one-sided P-value for the alternative $\mu_{BA} > \mu_{BSc}$ is 0.0049 (= 0.009767/2). The null is even more strongly rejected when the alternative is one-sided.

The assumptions of the two-sample problem were examined in Example #1 of the two-sample CI module. The assumptions of normality and equality of variances were both violated. However, it is likely that rejection of the null would be upheld using a more appropriate test since the P-value here is quite small and thus the evidence in favour of the alternaive is strong.

13

Analysis of Variance and MANOVA

Analysis of variance (ANOVA) is a collection of statistical models, and their associated procedures, in which the observed variance is partitioned into components due to different explanatory variables. In its simplest form ANOVA gives a statistical test of whether the means of several groups are all equal, and therefore generalizes Student's two-sample *t*-test to more than two groups.

ANALYSIS OF VARINCE AND COVARIANCE

The data can be from two different study desings.

Desing 1. We take 20 persons to the experiment. The persons are randoimized into two groups. We give the SLEEP1 pills for the group1 and SLEEP1 pills for the group2 ($n_1 = n_2 = 10$) and ask the length of the sleep after taking the pill.

If the sleepingtime is almost normally distributed and the groups are independent, we can compare the means with independent group t-test, where nullhypothese is H_0: $\mu_1 = \mu_2$

The test bases the difference of the groupmeans and comparing the difference to the standard error of the difference. If the variances in the groups do not differ, the standard error of the difference is

$$SE(\overline{x_1} - \overline{x_2}) = S\sqrt{\frac{1}{n_1} + \frac{1}{n_2}}$$

where s the standard deviation of the all observations. Here s = 1.96, so the standard error of the difference is

$$SE(\overline{x_1} - \overline{x_2}) = 0.877.$$

If the variances in the groups differ, the standard error of the difference is:

$$SE(\overline{x_1} - \overline{x_2}) = \sqrt{\frac{S_1^2}{n_1} + \frac{S_2^2}{n21}}$$

We get the test value t by deviding the difference with the standard error of the difference. Here the test value t = 1.0/0.877 = 1.14 is very small and from the t(18)-distribution, the probability is p = P(|t(18)| > 1.14) = 0.269 We must accept the H_0, because the risk to make an error when we reject H_0 is too large.

Design 2. We take 10 persons, witch take both pills. Half of the persons takes first the SLEEP1 pill and after a week the SLEEP2. An other half takes first the SLEEP2 and after a week the SLEEP1. Now the observation depend pairwise, and we can use paired t-test. The idea is to calculate the difference between the sleepingtimes after the pills and the test if the mean of the difference is zero

The differences can be seen in the table and the mean of the differences is 1.0 with standard deviation s = 0.47. The standard error of the mean is s/ $\sqrt{n}$, if the difference is normal distributed.

Here the,

$$\text{SE(x)} = 0.47/\sqrt{10 = 0.15}\ 10 = 0.15.$$

The test value t = 1.0/0.15 = 6.667 is large and the risk to make an error to reject the correct H_0 is p = P(|t(9)| > 6.667) = 0.000092 small enough to reject. The advantage in the first design is that the groups are independent and the treatment cannot effect to the other treatment (for exaple, residual of the SLEEP1 might affect to the sleepingtime after SLEEP2).

There is also designs, where the treatment can be done only once for one unit (for exaple learning experiments and the treatments, where an animal is hurt). The advantage in the second design is seen in the standard error of the measured statistic (mean). Here it is 0.15, when the independent groups gives 0.877. The longitudinal effect of the treatment is taken care varying the treatment order.

Some of the criteria for good experinmental designs are as follows:

- The analyses resulting from the design should probvide unambigous information on the primary objectives of the experiment. In particular the design should lead to unbiased estimates.
- The model and its underlying assumptions should be appropriate for the experimental material.
- The design should provide the maximum information with respect to the major objectives of the experiment per minimum amount of experimental effort.
- The design should provide some information with respect to all the objectives of the experiment.
- The design must be feasible within the working conditions that exist for the experimenter.

J.B. Wiener (1971) presents following picture:

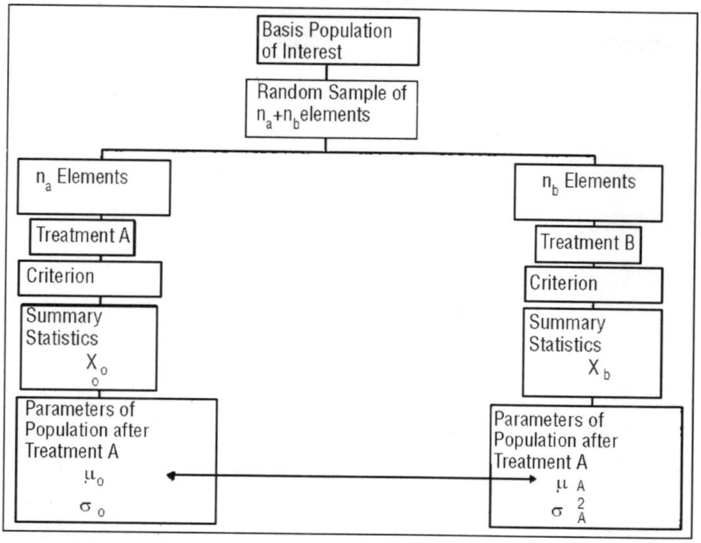

ONEWAY ANALYSIS OF VARIANCE

If the observations of the response variable can be assumed to be normal distributed, a model for an obseration in the saple is given by:

$$X_\mu = \mu + S\mu$$

Wher μ = Fixed but unknown Constant

ε_μ = Random Variable Distributed as $N(0, \sigma^2)$

We Can add the differencs between groups (treatments) into the model

$$X_\mu = \mu + j_\mu + \varepsilon_\mu$$

Where τ_j = Effect of treatment j.

We can compare two previous structural models with the likelihood ratio test.

If the variances in the groups (treatments) are similar, we can devide the variation of the observations into the variation of the groups (variation of the means) and the variation in the groups. The variation is measured with the sum of the squares: SS (Total) = SS (Between) SS (Within)

$$SS(Total) = \sum_{j-1}^{k} \sum_{j-1}^{ri} (Xij - \overline{X})^2$$

$$SS(Between) = \sum_{j-i}^{k} (\overline{X}ij - \overline{X}_j)^2$$

$$SS(Within) = \sum_{j-1}^{k} \sum_{j-1}^{ri} (Xij - \overline{X}_j)^2$$

The idea is to measure the variation of the groupmeans. If the the variation of the means is large compared to the variation in the groups (Within), the groups differ. We must take care of the number of the observations deviding the sum of squares with the degreece of freedoms:

$$MS(Within)\frac{SS(Within)}{n-k}\ MS(Between)=\frac{SS(Between)}{k-1}$$

The Mean sum of squares are Comparable and the test Value

$$\widetilde{F}\frac{MS(Between)}{MS(Within)}\sim F(k-1,n-k)$$

is Large, if the variation between the groupmeans is larger than than the variation in the groups. The significance of the test,

$$\mathrm{P}=P(F>\widetilde{F})$$

tells the Probability of the,

$$H_0:\mu_1=\mu_2=\ldots=\mu_k$$

COMPARISONS AMONG TREATMENT MEANS

The analysis of variance tells only if the groupmeans differ. It does not tell how the means differ. We compared two means with independent samples t-test, but it des not fit here, because the t-test does not take into consideration the variation of all groups and using the t-tests, we make an error, when we use unadjusted p-values.

Taking into consideration the variation of all observations, will give more power into the test (smaller p-values). Testing the same variable with several tests is like tossing a coin several times: with one toss the probability of tail is 1/2, but with 3 tosses the probability to get at least one tai is not 1/2.

If we use t-test comparing the means pairwise, the p-value should be adjusted with Bonferroni correction:

$$p_{adjusted}=1-(1-p_{test})^{\text{number of the comparisons}}$$

The main idea of the pairwise tests is to use the Bonferroni adjustment and replace the standard error of the difference between means with the standard error term from the all groups. Here is two exaples for the pairwise comparisons formulas:

$$q=\frac{\overline{X}_A-\overline{X}_B}{\sqrt{\frac{S^2}{2}\left(\frac{1}{n_A}+\frac{1}{n_B}\right)}}\ or\ q=\frac{\overline{X}_A-\overline{X}_B}{\sqrt{mMS(within)}}$$

where q is F -distributed with degreece of freedom number of treatments (k) and MS(Within) (n-k).

Several persons have presented the comparisons (for example Duncan, Sheffe, Tukey and Dunnet). Their methods bases on the algorithms to not compare the means, witch we already know to differ or not differ.

If the researcher can formulate a hypothese (and is interested in) to compare the groups of the groups, we can use the contrasts. For example the hypothese can be to compare two first groups to two second groups.

$$\frac{\overline{X}_1 - \overline{X}_2}{2} - \frac{\overline{X}_3 - \overline{X}_4}{2}$$

The comparison is usually presented with the coefficients (1/2, 1/2, -1/2 and -1/2). The result is close the zero, if the means do not differ. We can test the difference deviding the reslut by the MS(Within). This comparison method is called as contrasts. The researcher can test also if the polynom explains the difference between the groups. For exaple coefficients for the linear contrast can be 1, 2, 3 and 4.

BLOCKS AND COVARIATES

Often the researcher knows the factors, that affects to the response varible. In the study desing the researcher should make the treatmen groups equal due these factors. In the analysis of variance the effect of the confounding factors can be adjusted and therefore we get the test for the pure treatment effect. The confounding factors grow the variaten in the groups (MS(Within)) and it can be taken care usingblock design or covariance anaysis. If the confoundin factor is noncontinous, we can use the block desing and if it is continous, we can use covariance analysis.

The sum of squares in the block effect anova is:

SS(Total) = SS(Between) + SS(Block) + SS(Within).

Where the SS(Block) is from the SS(Within) in the simple anova. The idea of the covariance analysis to explain the response variable by the confounding covariate with the regression analysis and then we do the anova for the regression residuals.

Exaple Following SPSS listing is from the block desing covariance analysis, where we compare the differences between (tratment) groups. To get the "pure" effect of the treatment, we adjust the response with age (continous)and sex (noncontinous).

	Sum of		**Mean**		**Sig**
Source of Variation	Squares	DF	Square	F	of F
Covariates	44.491	1	44.491	34.291	.000
AGE	44.491	1	44.491	34.291	.000
Main Effects	15.718	2	7.859	6.057	.011

SEX	15.695	1	15.695	12.097	.003
GROUP	.026	1	.026	.020	.890
Explained	75.791	3	25.264	19.472	.000
Residual	20.759	16	1.297		
Total	96.550	19	5.082		

Here we can see, that the age affect significantly to the response variable (Sif of F = p =.000) and the sex affect too (Sig of F = p =.003). Whet the effect of the age and sex has been adjusted the groups do not differ (Sig of F = p =.890). The one-way anova table between groups:

Sum of Mean F F Source D.F. Squares Squares Ratio Prob. Between Groups 1.0500.0500.0093.9241. Within Groups 18 96.5000 5.3611 Total 19 96.5500.

MULTI-FACTOR ANALYSIS OF VARIANCE

If in the previous exaple the study question conserns also testing the effect of the sex (not just blocking variable), we can use two-way anova. With two-way anova we can get also an interaction effect, that tells us in thin exaple if the treatment effects differently to male than to female.

The SPSS listing from the two-way anova:

	Sum of		**Mean**		**Sig**
Source of	Squares	DF	Square	F	of F
Main Effects	31.300	2	15.650	3.913	.041
SEX	31.250	1	31.250	7.813	.013
GROUP	.050	1	.050	.013	.912
2-Way	1.250	1	1.250	.313	.584
Interactions					
SEX GROUP	1.250	1	1.250	.313	.584
Explained	32.550	3	10.850	2.713	.080
Residual	64.000	16	4.000		
Total	96.550	19	5.082		

Here we can se that the sex effects to the response variable (p =.013), the treatment (GROUP) does not (p =.912) and the treatment does not effect differently for sexes (p =.584).

The sum of squares in the two-way anova can be written

$$SS(Total) = SS(A) + SS(B) + SS(AB) + SS(Within),$$

where A and B are the factors and AB is the interaction term.

This can be generalized into the several factors design, where we get the multiway interaction terms. There is two kind of problems in multiway anova: there must be enough observations in the all groups and the intrpretation can be difficult or the multiway interaction can be meningless for the study problem. Example from Armitage & Berry. The response variable is the relative weight of right adrenal in mice obtained by crossing parents of four strains.

For each of the 16 combinations of parental strains, four mice were used. This is s three-factor design. The factors - mother's strain, father's strain and are not, of course, experimental treatments imposed by random allocaion.

Nevertheless they represent potential sources of variation whose main effects and interactions may be studied. Here is the variance table for the analysis:

	Sum of		**Mean**		**Signif**
Source of Variation	Squares	DF	Square	F	of F
Main Effects	15.470	7	2.210	55.915	.000
Sex	14.890	1	14.890	376.737	.000
Mother	.340	3	.113	2.864	.052
Father	.240	3	.080	2.025	.130
2way Interactions	1.718	15	.115	2.897	.006
Sex Mother	.394	3	.131	3.327	.032
Sex Father	.024	3	.008	.206	.891
Mother Father	1.299	9	.144	3.651	.003
3way Interactions	.261	9	.029	.735	.675
Sex Father Mother	.261	9	.029	.735	.675
Explained	17.449	31	.563	14.241	.000
Residual	1.265	32	.040		
Total	18.713	63	.297		

The sex affect to the adrenal (p =.000) and the effect of the mother's strain is almost significant (p =.052), but the father's strain does not effet (p =.130).

From the two-way interactions we can see, that the mother's strain effects differently the sexes (p =.032) and mother's strain has an interaction with the father's strain (p =.003) but the father's stain effects similar both sexes (p =.891). There is no three-way interaction (p =.675).

To closer analyse of the effects, we must draw a graph from the means:

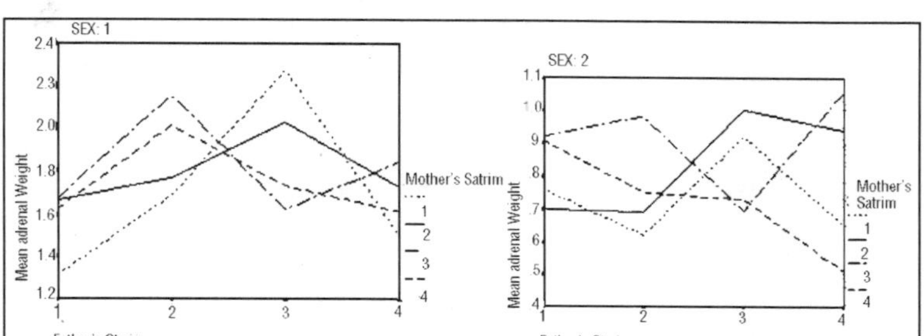

The means for the females (sex = 2, 0.5 - 1.1) is smaller than the means for males (sex = 1, 1.2 - 2.2). Effect of the mother's strain can be seen in the high values in the strain 3 and the small values in the strain 1. The interaction of the parents can bee seen in the crossing lines.

REPEATED MEASURES ANOVA

When the same units (animals, persons, patients) have been measured several times, the observations depend and the difference between the means should be tested with the repeated measures anova. The variation of the data can be devided into between persons and within people variation:

SS(Total) = SS(Between people) + SS(Within people),

where the Within people variation can be devided in to repeated and residual varition:

SS(Within people) = SS(Repeated) + SS(Residual).

The idea is to compre the repeated variation to the residual variation, when the between people variation is taken from the total variation. Example From the earlier exaple for the pairet t-test about the sleepin pills with repeated measures anova.

Within people sum of squares can be calculated subtracting the between people SS from the total SS:

$$\frac{\sum_{i=1}^{10}(y_{11} + y_{12})}{2}$$

In this example it is:

SS(Within people) = (72+62+32+32+62+52+...+52) – (132+62+... +112)/2 = 6.0,

witch is devided into repeated SS and residual SS:

$$\text{SS(Repeated)} = \frac{57^2 + 47^2}{10} - \frac{104^2}{2 \cdot 10} = 5.0$$

SS(Residual) = 6.0 – 5.0 = 1.0

The sum of squares are devided by the degreece of freedoms 5.0/1 = 5.0 and 1.0/9 = 0.111 and we get the mean sum of squares (MS). The ratio of the mean squares F = 5.0/0.111 = 45 is F-distributed with degreece of freedom 1 and 9. If the test value F is small, the means do not differ, but if F is large, the means differ.

From the F-distribution we get p = P(F > 45) = 0.000087. The result is same as in the paired t-test and if we had larger calculation accuracy, the p-value would be the same. We can do the repeated measures anova in the SPSS choosing SCALE (the first listing) or choosing Anova Models Repeated measures (the second listing):

Source of Variation	Sum of Sq.	DF	Mean Square	F	Prob.
Between People	67.2000	9	7.4667		
Within People	6.0000	10	.6000		
Between Measures	5.0000	1	5.0000	45.0000	.0001
Residual	1.0000	9	.1111		
Total	73.2000	19	3.8526		

Tests of Significance for T1 using UNIQUE sums of squares. Source of Variation SS DF MS F Sig of F WITHIN + RESIDUAL 67.20 9 7.47 CONSTANT 540.80 1 540.80 72.43.000

Tests of Significance for T2 using UNIQUE sums of squares. Source of Variation SS DF MS F Sig of F WITHIN +RESIDUAL 1.00 9.11 FACTOR1 5.00 1 5.00 45.00.000. The first is from the SCALE listing, where we can see all the sums. The second is ANOVA listing a test if the allover mean (CONSTANT) differs from zero. The third is also ANOVA listing.

Schematic representation of the analysis:

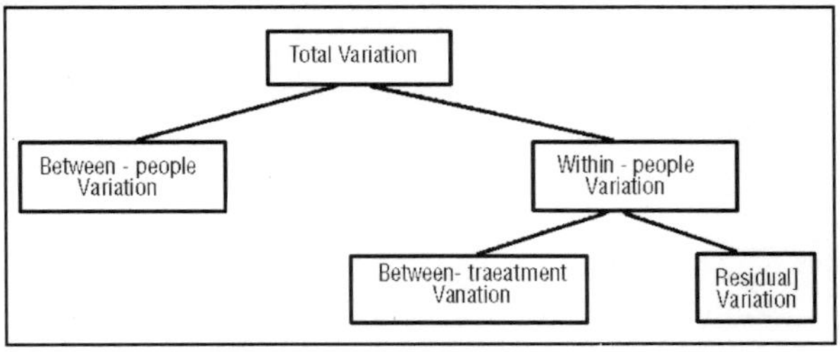

COMPARISONS AMONG REPEATED MEANS

There is all the same problems and possibilities in the repeated measurements pairwise comprisons as in the independendent groups anova. Unfortunately the "usual" statistical packages (like SPSS and SAS) do not offer the pairwise prosedures in the repeated anova like in the independent one-way anova.

The easiest way to compare the means in the dependent measurements is to use t-tests with Bonferroni correction. Neuman - Keuls method for the pairwise comparison is to calculate the difference between the means and devide it with the adjusted residual SS term:

$$q_1 = \frac{\overline{X}_j - \overline{X}_j}{\sqrt{nMS(\mathrm{Re}\,sidual)}}$$

The statistic q_r is F -distributed with degreese of reedom number of measurement and MS (Residual). Example Three repeated measurements in the hart rate with SPSS (repeated anova):Orthonormalized Transformation Matrix (Transposed)

	T1	T2	T3
RHR0	.577	.816	.000
RHR1	.577	.408	.707
RHR2	.577	.408	.707

Univariate F tests with (1,39) D. F.

Variable Hypoth. SS Error SS Hypoth. MS Error MS F Sig. of F T2 212.81667 1528.18333 212.81667 39.18419 5.43119.025 T3 96.80000 2244.20000 96.80000 57.54359 1.68220.202

AVERAGED Tests of Significance for RHR using UNIQUE sums of squares. Source of Variation SS DF MS F Sig of F WITHIN CELLS 3772.38 78 48.36 FACTOR1 309.62 2 154.81 3.20.046. Variable Mean Std Dev Minimum Maximum N Label RHR0 68.55 11.62 47 97 40 RHR1 66.82 12.04 44 92 40 RHR2 64.63 10.11 50 98 40.

We can see from the anova table that the means differ with the significant level p = 0.046. For the contrasts there is printed the transformation matrix, that shows that the cantrast T2 compares the 1. measurement to the others and the contrast T3 compares 2. and 3. measurements. Here the first measurement (mean) differs from the others (p = 0.025). The repeated measurements anova assumes the variables distributed with normal distribution and the variaces to be equal.

The researcher can test the normal distribution asuumption with Kruskall-Wallis test and the equality of the variances with Mauchly spericity test. The SPSS repeated measurements anova presents the Mauchly test:

Tests involving 'FACTOR1' WithinSubject Effect.

Mauchly sphericity test,

W =.93476 Chisquare approx. = 2.56370 with 2 D. F. Significance =.278

GreenhouseGeisser Epsilon =.93876 HuynhFeldt Epsilon =.98458 Lowerbound Epsilon =.50000 Averaged Tests of Significance that follow multivariate tests are equivalent to univariate or splitplot or mixedmodel approach to repeated measures.Epsilons may be used to adjust d.f. for the Averaged results.

The variances are equal with p = 0.278. If the variances would be unequal (p < 0.05), we could adjust the degreece of freedoms in the anova table with the epsilon coefficient with multiplying the degreece of freedoms with epsilon.

MIXED-MODEL ANOVA

If the researcher has the independent groups and the repeated measurements, the most important hypothese is to test if the change is different in the groups. Here we can use the mixed model anova, where the model is mixed from the independent factors and dependent factors. Example Partly prepared data, where rats has three groups (control and two treatments) and three measurements. The response variables is a latens in the labyrint: Tests of BetweenSubjects Effects. Tests of Significance for T1 using UNIQUE sums of squares Source of Variation SS DF MS F Sig of F WITHIN CELLS 2332270.92 122 19116.97 CONSTANT 7818915.35 1 7818915.3 409.00.000 GROUP 141934.33 2 70967.16 3.71.027

Tests involving 'FACTOR1' WithinSubject Effect. Mauchly sphericity test, W =.89427 Chisquare approx. = 13.52150 with 2 D. F. Significance =.001 GreenhouseGeisser Epsilon =.90438 HuynhFeldt Epsilon =.93224 Lowerbound Epsilon =.50000

Averaged Tests of Significance that follow multivariate tests are equivalent to univariate or splitplot or mixedmodel approach to repeated measures.Epsilons may be used to adjust d.f. for the Averaged results. Averaged Tests of Significance for LAT using UNIQUE sums of squares Source of Variation SS DF MS F Sig of F WITHIN CELLS 1989646.23 244 8154.29 FACTOR1 397285.84 2 198642.92 24.36.000 GROUP BY FACTOR1 62465.36 4 15616.34 1.92.109 In the first we can see that the groups differ (p = 0.027) over all the measurements.

The variance test (Mauchly) tells that the variances differ and we must use the adjustments (or to use MANOVA). In the last is the mixed model anova listing, where we must adjust the df:s (0.90438 × 244 = 220.669, 0.90438 × 2 = 1.80856 and 0.90438 × 4 = 3.618) and we get p < 0.000001 and p = 0.115. So there has been statistically significant change in heart rate, but the cange has not been different in the groups.

Here is a graph from the previous means:

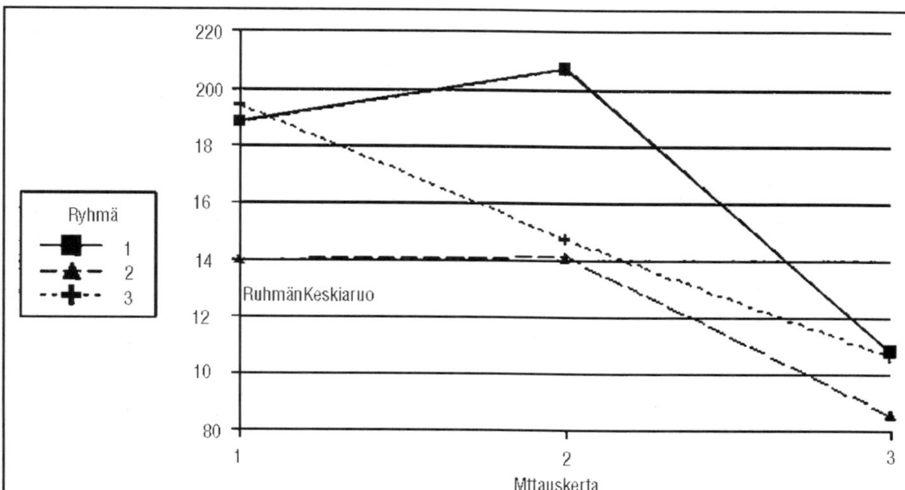

1	18	207	10
2	14	14	86
3	19	14	10

The graph shows, that the last measurement has the smallest mean. The group 1 seems to have largest means and the group 3 the smallest. Event the trens looks to be different, the interaction effect is not statistically significant. We can compare the trend of the group 1 to the other group trend with contrasts:

Estimates for T3 (CONT.)

GROUP BY FACTOR1

Parameter Coeff. Std. Err. t Value Sig. t Lower 95% CL Upper

2 25.614178 16.85742 1.51946.131 58.98513 7.75677 3 37.564796 16.65225 2.25584.026 70.52959 4.60000

The parameter 3 (can bee seen in the transformation matrix) compares the first group (control group) to the others and the the estimate is the interaction effect. The p-value 0.025 tells, that the change in the group 1 is different from the othser groups.

ABOUT MANOVA

If the variances in the repeated measurements anova are not equal (Maucly test) we can use the multivariate analysis of variance model to test the differences.

The MANOVA is not also so sensitive to the normal distribution assumption as anova. The MANOVA in not only a alternative to anova.

We can explain several response variables in one MANOVA and to do several kind of analysis. The basic idea of MANOVA is linear model.

For exaple a model for repeated measurements with several groups can be written:

$$X_{ijk} = \mu + T_j \pi_{kj} + \beta_j + \alpha\beta_{ij} + \beta\pi_{jki} + \varepsilon_{n(ijk)}$$

where the parameters μ, τ, π, ß, αß... tells the difference between the means in the groups and the measurements. The we just test the significance of the parameter (if the parameter differs from the zero).

The tests are called with the names of the persons, who have found the test (Pillais, Hotellings and Wilks). The assumption of the tests is the normal distribution of the residual.

Here is MANOVA listing from the previous rat example:

Multivariate Tests of Significance (S = 2, M = 1/2, N = 59 1/2)

Test Name Value Approx. F Hypoth. DF Error DF Sig. of F

Pillais.07250 2.29456 4.00 244.00.060 Hotellings.07668 2.30054 4.00 240.00.059 Wilks.92816 2.29773 4.00 242.00.060 Roys.06175

EFFECT.. FACTOR1

Multivariate Tests of Significance (S = 1, M = 0, N = 59 1/2)

Test Name Value Approx. F Hypoth. DF Error DF Sig. of F

Pillais.32139 28.65220 2.00 121.00.000 Hotellings.47359 28.65220 2.00 121.00.000 Wilks.67861 28.65220 2.00 121.00.000 Roys.32139

The first is the test of the interaction effect and it gives $p = 0.06$, so the canges has been closely statistically different. This result is closer to the previous analyse form the graph. The small different in the results may be because the response variable (latent) in not very normal distributes and the MANOVA works better here. The second is the test of the repeated measurement parameter and it gives the same result ($p < 0.001$) as the mixed model anova.

MANOVA procedures are multivariate, significance test analogues of various univariate ANOVA experimental designs. MANOVA, as with its univariate counterparts typically involve random assignment of participants to levels of one or more nominal independent variables; however, all participants are measured on several continuous dependent variables.

There are three basic variations of MANOVA:

- *Hotelling's T*: This is the MANOVA analogue of the two group T-test situation; in other words, one dichotomous independent variable, and multiple dependent variables.
- *One-Way MANOVA*: This is the MANOVA analogue of the one-way F situation; in other words, one multi-level nominal independent variable, and multiple dependent variables.
- *Factorial MANOVA*: This is the MANOVA analogue of the factorial ANOVA design; in other words, multiple nominal independent variables, and multiple dependent variables.

While all of the above MANOVA variations are used in somewhat different applications, they all have one feature in common: they form linear combinations of the dependent variables which best discriminate among the groups in the particular experimental design.

In other words, MANOVA is a test of the significance of group differences in some m-dimensional space where each dimension is defined by linear combinations of the original set of dependent variables. This relationship will be represented for each design in the following sections.

Why does MANOVA have to be so complicated? Why can't you just do separate ANOVA's for each dependent variables rather than form linear combinations of all dependent variables? There are several primary concerns to consider. First, very often and most likely, the dependent variables will be correlated with each other; thus, your findings from separate ANOVA's will be redundant and difficult to integrate. Second, the family-wise error rate becomes high; the odds of finding something significant simply because of chance rises with repeated use of the same sample of data.

Two Group Discrimination: Hotelling's T

The first diagram below represents the situation of two groups on a univariate dimension (y) where population differences are"real.

" The second diagram represents"real" population differences between group centroids--points defined by the y_1 and y_2 means for each group--of the two groups onyl and y_2.

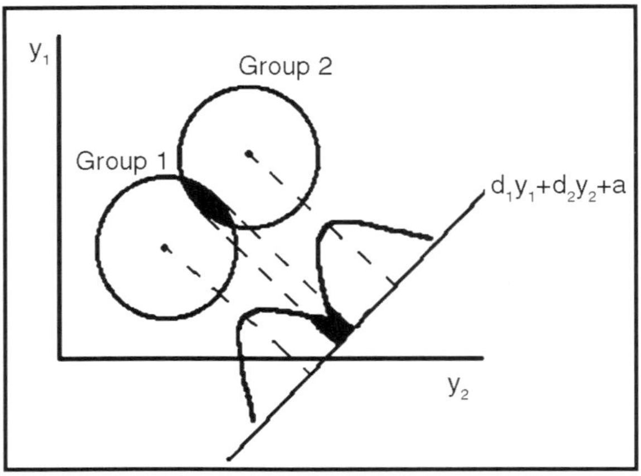

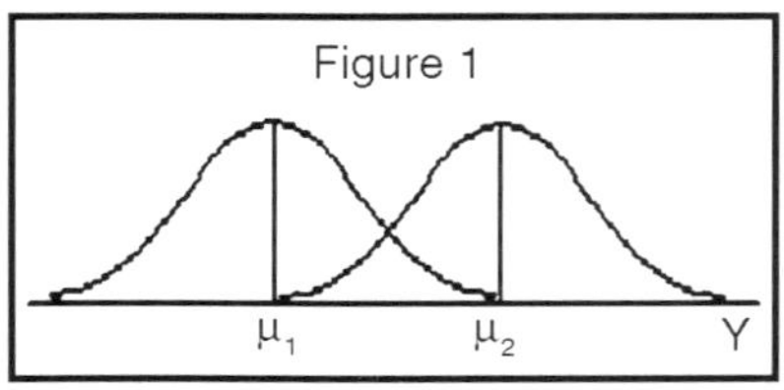

Figure 1

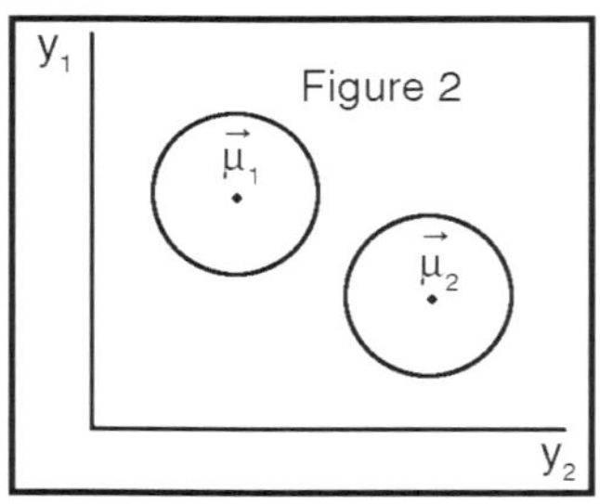

Figure 2

Now the task becomes the formation of linear combinations ofy1 and y_2 in order to:

- Correct for redundancy
- Maximally discriminate amongst the groups.

The discriminant weights of this composite (d_1 and d_2) are mathematically derived such that if we were to calculate a composite score for each participant, then the weights yield composite scores that will give the maximum F Ratio value. Essentially, this minimizes within-group variance and maximizes between-group variance. The new composite dimension (a linear combination) can be plotted against y_1 and y_2 to examine the univariate frequency distributions of the groups were overlap is minimized: With Hotelling's T we can construct only one dimension, and the test is basically checking whether the differences between the centroids are significantly different on the composite dimension. The statistic is distributed as an F, with q and n1 + n2 – q – 1 degrees of freedom, where q is the number of dependent variables.

The One-Way MANOVA

This MANOVA application is simply an extension of Hotelling's T to more than two groups. We have a single independent variable with more than two levels, and each participant is measured on several dependent variables. Rather than being limited to constructing a single dimension we can, the maximum number of dimensions that can be constructed in always the smaller of the following two values:

- The number of groups minus one,
- The number of continuous dependent variables.

The test statistic in this situation determines whether the whole set of composites can significantly discriminate the groups.

If more than one composite is constructed by the MANOVA procedure, all composite dimensions are uncorrelated. Therefore, information offered by the first composite is independent of that offered by the second, and so on. This occurs because the construction of each composite is built by using the residual of the previous composite.

Factorial MANOVA

This MANOVA application is truly a super-factorial design. Participants are nested under multiple treatment combinations (multiple independent variables) and are measured using several continuous dependent variables.

It maintains the advantages that factorial designs have over simple one-way designs (*i.e.*, interaction information) plus it can form composite dimensions specific to each effect in the design which optimally separate the groups being evaluated for each effect. In other words, factorial MANOVA involves the calculation of several sets of composite variables and each set is specific to a particular effect.

For factorial MANOVA, we can form a total number of uncorrelated linear combinations of all dependent variables for each effect that is equal to the smaller of the number of degrees of freedom for that effect (Number of cells minus one) or the number of dependent variables. For example, in a 3 x 4 design with 20 dependent variables we can examine the following:

- *The A Effect*: As in any factorial design, we examine the A main effect by collapsing across all other variables. Since we have three levels of A (dfA = 2), we can form a maximum of 2 independent linear composite dimensions (like those in Hotelling's T). Then calculate Lambda to evaluate whether these two dimensions as a set significantly discriminate the A groups.
- *The B Effect*: By the same logic as above, we can form a total of 3

linear combinations. Again, calculate Lambda to determine whether the B groups differ significantly on all three dimensions.

- *The AB Interaction*: Since the degrees of freedom for the interaction equals six, we can calculate six independent composite dimensions on which we can calculate Lambda to determine if we have a significant interaction.

Solving the RMD Problem: The Poor Technique

The MANOVA procedure does have another application. The Repeated Measures design and the mixed design both assume compound symmetry (*i.e.* the variances are equal among groups and that the covariances among levels are equal). When this is violated, each independent variable can be treated as a separate dependent variable (using dummy coding). A MANOVA is then performed in order to look for effects, and a significant linear combination of variables would indicate a significant difference between the original levels. This can also be extended to the violation of compound symmetry for several dependent variables; in this case, the procedure is known as a doubly multivariate analysis.

14

Nonparametric Tests

Occasionally, the assumptions of the t-tests are seriously violated. In particular, if the type of data you have is ordinal in nature and not at least interval. On such occasions an alternative approach is to use nonparametric tests. We are not going to place much emphasis on them in this unit as they are only occasionally used. But you should be aware of them and have some familiarity with them. Nonparametric tests are also referred to as distribution-free tests. These tests have the obvious advantage of not requiring the assumption of normality or the assumption of homogeneity of variance. They compare medians rather than means and, as a result, if the data have one or two outliers, their influence is negated. Parametric tests are preferred because, in general, for the same number of observations, they are more likely to lead to the rejection of a false hull hypothesis. That is, they have more power. This greater power stems from the fact that if the data have been collected at an interval or ratio level, information is lost in the conversion to ranked data (*i.e.*, merely ordering the data from the lowest to the highest value).

The following table gives the non-parametric analogue for the paired sample t-test and the independent samples t-test. There is no obvious comparison for the one sample t-test. Chi-square is a one-sample test and there are alternatives to chi-square but we will not consider them further. Chi-square is already a non-parametric test. Pearson's correlation also has non-parametric alternative (Spearman's correlation) but we will not deal with it further either.

There are a wide range of alternatives for the two group t-tests, the ones listed are the most commonly use ones and are the defaults in SPSS. Generally, running nonparametric procedures is very similar to running parametric procedures, because the same design principle is being assessed in each case. So, the process of identifying variables, selecting options, and running the procedure are very similar. The final p-value is what determines significance or not in the same way as the parametric tests. SPSS gives the option of two or three analogues for each type of parametric test, but you need to know only the ones cited in the table. Same practice with these tests is given in Assignment II.

Parametric test	Non-parametric analogue
One-sample t-test	Nothing quite comparable
Paired sample t-test	Wilcoxon T Test
Independent samples t-test	Mann-Whitney U Test
Pearson's correlation	Spearman's correlation

BRIEF REVIEW OF THE IDEA OF SIGNIFICANCE TESTING

To understand the idea of *nonparametric* statistics (the term *nonparametric* was first used by Wolfowitz, 1942) first requires a basic understanding of parametric statistics. The *Elementary Concepts* chapter of the manual introduces the concept of statistical significance testing based on the sampling distribution of a particular statistic (you may want to review that chapter before reading on).

In short, if we have a basic knowledge of the underlying distribution of a variable, then we can make predictions about how, in repeated samples of equal size, this particular statistic will "behave," that is, how it is distributed.

For example, if we draw 100 random samples of 100 adults each from the general population, and compute the mean height in each sample, then the distribution of the standardized means across samples will likely approximate the normal distribution (to be precise, Student's *t* distribution with 99 degrees of freedom; see below).

Now imagine that we take an additional sample in a particular city ("Tallburg") where we suspect that people are taller than the average population.

If the mean height in that sample falls outside the upper 95% tail area of the *t*distribution then we conclude that, indeed, the people of Tallburg are taller than the average population.

ARE MOST VARIABLES NORMALLY DISTRIBUTED?

In the above example we relied on our knowledge that, in repeated samples of equal size, the standardized means (for height) will be distributed following the *t*distribution (with a particular mean and variance).

However, this will only be true if in the population the variable of interest (height in our example) is normally distributed, that is, if the distribution of people of particular heights follows the normal distribution (the bell-shape distribution).

For many variables of interest, we simply do not know for sure that this is the case. For example, is income distributed normally in the population? — probably not. The incidence rates of rare diseases are not normally distributed in the population, the number of car accidents is also not normally distributed, and neither are very many other variables in which a researcher might be interested.

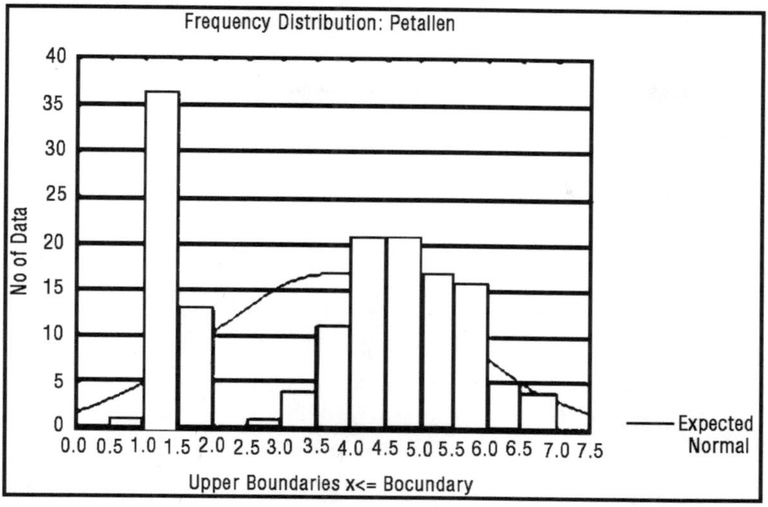

SAMPLE SIZE

Another factor that often limits the applicability of tests based on the assumption that the sampling distribution is normal is the size of the sample of data available for the analysis (*sample size;n*).

We can assume that the sampling distribution is normal even if we are not sure that the distribution of the variable in the population is normal, as long as our sample is large enough (*e.g.*, 100 or more observations). However, if our sample is very small, then those tests can be used only if we are sure that the variable is normally distributed, and there is no way to test this assumption if the sample is small.

PROBLEMS IN MEASUREMENT

Applications of tests that are based on the normality assumptions are further limited by a lack of precise measurement. For example, let us consider a study where grade point average (*GPA*) is measured as the major variable of interest.

Is an A average twice as good as a C average? Is the difference between a B and an A average comparable to the difference between a D and a C average? Somehow, the GPA is a crude measure of scholastic accomplishments that only allows us to establish a rank ordering of students from "good" students to "poor" students.

This general measurement issue is usually discussed in statistics textbooks in terms of *types of measurement* or *scale of measurement*. Without going into too much detail, most common statistical techniques such as analysis of variance (and *t*- tests), regression, etc.

Assume that the underlying measurements are at least of *interval,* meaning that equally spaced intervals on the scale can be compared in a meaningful manner (e.g, *B* minus *A* is equal to *D* minus *C*). However, as in our example, this assumption is very often not tenable, and the data rather represent a *rank* ordering of observations (ordinal) rather than precise measurements.

PARAMETRIC AND NONPARAMETRIC METHODS

Hopefully, after this somewhat lengthy introduction, the need is evident for statistical procedures that allow us to process data of "low quality," from small samples, on variables about which nothing is known (concerning their distribution).

Specifically, nonparametric methods were developed to be used in cases when the researcher knows nothing about the parameters of the variable of interest in the population (hence the name *nonparametric*).

In more technical terms, nonparametric methods do not rely on the estimation of parameters (such as the mean or the standard deviation) describing the distribution of the variable of interest in the population. Therefore, these methods are also sometimes (and more appropriately) called *parameter-free* methods or *distribution-free* methods.

BRIEF OVERVIEW OF NONPARAMETRIC METHODS

Basically, there is at least one nonparametric equivalent for each parametric general type of test. In general, these tests fall into the following categories:

- Tests of differences between groups (independent samples);
- Tests of differences between variables (dependent samples);
- Tests of relationships between variables.

Differences Between Independent Groups

Usually, when we have two samples that we want to compare concerning their mean value for some variable of interest, we would use the *t*-test for independent samples); nonparametric alternatives for this test are the *Wald-Wolfowitz runs test*, the *Mann-Whitney U test*, and the *Kolmogorov-Smirnov two-sample test*. If we have multiple groups, we would use analysis of variance.

Differences Between Dependent Groups

If we want to compare two variables measured in the same sample we would customarily use the *t-test for dependent samples* (in Basic Statistics for example, if we wanted to compare students' math skills at the beginning of the semester with their skills at the end of the semester).

Nonparametric alternatives to this test are the *Sign* test and *Wilcoxon's matched pairs* test. If the variables of interest are dichotomous in nature (*i.e.*, "pass" vs. "no pass") then *McNemar's Chi-square*http://www.statsoft.com/textbook/glosc.html - Chi-square Distribution test is appropriate. If there are more than two variables that were measured in the same sample, then we would customarily use repeated measures ANOVA.

Nonparametric alternatives to this method are *Friedman's two-way analysis of variance* and *Cochran Q* test (if the variable was measured in terms of categories, *e.g.*, "passed" vs. "failed"). Cochran Q is particularly useful for measuring changes in frequencies (proportions) across time.

Relationships Between Variables

To express a relationship between two variables one usually computes the correlation coefficient. Nonparametric equivalents to the standard correlation coefficient are*Spearman R, Kendall Tau,* and coefficient Gamma. If the two variables of interest are categorical in nature (*e.g.*, "passed" vs. "failed" by "male" vs. "female") appropriate nonparametric statistics for testing the relationship between the two variables are the *Chi-square* test, the *Phi* coefficient, and the *Fisher exact* test.

In addition, a simultaneous test for relationships between multiple cases is available: *Kendall coefficient of concordance*. This test is often used for expressing inter-rater agreement among independent judges who are rating (ranking) the same stimuli.

DESCRIPTIVE STATISTICS

When one's data are not normally distributed, and the measurements at best contain rank order information, then computing the standard descriptive statistics (*e.g.*, mean, standard deviation) is sometimes not the most informative way to summarize the data.

For example, in the area of psychometrics it is well known that the *rated* intensity of a stimulus (*e.g.*, perceived brightness of a light) is often a logarithmic function of the actual intensity of the stimulus (brightness as measured in objective units of *Lux*). In this example, the simple mean rating (sum of ratings divided by the number of stimuli) is not an adequate summary of the average actual intensity of the stimuli.

(In this example, one would probably rather compute the geometric mean.). Nonparametrics and Distributions will compute a wide variety of measures of location (mean, median, mode, etc.) and dispersion (variance, average deviation, quartile range, etc.) to provide the "complete picture" of one's data.

WHEN TO USE WHICH METHOD

It is not easy to give simple advice concerning the use of nonparametric procedures. Each nonparametric procedure has its peculiar sensitivities and blind spots. For example, the Kolmogorov-Smirnov two-sample test is not only sensitive to differences in the location of distributions (for example, differences in means) but is also greatly affected by differences in their shapes. The Wilcoxon matched pairs test assumes that one can rank order the magnitude of differences in matched observations in a meaningful manner.

If this is not the case, one should rather use the Sign test. In general, if the result of a study is important (*e.g.*, does a very expensive and painful drug therapy help people get better?), then it is always advisable to run different nonparametric tests; should discrepancies in the results occur contingent upon which test is used, one should try to understand why some tests give different results.

On the other hand, nonparametric statistics are less statistically powerful (sensitive) than their parametric counterparts, and if it is important to detect even small effects (*e.g.*, is this food additive harmful to people?) one should be very careful in the choice of a test statistic.

Large Data Sets and Nonparametric Methods

Nonparametric methods are most appropriate when the sample sizes are small. When the data set is large (*e.g.*, $n > 100$) it often makes little sense to use nonparametric statistics at all.

The Elementary Concepts chapter of the manual briefly discusses the idea of the *central limit theorem*. In a nutshell, when the samples become very large, then the sample means will follow the normal distribution even if the respective variable is not normally distributed in the population, or is not measured very well.

Thus, parametric methods, which are usually much more sensitive (*i.e.*, have more *statistical power*) are in most cases appropriate for large samples. However, the tests of significance of many of the nonparametric statistics described here are based on asymptotic (large sample) theory; therefore, meaningful tests can often not be performed if the sample sizes become too small. Please refer to the descriptions of the specific tests to learn more about their power and efficiency.

Nonparametric Correlations

The following are three types of commonly used nonparametric correlation coefficients (Spearman R, Kendall Tau, and Gamma coefficients). Note that the chi-square statistic computed for two-way frequency tables, also provides a careful measure of a relation between the two (tabulated) variables, and unlike the correlation measures listed below, it can be used for variables that are measured on a simple nominal scale.

Spearman R

Spearman R assumes that the variables under consideration were measured on at least an ordinal (rank order) scale, that is, that the individual observations can be ranked into two ordered series. Spearman R can be thought of as the regular Pearson product moment correlation coefficient, that is, in terms of proportion of variability accounted for, except that Spearman R is computed from ranks.

Kendall Tau

Kendall tau is equivalent to Spearman R with regard to the underlying assumptions. It is also comparable in terms of its statistical power. However, Spearman R and Kendall tau are usually not identical in magnitude because their underlying logic as well as their computational formulas are very different. Siegel and Castellan (1988) express the relationship of the two measures in terms of the inequality:

-1 £ 3 * Kendall Tau – 2 * Spearman R £ 1

More importantly, Kendall tau and Spearman R imply different interpretations: Spearman R can be thought of as the regular Pearson product moment correlation coefficient, that is, in terms of proportion of variability accounted for, except that Spearman R is computed from ranks.

Kendall tau, on the other hand, represents a probability, that is, it is the difference between the probability that in the observed data the two variables are in the same order versus the probability that the two variables are in different orders.

Gamma

The Gamma statistic is preferable to Spearman R or Kendall tau when the data contain many tied observations. In terms of the underlying assumptions, Gamma is equivalent to Spearman R or Kendall tau; in terms of its interpretation and computation it is more similar to Kendall tau than Spearman R. In short, Gamma is also a probability; specifically, it is computed as the difference between the probability that the rank ordering of the two variables agree minus the probability that they disagree, divided by 1 minus the probability of ties. Thus, Gamma is basically equivalent to Kendall tau, except that ties are explicitly taken into account.

A gamma test tests the strength of association of the cross tabulated data when both variables are measured at the ordinal level. It makes no adjustment for either table size or ties. Values range from -1 (100% negative association, or perfect inversion) to +1 (100% positive association, or perfect agreement). A value of zero indicates the absence of association. This test statistic is also known as Goodman and Kruskal's gamma (which is distinct from Goodman and Kruskal's lambda).

The value of a gamma test statistic, G, depends on two quantities:

- Ns, the number of pairs of cases ranked in the same order on both variables (number of concordant pairs),
- Nd, the number of pairs of cases ranked differently on the variables (number of discordant pairs).

Then,

$$G = \frac{N_s - N_d}{N_s + N_d}$$

The test statistic can be regarded as estimating the theoretical quantity γ, where

$$\gamma = \frac{P_s - P_d}{P_s + P_d}$$

and where for example Ps is the probability that a randomly selected pair of observations will place in the same order by both variables.

Critical values for the gamma tests statistic are sometimes found by using an approximation, whereby a transformed value, Z of the test statistic is referred to a normal or Student t distribution, where

$$Z = G\sqrt{\frac{N_s + N_d}{N(1 - G^2)}},$$

and where N is the number of observations (not the number of pairs).

15

Quality Management

Quality: a customer's perception of the value of a product or service; organizations, theorists, and dictionaries define it differently.

Well-known definitions include:

- Conformance to requirements" (Crosby)
- The efficient production of the quality that the market expects" (Deming)
- Fitness for use"; "product performance and freedom from deficiencies" (Juran)
- The total composite product and service characteristics of marketing, engineering, manufacturing, and maintenance through which the product and service in use will meet the expectations of the customer" (Felgenbaum)
- Anything that can be improved" (Imal)
- Meeting or exceeding customer expectations at a cost that represents value to them" (Harrington)
- Does not impart loss to society" (Taguchi)
- The totality of features and characteristics of a product or service that bear on its ability to satisfy a given need" (American Society for Quality Control)
- Degree of excellence" (Webster's Third New International Dictionary)

Quality management is a method for ensuring that all the activities necessary todesign, develop and implement a product or service are effective and efficient withrespect to the system and its performance. Quality management can be consideredto have three main components: quality control, quality assurance and qualityimprovement. Quality management is focused not only on product quality, but alsothe means to achieve it. Quality management therefore uses quality assurance andcontrol of processes as well as products to achieve more consistent quality.

COMPONENT OF QUALITY MANAGEMENT

There are the main components of Quality Management.

Components:

- Quality Control
- Quality Assurance
- Quality Improvement
- Software Quality Factors

Quality Control

Quality control is a process employed to ensure a certain level of quality in a product or service. It may include whatever actions a business deems necessary to provide for the control and verification of certain characteristics of a product or service. The basic goal of quality control is to ensure that the products, services, or processes provided meet specific requirements and are dependable, satisfactory, and fiscally sound. Essentially, quality control involves the examination of a product, service, or process for certain minimum levels of quality. The goal of a quality control team is to identify products or services that do not meet a companyâ€™s specified standards of quality.

If a problem is identified, the job of a quality control team or professional may involve stopping production temporarily. Depending on the particular service or product, as well as the type of problem identified, production or implementation may not cease entirely. Usually, it is not the job of a quality control team or professional to correct quality issues. Typically, other individuals are involved in the process of discovering the cause of quality issues and fixing them.

Once such problems are overcome, the product, service, or process continues production or implementation as usual. Quality control can cover not just products, services, and processes, but also people. Employees are an important part of any company. If a company has employees that don't have adequate skills or training, have trouble understanding directions, or are misinformed, quality may be severely diminished. When quality control is considered in terms of human beings, it concerns correctable issues. However, it should not be confused with human resource issues.

Often, quality control is confused with quality assurance. Though the two are very similar, there are some basic differences. Quality control is concerned with the product, while quality assurance is process "oriented". Even with such a clear-cut difference defined, identifying the differences between the two can be hard. Basically, quality control involves evaluating a product, activity, process, or service. By contrast, quality assurance is designed to make sure processes are sufficient to meet objectives. Simply put, quality assurance ensures a product or service is manufactured, implemented, created, or produced in the right way; while quality control evaluates whether or not the end result is satisfactory.

Example: Quality Control refers to quality related activities associated with the creation of project deliverables. Quality control is used to verify that deliverables are of acceptable quality and that they are complete and correct. Examples of quality control activities include deliverable peer reviews and the testing process.

Quality Assurance refers to the process used to create the deliverables, and can be performed by a manager, client, or even a third-party reviewer. Examples of quality assurance include process checklists and project audits. If your project gets audited, for instance, an auditor might not be able to tell if the content of a specific deliverable is acceptable (quality control). However, the auditor should be able to tell if the deliverable seems acceptable based on the process used to create it (quality assurance).

That's why project auditors can perform a quality assurance review on your project, even if they do not know the specifics of what you are delivering. They don't know your project, but they know what good processes look like. Here's an example to drive home the point. Let's say a project manager asked the sponsor to approve the Business Requirements Report. If you were the sponsor, how would you validate that the business requirements seemed complete and correct? One solution would be for you to actually review the document and the business requirements. If you did that, you would be performing a quality control activity, since your actions would be based on validating the deliverable itself. However, let's say the document was thirty pages long and that you (as the sponsor) did not have the expertise, the time, or the inclination to do a specific content review. In that case, you wouldn't ask to review the document itself. Instead, you would ask the project manager to describe the process used to create the document. Let us say you received the following reply:

Project manager - "I gathered eight of your major users in a facilitated session. After the meeting, I documented the requirements and asked the group for their feedback, modifications, etc. I then took these updated requirements to representatives from the Legal, Finance, Manufacturing and Purchasing groups and they added requirements that were needed to support company standards. We then had a meeting with the four managers in your area that are most impacted by this system. These managers added a few more requirements. I then asked your four managers to sign off on the requirements and you can see their signatures on the last page." If you were the sponsor, would you now feel comfortable to sign the requirements? If it were me, I would feel pretty comfortable. That's the difference. Quality control activities are focused on the deliverable itself. Quality assurance activities are focused on the process used to create the deliverable. They are both powerful techniques and both must be performed to ensure that the deliverables meet your customers quality requirements.

Quality Assurance

Quality assurance, or QA for short, is the activity of providing evidence needed to establish quality in work, and that activities that require good quality are being performed effectively. All those planned or systematic actions necessary to provide enough confidence that a product or service will satisfy the given requirements for quality.

Quality Assurance Activities

Quality assurance covers all activities from design, development, production, installation, servicing and documentation. This introduced the rules: "fit for purpose" and "do it right the first time". It includes the regulation of the quality of raw materials, assemblies, products and components; services related to production; and management, production, and inspection processes. One of the most widely used paradigms for QA management is the PDCA (Plan-Do-Check-Act) approach, also known as the Shewhart cycle.

- *Failure testing:* Quality assurance covers all activities from design, development, production, installation, servicing and documentation. This introduced the rules: "fit for purpose" and "do it right the first time". It includes the regulation of the quality of raw materials, assemblies, products and components; services related to production; and management, production, and inspection processes.
- *Statistical control:* Many organizations use statistical process control to bring the organization to Six Sigma levels of quality, in other words, so that the likelihood of an unexpected failure is confined to six standard deviations on the normal distribution. This probability is less than four one-millionths. Items controlled often include clerical tasks such as order-entry as well as conventional manufacturing tasks.

Traditional statistical process controls in manufacturing operations usually proceed by randomly sampling and testing a fraction of the output. Variances of critical tolerances are continuously tracked, and manufacturing processes are corrected before bad parts can be produced.

- *ISO 17025:* ISO 17025 is an international standard that specifies the general requirements for the competence to carry out tests and or calibrations. There are 15 management requirements and 10 technical requirements. These requirements outline what a laboratory must do to become accredited.

Management system refers to the organization's structure for managing its processes or activities that transform inputs of resources into a product or service which meets the organization's objectives, such as satisfying the customer's quality requirements, complying with regulations, or meeting environmental objectives.

For software development organization, CMMI (Capability Maturity Model Integration) standards are widely used to measure the Quality Assurance. These CMMI standards can be divided in to 5 steps, which a software development company can achieve by performing different quality improvement activities within the organization.

Company Quality

During the 1980s, the concept of "company quality" with the focus on management and people came to the fore. It was realised that, if all departments approached quality with an open mind, success was possible if the management led the quality improvement process.

The company-wide quality approach places an emphasis on four aspects:

- Elements such as controls, job management, adequate processes, performance and integrity criteria and identification of records
- Competence such as knowledge, skills, experience, qualifications
- Soft elements, such as personnel integrity, confidence, organizational culture, motivation, team spirit and quality relationships.
- Infrastructure (as it enhances or limits functionality)

  The quality of the outputs is at risk if any of these aspects is deficient in any way.

The approach to quality management given here is therefore not limited to the manufacturing theatre only but can be applied to any business activity:

- Design work
- Administrative services
- Consulting
- Banking
- Insurance
- Computer software
- Retailing
- Transportation

It comprises a quality improvement process, which is generic in the sense it can be applied to any of these activities and it establishes a behaviour pattern, which supports the achievement of quality. This in turn is supported by quality management practices which can include a number of business systems and which are usually specific to the activities of the business unit concerned. In manufacturing and construction activities, these business practices can be equated to the models for quality assurance defined by the International Standards contained in the ISO 9000 series and the specified Specifications for quality systems. Still, in the system of Company Quality, the work being carried out was shop floor inspection which did not control the major quality problems. This led to quality assurance or total quality control, which has come into being recently.

Concepts and Definitions of Software Quality Assurance (SQA)

Software Quality Assurance (SQA) is defined as a planned and systematic approach to the evaluation of the quality of and adherence to software product standards, processes, and procedures. SQA includes the process of assuring that standards and procedures are established and are followed throughout the software acquisition life cycle. Compliance with agreed-upon standards and procedures is evaluated through process monitoring, product evaluation, and audits. Software development and control processes should include quality assurance approval points, where an SQA evaluation of the product may be done in relation to the applicable standards.

Standards and Procedures

Establishing standards and procedures for software development is critical, since these provide the framework from which the software evolves. Standards are the established criteria to which the software products are compared. Procedures are the established criteria to which the development and control processes are compared.

Standards and procedures establish the prescribed methods for developing software; the SQA role is to ensure their existence and adequacy. Proper documentation of standards and procedures is necessary since the SQA activities of process monitoring, product evaluation and auditing rely upon unequivocal definitions to measure project compliance. Types of standards include:

Documentation Standards specify form and content for planning, control, and product documentation and provide consistency throughout a project. The NASA Data Item Descriptions (DIDs) are documentation standards. Design Standards specify the form and content of the design product. They provide rules and methods for translating the software requirements into the software design and for representing it in the design documentation.

Code Standards specify the language in which the code is to be written and define any restrictions on use of language features. They define legal language structures, style conventions, rules for data structures and interfaces, and internal code documentation. Procedures are explicit steps to be followed in carrying out a process. All processes should have documented procedures. Examples of processes for which procedures are needed are configuration management, nonconformance reporting and corrective action, testing, and formal inspections. If developed according to the NASA DID, the Management Plan describes the software development control processes, such as configuration management, for which there have to be procedures, and contains a list of the product standards. Standards are to be documented according to the Standards and Guidelines DID in the Product Specification. The planning activities required to assure that both products and processes comply with designated standards and procedures are described in the QA portion of the Management Plan.

Software Quality Assurance Activities

Product evaluation and process monitoring are the SQA activities that assure the software development and control processes described in the project's Management Plan are correctly carried out and that the project's procedures and standards are followed. Products are monitored for conformance to standards and processes are monitored for conformance to procedures. Audits are a key technique used to perform product evaluation and process monitoring. Review of the Management Plan should ensure that appropriate SQA approval points are built into these processes. Product evaluation is an SQA activity that assures standards are being followed. Ideally, the first products monitored by SQA should be the project's standards and procedures.

SQA assures that clear and achievable standards exist and then evaluates compliance of the software product to the established standards. Product evaluation assures that the software product reflects the requirements of the applicable standard(s) as identified in the Management Plan. Process monitoring is an SQA activity that ensures that appropriate steps to carry out the process are being followed. SQA monitors processes by comparing the actual steps carried out with those in the documented procedures. The Assurance section of the Management Plan specifies the methods to be used by the SQA process monitoring activity.

A fundamental SQA technique is the audit, which looks at a process and/ or a product in depth, comparing them to established procedures and standards. Audits are used to review management, technical, and assurance processes to provide an indication of the quality and status of the software product. The purpose of an SQA audit is to assure that proper control procedures are being followed, that required documentation is maintained, and that the developer's status reports accurately reflect the status of the activity. The SQA product is an audit report to management consisting of findings and recommendations to bring the development into conformance with standards and/or procedures.

SQA RELATIONSHIPS TO OTHER ASSURANCE ACTIVITIES

Some of the more important relationships of SQA to other management and assurance activities are described below.

- *Configuration Management Monitoring:* SQA assures that software Configuration Management (CM) activities are performed in accordance with the CM plans, standards, and procedures. SQA reviews the CM plans for compliance with software CM policies and requirements and provides follow-up for nonconformances. SQA audits the CM functions for adherence to standards and procedures and prepares reports of its findings.

The CM activities monitored and audited by SQA include baseline control, configuration identification, configuration control, configuration status accounting, and configuration authentication. SQA also monitors and audits the software library. SQA assures that: Baselines are established and consistently maintained for use in subsequent baseline development and control. Software configuration identif-ication is consistent and accurate with respect to the numbering or naming of computer programs, software modules, software units, and associated software documents.

Configuration control is maintained such that the software configuration used in critical phases of testing, acceptance, and delivery is compatible with the associated documentation. Configuration status accounting is performed accurately including the recording and reporting of data reflecting the software's configuration identification, proposed changes to the configuration identification, and the implementation status of approved changes. Software configuration authentication is established by a series of configuration reviews and audits that exhibit the performance required by the software requirements specification and the configuration of the software is accurately reflected in the software design documents. Software development libraries provide for proper handling of software code, documentation, media, and related data in their various forms and versions from the time of their initial approval or acceptance until they have been incorporated into the final media. Approved changes to baselined software are made properly and consistently in all products, and no unauthorized changes are made.

- *Verification and Validation Monitoring:* SQA assures Verification and Validation (V&V) activities by monitoring technical reviews, inspections, and walkthroughs. The SQA role in formal testing is described in the next section. The SQA role in reviews, inspections, and walkthroughs is to observe, participate as needed, and verify that they were properly conducted and documented. SQA also ensures that any actions required are assigned, documented, scheduled, and updated.

Formal software reviews should be conducted at the end of each phase of the life cycle to identify problems and determine whether the interim product meets all applicable requirements. Examples of formal reviews are the Preliminary Design Review (PDR), Critical Design Review (CDR), and Test Readiness Review (TRR).

A review looks at the overall picture of the product being developed to see if it satisfies its requirements. Reviews are part of the development process, designed to provide a ready/not-ready decision to begin the next phase. In formal reviews, actual work done is compared with established standards. SQA's main objective in reviews is to assure that the Management and Development Plans have been followed, and that the product is ready to proceed with the next phase of development. Although the decision to proceed is a management decision, SQA is responsible for advising management and participating in the decision.

An inspection or walkthrough is a detailed examination of a product on a step-bystep or line-of-code by line-of-code basis to find errors. For inspections and walkthroughs, SQA assures, at a minimum, that the process is properly completed and that needed follow-up is done. The inspection process may be used to measure compliance to standards.

- *Formal Test Monitoring:* SQA assures that formal software testing, such as acceptance testing, is done in accordance with plans and procedures. SQA reviews testing documentation for completeness and adherence to standards. The documentation review includes test plans, test specifications, test procedures, and test reports. SQA monitors testing and provides follow-up on nonconformances. By test monitoring, SQA assures software completeness and readiness for delivery.

The objectives of SQA in monitoring formal software testing are to assure that:

- The test procedures are testing the software requirements in accordance with test plans.
- The test procedures are verifiable.
- The correct or "advertised" version of the software is being tested (by SQA monitoring of the CM activity).
- The test procedures are followed.
- Nonconformances occurring during testing (that is, any incident not expected in the test procedures) are noted and recorded.
- Test reports are accurate and complete.
- Regression testing is conducted to assure nonconf-ormances have been corrected.
- Resolution of all nonconformances takes place prior to delivery.

Software testing verifies that the software meets its requirements. The quality of testing is assured by verifying that project requirements are satisfied and that the testing process is in accordance with the test plans and procedures.

TOTAL QUALITY MANAGEMENT

In the global marketplace increased levels of competition have resulted in quality becoming of increasing importance to organizations and consequently total quality management (TQM) has become a key management issue.

A considerable number of companies are applying TQM and the topic is the subject of many books and papers. As the end of the twentieth century approaches, TQM appears to be a well-accepted system of management. Yet two decades ago the term was not used. What has been the process of development of TQM theory and practice and when and why did the term come into being? This paper attempts to answer these questions. Before discussing the origins of TQM it is necessary to examine definitions of the term.

This is not an easy task as almost every writer on the subject has their own definition, by and large devising it to suit their own beliefs, prejudices and business and academic experiences. To some degree this is also true in the organizations which have introduced a TQM approach to managing the business. The result is a proliferation of unique definitions which confounds comparisons and adds to the difficulties of understanding and analysis. Even with the publication of an international definition of TQM in ISO 8402(1994) there is ample evidence that writers and researchers do not stick to this definition and create their own unique offering.

Moreover, as Hackman and Wageman (1995) state, a large number of interventions not related with TQM are being encompassed under the TQM banner; this further complicates the issue of definition and understanding. Despite the divergence of views on what constitutes TQM there are a number of common elements running through the various definitions (*e.g.* top management support, customer and supplier relationships and employee involvement). Several writers have tried to define the different dimensions that shape TQM.

Table contains an analysis by the authors of the common dimensions. In this paper the discussion about the development of TQM begins with a brief historical review of the different stages that preceded the birth of TQM. A comparative analysis of the Japanese approach to quality management and an examination of Feigenbaum's (1961) concept of total quality control is made, these constitute two of the major inputs into the development of TQM. The visions of the quality management gurus are also examined.

A HISTORICAL PERSPECTIVE

Powell (1995) makes the points that: "TQM's origins can be traced to 1949, when the Union of Japanese Scientists and Engineers formed a committee of scholars, engineers, and government officials devoted to improving Japanese productivity, and enhancing their post-war quality of life" and "American firms began to take serious notice of TQM around 1980". It can be argued that many of the TQM dimensions outlined in Table I were being applied by organisations before the TQM movement appeared; consequently, it is not easy to establish the exact date of birth of the term TQM. Stuelpnagel (1993) considers that in Ford and Crowter's book *My Life and Work,* published in 1926, the origins of TQM can be found.

Nevertheless, it is clear that the term and the philosophy as a whole appeared around the mid 1980s. Bemowski (1992) states that the term TQM was initially coined in 1985 by the Naval Air Systems Command to describe its Japanese-style management approach to quality improvement. Perhaps, the main reason for the origin of the term TQM could be a substitution in the previously used term of total quality control (TQC), the word "control" by "management" with the reasoning that quality is not just a matter of control, it has to be managed. This is reinforced by Deming's (1982) view that sampling inspection should be suppressed and also by Crosby (1979) who makes the point that control is not necessary when a zero defects level is achieved. The term "control" is sometimes understood as meaning control over the workforces activities, and this is clearly not the aim of TQM. In the USA the development of quality management resulted from the penetration of its markets by Japanese products which started in the 1970s, together with the impact of the writings of Crosby, Deming, Feigenbaum and Juran. Consequently, companies and academics studied the works of these authors and others, such as Ishikawa, and, integrating their approaches with quality management, gave rise to the concept of TQM. This movement was exported to other countries, the UK being one of the first.

Dale, who started his research in quality management back in 1981, believes that the term TQM arose in the UK from the activities of the Department of Trade and Industry National Quality Campaign which was launched in 1983 and the pioneering work of organisations such as IBM. He relates a discussion with John MacDonald (one of the stalwarts of the UK quality management and the first managing director of Crosby Associates UK Ltd) who mentioned that around mid 1986 he was using the term TQM in his cross-Atlantic communication with Philip Crosby, who responded with the retort "what is TQM"? It is also worth mentioning that in the early to mid-1980s the use of qualityrelated terms and acronyms was nothing like as pronounced as it is today.

Table has been created from an analysis of the ABI-INFORM database, which includes brief summaries of business articles published since 1986. The number of references with the terms TQM, quality management (QM) and total quality (TQ) included in them has been searched. As Table II shows, the number of papers including the term TQM in 1986, 1987 and 1988 is small, which confirms the view already expressed that the term only started to be used in the literature since the mid-1980s.

It can be seen that at the beginning of the 1990s, the use of the term was already widespread, reaching a peak in 1993. Since then, the number of papers using the term has been in decline, although maintaining some importance in relation to volume of material. It is the authors' opinion that this decrease in the number of papers is because TQM is widely known and accepted and is not attracting the attention from writers as it once did. However, some of the most recent incorporations into TQM, such as benchmarking and self assessment, have been the subject of further treatment in the management literature. If the origins of the TQM dimensions in Table I are traced and analysed, the following key points emerge:

- Those related with workforce management and the need for top management leadership have their origins in the USA, arising from the Hawthorne studies.

- With respect to process flow management, SPC has its roots in the USA with Shewhart (1931) and the UK with Dudding (BS 600 (1935)). On the other hand, mistake proofing systems are a Japanese idea, as is the importance of cleanliness and organisation of tools and housekeeping using the fives and CANDO (cleanliness, arrangement, neatness, discipline and orderliness) principles.
- The concern about consumers needs has been of inherent interest to marketing theorists since it first appeared, the maindevelopment work on this subject has beenconducted in the USA. The increase in competition and demanding consumers have been the main reasons for companies treating this need to listen to "customers' voices" in a serious manner.
- Most of the recommendations about design processes have arisen from observation of Japanese procedures and best practices. Taguchi methods were developed by Genichi Taguchi, a statistician and electrical engineer who was involved in rebuilding the Japanese telephone system. Quality function deployment (QFD) methods were also developed in Japan, but, as with the case of many other Japanese management tools and techniques, they have been popularized world-wide by North American writers such as Hauser and Clausing (1988).
- The grounds of the supplier relationship dimension can be found mostly in JIT theories, which were first developed in Toyota.
- The role of the quality department has been widely analysed by American writers such as Feigenbaum (1991) and Juran *et al.* (1974).
- Benchmarking was first developed in Xerox, an American company and popularised by the work of Camp (1989).

A brief résumé of the historical events that have influenced the development of TQM theory and practice is provided in Table III, indicating a gradual emergence of TQM.

The use of statistical methods and the fundamentals of the system of workforce management began to be developed early in the century and Japan developed its TQM approach gradually from the end of the Second World War. At the end of the 1970s and the beginning of the 1980s, Japanese pressure and the success of some American writers created a general concern about the focus on quality management in the USA, and from this country to the rest of the world.

The publication of the Malcolm Baldrige National Quality Award and other similar awards in other countries was the official recognition of the importance of TQM.

COMPARISONS BETWEEN JAPANESE AND AMERICAN TQC

Feigenbaum (1956, 1961) was the first author who used the term TQC. In his first book on TQC (a revision of the book original published under the title *Quality Control* in 1951), he defined TQC as "an effective system for integrating the qualitydevelopment, quality maintenance, and quality-improvement efforts of the various groups in an organisation so as to enable production and service at the most economical levels which allow for full customer satisfaction".

He considered that "control must start with the design of the product and end only when the product has been placed in the hands of a customer who remains satisfied". In this book Feigenbaum recognised that all departments in a company have some responsibility for the achievement of quality, as it was originally perceived by Feigenbaum. However, TQC did not include many of the elements (*e.g.* supplier developmental relationships, people empowerment and teamwork) that are now considered part of the TQM concept.

Japanese companies have developed their own approach to TQC, based on the teachings of Deming and Juran, shaping it to suit their own culture and operating environment along with the development of a new set of tools, techniques and operating systems. In the authors' opinion Ishikawa was mainly responsible for shaping Japanese style TQC. His definition of TQC or company wide quality control (CWQC) is: "Quality control consists of developing, designing, producing, marketing, and servicing products and services with optimum cost-effectiveness and usefulness, which customers will purchase with satisfaction. To achieve these aims, all the separate parts of a company must work together".

Analysing Feigenbaum's and Ishikawa's definitions, it can be seen that there are no major differences. However, the difference between CWQC and Feigenbaum's approach is that, while Feigenbaum advocates that TQC is conducted essentially by QC specialists, CWQC has never been an exclusive domain of such specialists. It can be seen that the focus on the participation of employees is weak and the task of improving quality is given to managers.

According to Garvin (1988), the term CWQC was introduced in Japan in 1968, some ten years after Feigenbaum introduced the term TQC. Garvin (1988) states that "CWQC includes four principal elements: the involvement of functions other than manufacturing in quality activities; the participation of employees at all levels; the goal of continuous improvement; and careful attention to customers' definitions of quality". He considers the confusion between CWQC and TQC to be widespread because "whereas some experts use the terms interchangeably others see CWQC as a more advanced and comprehensive concept".

It is interesting that in Japan for the last three years there has been discussion of the differences between TQC and TQM and the latter term is now starting to be used by both organisations and academics. The differences in Japanese and Western views may relate to differences in culture, politics and company philosophy. Ishikawa (1989) identified 14 areas of difference between Japan and the West, including:

- In the USA and Western Europe, great emphasis is placed on professionalism and specialisation; "QC only for QC specialists".
- In the USA and Western Europe, great emphasis is placed on the Taylor system.
- The pay system in the USA and Western Europe is based on merit (to motivate people by money alone). Japan uses a system of seniority and ranking.
- High turnover rates and layoffs are found in the West; Japan has a lifetime employment system.
- Relationships with subcontractors – 70 per cent of a product's manufacturing costs are contributed by outside suppliers in Japan, and only 50 per cent in the USA. Subcontractors are treated as friends not enemies as in the case in the West.
- Old-style capitalism versus democratization of capital: short-term profits versus long-term profits. These six differences, together with political and cultural differences have meant that the TQM approaches in Japan, the USA and Europe are different.

Although the Japanese model has a proven successful track record, the existence of differences is not necessarily an indicator that the Western model is inferior, since, as Ishikawa (1989) advocates, companies must adapt CWQC to the country or company according to differences of social background. In the last decade numerous success stories have emerged of TQM applications in Europe and America. Abo (1995) demonstrates how the management of manufacturing systems of Japanese multinationals is different in Asia, Europe and the USA. These differences indicate that Japanese multinationals have had to adapt their management systems to the different conditions of countries. On the other hand, Ebrahimpour (1988) and Garvin (1986) examine how Japanese companies operating in the USA have successfully applied some of the features of the quality management approach they employ in Japan.

The authors' consider that the way in which TQM has developed from the Japanese and Feigenbaum's concepts has been the inclusion of appropriate management theory as demonstrated by the TQM dimensions. Examining the ISO 8402 (1994) definition of TQM, it is clear that TQC and CWQC are essentially TQM. However, differences in its application in companies, due partially to the differences that Ishikawa (1989) identified, still exist and this will always be the case.

TQM: VIEWS OF THE QUALITY MANAGEMENT GURUS

Crosby, Deming, Feigenbaum, Ishikawa and Juran can be considered the most important gurus of the quality management movement. However, this does not mean that their approaches are the same. The views of Feigenbaum and Ishikawa have already been considered and the focus of attention is now turned to Crosby, Deming and Juran. Deming achieved great popularity in 1980 after the NBC television documentary about success in Japan where he was considered a key element.

Although Deming maintained a contrary position with respect to some of the TQM elements (*e.g.* zero defects and quality costing), a considerable number of authors consider him as one of the main supporters ofthe TQM concept. English (1996) considersthat Juran is related with TQM and Drensek and Grubb (1995) and English (1996) also consider that Crosby is a TQM theorist. Hackman and Wageman (1995) state that Deming, Ishikawa and Juran can be considered the founders of the TQM philosophy, "since TQM drinks in their works". Surprisingly, they do not mention Feigenbaum, the originator of the term TQC.

CAPABILITY MATURITY MODEL (CMM)

History of CMM

The Capability Maturity Model was initially funded by military research. The United States Air Force funded a study at the Carnegie-Mellon Software Engineering Institute to create an abstract model for the military to use as an objective evaluation of software subcontractors. The result was the Capability Maturity Model, published as Managing the Software Process in 1989. The CMM is no longer supported by the SEI and has been superseded by the more comprehensive Capability Maturity Model Integration (CMMI), of which version 1.2 has now been released.

Context

In the 1970s, technological improvements made computers more widespread, flexible, and inexpensive. Organizations began to adopt more and more computerized information systems and the field of software development grew significantly.

This led to an increased demand for developers—and managers—which was satisfied with less experienced professionals. Unfortunately, the influx of growth caused growing pains; project failure became more commonplace not only because the field of computer science was still in its infancy, but also because projects became more ambitious in scale and complexity.

In response, individuals such as Edward Yourdon, Larry Constantine, Gerald Weinberg, DeMarco, and David Parnas published articles and books with research results in an attempt to professionalize the software development process. Watts Humphrey's Capability Maturity Model (CMM) was described in the book Managing the Software Process (1989). The CMM as conceived by Watts Humphrey was based on the work a decade earlier of

Phil Crosby who published the Quality Management Maturity Grid in his book Quality is Free in Active development of the model by the SEI (US Dept. of Defence Software Engineering Institute) began in 1986.

The CMM was originally intended as a tool to evaluate the ability of government contractors to perform a contracted software project. Though it comes from the area of software development, it can be, has been, and continues to be widely applied as a general model of the maturity of processes (*e.g.*, IT Service Management processes) in IS/IT (and other) organizations.

The model identifies five levels of process maturity for an organisation:

- Initial (chaotic, ad hoc, heroic) the starting point for use of a new process.
- Repeatable (project management, process discipline) the process is used repeatedly.
- Defined (institutionalized) the process is defined/confirmed as a standard business process.
- Managed (quantified) process management and measurement takes place.
- Optimising (process improvement) process management includes deliberate process optimization/improvement.

Within each of these maturity levels are KPAs (Key Process Areas) which characterise.

That level, and for each KPA there are five definitions identified:

- Goals
- Commitment
- Ability
- Measurement
- Verification

The KPAs are not necessarily unique to CMM, representing — as they do — the stages that organizations must go through on the way to becoming mature. The assessment is supposed to be led by an authorised lead assessor. One way in which companies are supposed to use the model is first to assess their maturity level and then form a specific plan to get to the next level. Skipping levels is not allowed. The CMM was originally intended as a tool to evaluate the ability of government contractors to perform a contracted software project.

It may be suited for that purpose. When it became a general model for software process improvement, there were many critics. "Shrinkwrap" companies are also called "COTS" or commercial-off-the-shelf firms or software package firms. They include Claris, Apple, Symantec, Microsoft, and Lotus, amongst others. Many such companies rarely if ever managed their requirements documents as formally as the CMM described in order to achieve level 2, and so all of these companies would probably fall into level 1 of the model.

Origins

In the 1980s, several military projects involving software subcontractors ran overbudget and were completed much later than planned, if they were completed at all. In an effort to determine why this was occurring, the United States Air Force funded a study at the SEI. The result of this study was a model for the military to use as an objective evaluation of software subcontractors. In 1989, the Capability Maturity Model was published as Managing the Software Process. The basis for the model is the Quality Management Maturity Grid introduced by Philip Crosby in his 1979 book 'Quality is Free'.

Timeline

- 1987: SEI-87-TR-24 (SW-CMM questionnaire), released.
- 1989: Managing the Software Process, published.
- 1990: SW-CMM v0.2, released (first external issue see Paulk handout).
- 1991: SW-CMM v1.0, released.
- 1993: SW-CMM v1.1, released.
- 1997: SW-CMM revisions halted in support for CMMI.
- 2000: CMMI v1.02, released.
- 2002: CMMI v1.1, released.
- 2006: CMMI v1.2, released.

Current State

Although these models have proved useful to many organizations, the use of multiple models has been problematic. Further, applying multiple models that are not integrated within and across an organization is costly in terms of training, appraisals, and improvement activities. The CMM Integration project was formed to sort out the problem of using multiple CMMs. The CMMI Product Team's mission was to combine three source models:

- The Capability Maturity Model for Software (SW-CMM) v2.0 draft C
- The Systems Engineering Capability Model (SECM)
- The Integrated Product Development Capability Maturity Model (IPD-CMM) v0.98
- Supplier sourcing

Index